ogy

NEW LINES IN CRIMINOLOGY

An Aldine de Gruyter Series of Texts and Monographs

SERIES EDITOR

Thomas G. Blomberg, *Florida State University*

Thomas G. Blomberg and Karol Lucken
American Penology
A History of Control

Bruce A. Jacobs
Robbing Drug Dealers
Violence Beyond the Law

American Penology
A History of Control

Thomas G. Blomberg

Karol Lucken

ALDINE DE GRUYTER
NEW YORK

About the Authors

Thomas G. Blomberg
Professor, School of Criminology and Criminal Justice, Florida State University.

Karol Lucken
Assistant Professor, Department of Criminal Justice, University of Central Florida.

ALDINE DE GRUYTER
A division of Walter de Gruyter, Inc.
200 Saw Mill River Road
Hawthorne, New York 10532

This publication is printed on acid free paper ∞

Library of Congress Cataloging-in-Publication Data

Blomberg, Thomas G.
    American penology : a history of control / Thomas G. Blomberg and Karol Lucken.
        p. cm. — (New lines in criminology)
    Includes bibliographical references and index.
    ISBN 0-202-30637-2 (cloth : alk. paper) — ISBN 0-202-30638-0 (pbk. : alk. paper)
    1. Prisons—United States—History. 2. Punishment—United States—History. I. Lucken, Karol. II. Title. III. Series.
    HV9466 .B55 2000
    365'.973—dc21   00-043031

Manufactured in the United States of America

10 9 8 7 6 5 4 3 2

*Dedicated to the
memory of*

*Mark R. Yeisley
(1971–2000)*

Contents

Acknowledgments

In writing this book, we have benefited from the contributions of a number of people. We wish to acknowledge the assistance of Laura Nemmersand, Alicia Vereen, Robert Neary, and Seresa Guild, who helped in conducting library research and historical data collection. Further, we want to acknowledge the editorial assistance provided by Valerie Johnson and Joan Murphy. Special acknowledgments are extended to Richard Koffler, Executive Editor, of Aldine de Gruyter for his assistance and support for a book that is aimed at providing students and instructors an alternative to traditional corrections textbooks. For their constructive criticisms and suggestions, we thank Stan Cohen and Dan Maier-Katkin. Finally, we wish to individually acknowledge and thank Barbara Lucken, Jeanine Blomberg, and Thomas G. Blomberg Jr. for their ongoing support and encouragement.

1

Introduction

THE PURPOSE OF *AMERICAN PENOLOGY* is to provide a story about punishment's past, present, and future. As with any story, the book contains a setting, many settings, in fact; a cast of characters, all of whom are involved in the problems of crime and punishment; and, finally, conclusions about punishment's past, present, and likely future. The story begins in the 1600s, in the setting of Colonial America. It ends in the year 2000, in what now is routinely termed millennial America. As the story evolves through various historical and contemporary settings, America's efforts to understand and control crime unfold. The context, ideas, practices, and consequences of various punishment reforms are described and examined. As these various punishment reforms evolve, patterns and relationships emerge, culminating in conclusions that may be disquieting to some—because of their Orwellian implications—but comforting to others—because of their prediction of greater order, convenience, and safety by whatever means necessary.

American Penology does not tell a new story about punishment. Rather, it offers a particular way of communicating the story that is intended to provide a more informed understanding of the patterns and relationships involved in America's punishment efforts. The contents are conceptualized in a way not found in correctional texts or the research literature. Most texts include compilation and description of a wide range of topics that are largely without an organizing theme. Employing a more "encyclopedic approach," texts provide selected descriptive information on numerous topics. Crime control, punishment, or corrections, as it is generally termed, is commonly portrayed as a blend of different people, ideas, events, programs, practices, facts, and figures, rather than as an evolving and interrelated process shaped by historical contingencies, ideas, and practices.

In contrast, the research literature provides contributions that are much more in-depth and narrow in focus. This is not to criticize the prior research literature, but instead to suggest that this is the nature of the research process, which is, necessarily focused and specialized. For example, Melossi and Pavarini (1981) examine the prison as a factory. Platt (1969) examines the juvenile court as a corporate class movement. Simon (1993) examines parole

1

as "poor discipline." Blomberg (1977) examines diversion as accelerated control. Petersilia and Turner (1990) examine intermediate punishment as a policy for overcrowded times. Greenberg (1977) correlates punishment rates with fluctuating business cycles.

Though this book's broader scope and purpose can be distinguished from the prior research literature, it necessarily incorporates many contributions from this literature. These many contributions are explicitly discussed in the book, and their relationship to the story of American penology is self-evident (e.g., the rise of prisons, reformatories, probation, parole, and juvenile courts, the origins and functions of prison subcultures, the needs of special inmate populations, the effectiveness of community-based alternatives to incarceration). Other theoretical contributions are incorporated and woven throughout the book and help frame the perspective from which the story is told.

It is important to acknowledge that while this book incorporates selected descriptions of historical contingencies in relation to particular eras and punishment ideas and practices, it does not provide individual "histories" of these eras. Rather than doing history, this book uses history to frame and help explain particular punishment ideas and practices in relation to the period and context from which they evolved. Doing such histories is beyond the scope of this book and would necessarily involve systematic collection, recording, and analysis of a broader range of numerous and complex historical data and then integrating, applying, and interpreting these data in relation to a particular historical era. However, a number of original historical studies are available and are referenced in the chapters that follow. The reader should consult these studies for more detailed histories of particular eras of interest. In contrast to such historical studies, this book focuses upon selected demographic, economic, political, religious, and intellectual contingencies that are associated with particular historical and contemporary eras to suggest how these contingencies shaped America's punishment ideas and practices. The purpose is to inform the reader about American penology's story as it evolved over several centuries. The focus, therefore, is purposely narrowed to major punishment reform eras and selected historical influences.

CONCEPTUAL FRAMEWORK

In the first half of the twentieth century, criminological inquiry was focused upon offender behavior and crime causation. The underlying assumption was that the behavior of formal crime control agents working in law enforcement, courts, or corrections was not problematic. It was assumed that these agents were merely operating in accordance with their formally prescribed goals and purposes. In the absence of an identifiable and acknowledged problem, their behavior did not capture the attention of criminological researchers.

During the 1960s, however, America witnessed firsthand the patterned inability of police, courts, and corrections personnel to effectively respond to the period's crime and civil disobedience. As public scrutiny increased, problems emerged that were directly connected to the underlying goals and purposes of the criminal justice system. Notions of "blind justice" or "disinterested professionalism" as accurate characterizations of criminal justice practices were quickly discarded. Criminal justice agencies were acknowledged to have taken on a self-interested "life of their own" and, in the process, to have displaced their law and order, due process, and offender treatment goals and purposes.

As these recognitions emerged, unprecedented interest in the critical study of the criminal justice system developed. Research shifted from a preoccupation with the offender and crime's causes to a preoccupation with the meaning and consequences of past and present crime control efforts. This book draws upon many of the themes that emerged from this critical literature over the past several decades. One particularly salient theme is what Cohen (1985) has termed the "demystification theme of penology," which emerged from critical examinations of the origins, operations, and outcomes of various penal strategies.

While different theoretical perspectives were employed in these various examinations, the work shared a singular curiosity—namely, the interface between penal ideas and consequences and a singular conclusion—the expansion of control over more of the population (Blomberg and Cohen, 1995). For many, the history of punishment was an unending cycle of good intentions gone bad, with the recurring disparity between ideas and consequences being attributed to a number of factors. For example, the implementation stage was perhaps flawed due to misunderstandings in program design or insufficient resources or staff (ibid.). Other perspectives held that the disparity between ideas and consequences was not so accidental. Organizational imperatives, such as maintenance, survival, and expansion, were systematically undermining the efforts of well-meaning reformers (Austin and Krisberg, 1981; Blomberg, 1977; Rothman, 1980).

Still others asserted that the intentions of penal reformers were themselves suspect from the outset. There were no *unintended* (negative) consequences associated with penal reform, just political and economic imperatives and interests being fulfilled. For example, seemingly benign attempts to decentralize corrections and thereby improve the chances of offender rehabilitation and societal reintegration were portrayed as actual efforts to alleviate state fiscal crises while still expanding offender control into the community (Scull, 1977). For other writers, penal reform initiatives were construed as an extension of economic preservation associated with class conflict and accompanying status panic by the rich and powerful (Platt, 1969; Simon, 1993). According to this interpretive theme, depending upon the needs of the labor market, the prison functioned as a factory by manufacturing disciplined and reliable workers, or, it functioned as a warehouse that controlled a surplus population of workers that threatened the existing social and economic order (Melossi and Pavarini, 1981; Rusche and Kirchheimer, 1939).

Despite these different interpretations of intent, motive, implementation, or practices, the reported consequences were consistent: more control over an ever-increasing proportion of the base population. This book assumes that each of these interpretative themes is useful. As a result, they have been incorporated, in part, to help frame and interpret the story of American penology. However, in contrast to some of the critical arguments, this book also assumes that motives related to civility, humanitarianism, progress, or what Schlossman (1977) termed "love of the American delinquent" to capture the motives of juvenile court reformers, should not be ignored. Following decades of discussion and debate, many scholars have now come to agree that some combination of historical contingencies have indeed influenced the course of penal change (Cohen, 1985; Garland, 1990; Lucken, 1997; Rothman, 1971). However, the order and weight of these various contingencies remain uncertain, as specific cause-and-effect relationships have not been identified. Rather, the combined forces, contingencies, and relationships are better understood as intermittent, not necessarily linear, and varying in degrees of priority (Lucken, 1998). Certain contingencies (e.g., religious, economic, etc.) are more prominent and meaningful to penal reform than others during different historical and contemporary eras.

In attempting to tell the story of American penology, then, an interrelated focus is employed. First, there are specific historical eras and contexts that are shaped by a number of different contingencies, in which particular ideas emerge to support and inform particular penal reforms. Second, there are the documented ways in which these reforms become implemented and practiced, thereby producing particular consequences. Moreover, it will be argued that these various penal reform and practice efforts have resulted in cumulative consequences over time. As new penal reforms were implemented, previous penal practices were seldom changed or discarded. It is in this regard that the concept of "net-widening" will be employed. Net-widening refers to the tendency of penal reforms to sequentially extend control over more of the base population, rather than to provide alternative control as generally claimed in the promotion of various penal reforms. The history of penal reform has been characterized by repeated efforts to modify, differentiate, or change previous penal practices through new or alternative strategies. However, in practice these reforms became implemented as supplements rather than alternatives to previous practices, thereby extending the overall proportion of the base population subject to some form of penal control or net-widening with little relationship to crime's fluctuating trends.

The conceptual framework for this book, therefore, will be eclectic. The framework is eclectic because it will employ critical, progressive, and bureaucratic perspectives, in its efforts to communicate a connection between historical and contemporary context, ideas, practice, and consequences of the major penal reforms that have constituted American penology over the past several centuries.

OUTLINE OF BOOK

The challenge this book faces in telling the story of American penology is a difficult one. To accomplish the book's purposes requires considerable focus, selection, and imposition upon historical and contemporary eras and related punishment ideas and practices. Actual time is not the same as time measured by research or what is often referred to as social or historical time (Friedman, 1993). To illustrate, this book condenses decades and sometimes centuries into a single reform era in the effort to capture what would otherwise be an overwhelming mass of data and details. Moreover, and as previously discussed, though chapters are devoted to the introduction of new penal reform strategies, this does not mean that previous strategies are replaced or discarded. For many decades and even centuries, old and new strategies coexisted, with the old sometimes gradually declining, and in many instances never declining and even reemerging later with greater popularity and influence.

Rossiter (1971) considers this historical trend when he notes that history is written but not made in chapters. Events unfold in an "untidy manner," and those seeking to interpret these events must proceed in a way that is neat and ordered. It is from an imposition of order that this book attempts to develop compelling arguments. Ultimately, the reader will have to determine the adequacy of the book's imposition of order and the related strength of its arguments. Certainly, this story is not the only story to be told, and, indeed, other stories of American penology have been told.

Though the book is entitled *American* penology, the story begins with the early history of punishment in Europe. Chapter 2 traces several centuries of European punishment practices. By tracing punishment from ancient society through the Middle Ages and into the Mercantilist Era, the conventional interpretation that throughout history man has become more humane, less brutal, and progressive is brought into question. The chapter argues that the punishment practices and changes occurring over these several centuries reflect much more than a civilizing process. Further, it argues that the emergence, decline, and reemergence of various punishment practices such as the death penalty reflects more than mere economic fluctuations and scarcities or surpluses of convict labor. Rather, the chapter contends that punishment ideas, reforms, and repetitions are shaped by interrelated factors that contribute to the particular historical context in which they emerge and to which they are relevant. These historical contexts are themselves complex and shaped by several often related factors and contingencies. The chapter concludes that historical context and punishment ideas and practices are necessarily interrelated. The subsequent chapters explore this interrelationship over the course of several centuries in the attempt to tell a story of American penology.

Chapter 3 begins the story of American penology. The chapter briefly describes Colonial America's strong English ties as related to criminal codes and punishments, the small, closely knit, and independent nature of individual colonial communities, their crime trends, their very strong religious views on what is crime and what causes it, and their related methods of punishment. Colonial punishment practices are portrayed as relevant and functional to the context, beliefs, and needs of the religious-laden and closely knit colonial community. As these influences and context began to change toward the end of the 1700s, America's punishment ideas and practices began to experience major transition.

Chapter 4 identifies selected economic, demographic, and intellectual influences that contributed to a set of distinct ideas about crime and punishment. During this approximately forty-year period, America experienced major reform of its legal codes, which were accompanied by the implementation of full-time police and incarceration as the dominant form of punishment. Under the combined influences of Enlightenment thought and postrevolution optimism, beginning industrialization, and associated urbanization, Colonial American ideas about crime's causes and punishment practices were no longer consistent with or functional to the rapidly changing needs and sensibilities of Americans during the period of transition. Crime became viewed as a consequence of free will and an accompanying pain vs. pleasure calculus rather than a product of grim determinism ordained by God. The reasoning was that if crime was made more painful than pleasurable, specific and general crime deterrence could be accomplished. The focus was upon reforming the laws, apprehending wrongdoers, and then providing swift and sure adjudication with imprisonment quickly becoming the punishment fashion. However, the rapid and makeshift development of prison facilities, or what were known as penitentiaries in the early nineteenth century, could not keep pace with the rising numbers of offenders sentenced to prison.

While Chapter 4 describes the formative beginnings of American prisons, Chapter 5 chronicles the nationwide proliferation and refinement of the penitentiary. Under the influence of a different combination of historical contingencies, notions of crime as a product of free will declined. A new deterministic explanation that connected crime to a moral disease that was itself connected to the socially disorganized and evil influences of the city became the theoretical idea guiding Jacksonian prison reformers. The resulting goals of prisons were twofold, namely, correct the wayward prisoner through regimen, discipline, and obedience, and provide the disorganized and depraved city with a model of proper social organization that it could emulate. The prison walls were not only to keep prisoners in, but to keep the city from contaminating the well-ordered prison environment. However, these lofty prison goals were not to be realized and the prison soon became characterized by organizational survival and managerial practices, prompting a new series of penal reforms.

Chapter 6 and Chapter 7 focus upon a period in which a major philosophical shift in American penology occurred, involving a broad and unquestioned embracing of individual treatment and offender rehabilitation. From the 1880s to the 1930s, America experienced an unprecedented call for increased government action to respond to increasing conditions of industrialization, urbanization, immigration, and an associated host of social problems that included most notably crime. Simultaneously occurring with this growing sense of urban disenchantment was an untempered optimism about the potential of the combined efforts of government and science to resolve crime and other urban social problems. The belief was that, by employing scientific principles, a more informed and effective governmental method of dealing with criminal offenders could be established. Individual treatment of offenders became the goal, and to realize this goal required a series of penal alternatives that came to include the reformatory, indeterminate sentencing, parole, probation, and the juvenile court. However, the implementation and actual practice of these interrelated reforms were far apart from their individual offender treatment and rehabilitation goals. Rather than providing more individualized treatment alternatives to the previous reliance upon prisons, these reform efforts became supplements to prisons serving a variety of managerial and offender control functions.

Chapter 8 traces how the combined science and government strategy of the progressive reform movement continued to guide American penology from the early 1900s to the 1960s. Specifically, as the scientific search for the causes of crime evolved, so evolved the penal system through major service proliferation and differentiation. Prisons, parole, probation, and the juvenile court, supported by the ideas of individual treatment and rehabilitation, experienced substantial organizational growth, differentiation, and bureaucratization. But while the penal system experienced unprecedented growth predicated on the unquestioned utility of the rehabilitative ideal, actual penal practices remained largely managerial, routinized, and control focused.

During this sixty-year period, numerous penal service expansions that were promoted as alternatives to previous practice became implemented as supplements, thereby expanding the overall proportion of population subject to some form of traditional or alternative penal control. This pattern of penal growth was viewed largely as a necessary response to the perceived growing problem of crime and was unquestioned until the turbulent decades of the 1960s and 1970s.

Chapter 9 shifts the previous chapters' focus upon the relationship between historical eras and changes in punishment ideas and practices to a more detailed consideration of the research and theory concerning the social organization of the prison. Such detail of the social organization of the prison is essential to grasp the full meaning of incarceration from those who know it best, namely, the inmates themselves. Beginning with Clemmer's 1940 contribution and subsequent contributions by Sykes (1958, 1995), Irwin and Cressey (1962), and Giallombardo (1966), a new appreciation is provided about life behind bars. The arguments presented by these authors are neither pleasant nor optimistic about the potential of prisons to deal humanely or effectively with inmates. Yet the prison emerges unscathed from these criticisms and continues to prosper and proliferate.

Chapter 10 addresses the rise of the prisoner rights movement in relation to the civil rights activism and civil disobedience of the 1960s and 1970s. The progressive agenda that had so dominated American penology for the first half of the century was under attack. Faith in the state and its agencies of crime control had waned. Different from previous reform efforts, which expanded the penal system, the new call was for restraint with specific checks aimed at narrowing the powers of the penal system. Following numerous lawsuits and consecutive legal victories, it appeared that America's prisoners had gained a number of important legal rights and privileges. However, many of the abuses the liberal Warren court decisions appeared to have remedied quickly reemerged. Further, the increasing conservative makeup of the U.S. Supreme Court over the past several decades has resulted in numerous reversals of the earlier court rulings on behalf of prisoners.

Chapter 11 examines several major penal reform efforts that characterized the decentralization of the correction's movement during the 1960s and 1970s. These reforms include deinstitutionalization, diversion, and community corrections programs, which were promoted as alternatives to the formal penal system altogether. The rationale underlying these program reforms was that providing offenders informal and voluntary forms of community treatment would avoid the negative labeling, stigmatization, and criminal associations that can occur with formal penal system contact and processing, thereby reducing the likelihood of subsequent criminal behavior. With legislative authority and funding, theoretical justification, and professional and public support, decentralized penal strategies proliferated throughout America. However, the chapter documents that while the goals of the various decentralized reforms appeared very different from preceding penal reforms, the practices and outcomes were not only similar but even more far-reaching. Specifically, the previous penal reforms of reformatories, parole, probation, and the juvenile court were promoted as alternatives that would reinforce and enable the penal system to provide more individualized offender treatment. In contrast, diversion, deinstitutionalization, and community corrections were promoted as alternatives to what was concluded to be a very negative penal system that was doing more harm to offenders than good. Nonetheless, and despite these seemingly different intentions, the decentralized reform efforts produced effects that were not only more of the same but were laden with more ominous implications. The decentralized reforms were implemented not as alternatives to prior practice but as supplements in which new levels of control were extended not only to unintended clients but often to their families as well. Further, when many of the families subject to these new control measures were unable to comply, a series of latent and negative consequences ensued, including the dissolution of some family units through the out-of-home placement of youth and sanctioning of parents, thereby potentially creating, perpetuating, or intensifying subsequent crime and delinquency.

By the end of the 1970s, declining faith in the rehabilitative ideal and decentralized correctional reforms peaked. Chapter 12 and Chapter 13 describe and assess some of the consequences of America's subsequent embrace of a "get tough on crime" ethos. In 1980, with the election of Ronald Reagan as president, there was a pervasive sense of cynicism that bordered on despair. The response was to abandon the liberalism of the past. As Reagan frequently stated in his early speeches following his election, "The problem with our liberal friends is not that they are ignorant, but that they know so much that isn't so!" Penal practices affected by this turning away from liberalism included parole, probation, and other seemingly soft-on-crime strategies. As these practices fell into disfavor, a series of get-tough strategies that together supported a new "zero tolerance on crime" orientation were quickly implemented. These chapters consider the context of the 1980s and 1990s in relation to this series of get-tough-on-crime ideas, practices, and consequences. Some of the emergent consequences included unprecedented numbers of offenders being incarcerated and for longer periods of time, prison overcrowding and associated cost explosions, with the problem of crime persisting. What followed were still other so-called intermediate punishment reforms, which attempted to blur getting-tough with community-based efforts that depended much less upon the costly use of imprisonment. But again, like previous liberal and get-tough penal reforms before and throughout the twentieth century, the cycle remained unbroken: more and more of the base population subject to control, with little if any connection to the occurrence of crime. Moreover, as we enter the new millennium with these cumulative and ever-expanding penal control patterns and with our unprecedented reliance upon prisons for not only the violent offender, but also nonviolent mothers, the mentally ill, the old and the infirm, the question looms ever so large: what does the future hold for not only penology and control but for our larger society and culture?

Chapter 14 extends the image of the prison as a total institution into mainstream culture and society. As some observers have claimed, we now live in a minimum- (Blomberg, 1987), medium-, or even maximum-"security" society (Marx, 1988) in which both criminal offenders and citizens alike are subject to new technologies and surveillance capacities that record and monitor their daily lives and movements. This concluding chapter considers the past, present, and future of penology and social control in relation to this growing culture of control that increasingly characterizes American society. The chapter explores how living in this culture of control subjects all citizens to the specter of an electronic panopticon (Gordon, 1990), in which their communities, homes, and bodies are becoming increasingly glasslike or transparent. Documentation of our individual histories, where we live, our physiological and psychological states, and behavior patterns are not only possible now but are compiled routinely and are readily accessible. Further, with such documentation come predictive profiles of our futures that are assembled invisibly, automatically, and generally without our consent. The individual is being described, explained, and predicted for various and sundry purposes. But is the future of American penology and the growing culture of control at once a new challenge that Americans with their commitment to democratic values can effectively confront? Or is the future to be characterized by even more far-reaching surveillance, visibility, regulation, and control that is beyond the control of democratically minded Americans?

2

Punishment in Ancient and Medieval Europe

INTRODUCTION

THIS CHAPTER EXAMINES punishment in Europe over several centuries. To accomplish the task of capturing several centuries of punishment, the chapter is organized into four historical eras. These eras include ancient society, early Middle Ages, late Middle Ages, and the Mercantilist Era. It should be recognized that while we specify when one era ends and another begins, such dating is approximate, at best. Historians themselves continue to debate the correct dating of these various eras.

Punishment in ancient and medieval society is routinely described as brutal. Numerous gruesome acts were administered in the name of truth and justice. Because disemboweling, drawing and quartering, and other forms of torture and mutilation are no longer practiced, scholars, and the public, in general, readily conclude that the evolution of punishment has been a "march of progress." Who could refute the claim that enlightenment, benevolence, and civility have replaced barbarism, cruelty, and ignorance in the administration of punishment? While many would accept this conclusion as commonsensical or self-evident, the "march of progress" interpretation does not capture the full complexity of punishment's history.

This chapter argues that punishment's developments, changes, and repetitions are complex and can only be understood in relation to the historical eras in which they emerged and to which they are relevant. The chapter concludes that the historical eras that have shaped various punishment ideas and practices are themselves shaped by an interrelated set of historical contingencies. As these historical contingencies changed over time, punishment ideas and practices changed and even reemerged with a renewed vigor.

11

ANCIENT SOCIETY

Private Vengeance

Primitive society (pre–700 A.D.) was characterized by roving tribal communities that resolved intertribal disputes through "blood feuds." The blood feud provided the method for private and/or free persons to settle conflicts. This warfare-style system of justice involved avenging wrongdoing through vendettas between members of the clans of the offender and the offended. Though the feud was a socially accepted form of private retaliation, a feud did not necessarily follow every crime. However, because the feud was common practice, the public peace could be threatened at the slightest provocation. Given the absence of third-party mediation, these blood feuds, like war, could erupt into indiscriminate killing, raping, and pillaging. Moreover, the blood feud could result in the ultimate decimation of the participating clans because there was no satisfactory method of bringing the quarrel or vendetta to an end. Violent retaliation as a standard means of resolving disputes served little purpose other than to exact vengeance. Consequently, the chief deterrent to crime was fear of vengeance from the injured party, though vengeful eruptions could be avoided through payment to the injured party.

As society became more agrarian, a less migrant and tumultuous form of existence emerged. Farming required more permanent residence and large numbers of people for labor. The chaos and destruction wrought by blood feuds was counterproductive in a society that increasingly depended upon stability and order to survive. These factors, and the emergence of rulers who were powerful enough to combat the feuds, contributed to the development of third-party mediation and a punishment system based increasingly on compensation.

Mediating Vengeance

Beginning in approximately 700 A.D., compensation became a preferred way of dealing with disputes. A form of tariff or financial penance existed for all offenses. In a world where every fighting and working man was a valuable asset, alternatives to death and debilitating forms of mutilation were necessary. An offender could buy back the peace he had disturbed by a system of fines that involved paying *bot* (betterment) to the offended party and *wite* to the king (Gorringe, 1996). Other penalty schedules included a fine of thirty shillings for cutting off an ear, a fine of sixty-six shillings for knocking out an eye, a fine of sixty shillings for raping a woman who was a virgin, and, if she was not a virgin, a fine of sixteen shillings was incurred. *Wergild* was the term given to the payment for the crime of homicide. The church advocated this system of penalties as a way to discourage the use of the death penalty (ibid.).

This apparent call for mercy through financial compensation was restricted to those who could pay and, as a result, had major social implications. Specifically, it was the imposition of fines and the inability of many to pay that contributed to the creation of a slave class. Individuals who were unable to pay their fines became indentured servants, often for life. Corporal punishments were generally reserved for the slave/lower class and involved bodily infliction of torture, mutilations, and branding. In Greece and Rome, debtors could be sentenced to hard labor in public works.

Some of the early penal codes that were influential at this time included the Burgundian Code of 500 A.D., the Justinian Code of 529 A.D., and the Laws of Ethelbert of 700 A.D. These codes were not the only penal codes of the time, but were representative of the period's penal codes. What these codes attempted to provide was a better-defined and scaled system of punishment. However, attempts to establish a more definitive system of justice should not be mistaken as attempts to establish a more equitable system of justice.

The new system of punishment was two-sided in the sense that one set of punishments existed for the free/upper class and another more severe set of punishments existed for the slave/lower class. These penal codes openly permitted discrimination against the slave/lower classes. For example, the Burgundian Code of 500 A.D. specified punishments in relation to the social class of the offender and victim. If the offender was a member of the slave/lower class and the victim a member of the upper class (e.g., in crimes such as manslaughter or assaults on freewomen, sexual relationships with freewomen, altering boundary markers, and aiding fugitives to escape), the offender was more severely punished. The slave/lower class was likely to receive some form of corporal punishment or death, while freemen or the upper class usually paid their way out of corporal punishment. For offenses such as murder, theft, and robbery, however, some degree of corporal punishment was unavoidable even for the upper class.

The most influential of these early penal codes was the Roman Justinian Code of 529 A.D. This code was the final formulation of law between the Ancient Roman Empire period and the Middle Ages. The Justinian Code represented one of the earliest attempts to equate severity of punishment with severity of offense. Although abandoned with the fall of the Roman Empire, the Justinian Code served as a precedent for subsequent laws throughout the Middle Ages.

The Laws of Ethelbert of 700 A.D., and other British variations, also used the social ranks of the accused and victim to determine the type and severity of punishment. Social status became the guide for assessing literally the value of life and limb. If a freeman raped the slave of a commoner, he had to pay no more than five shillings, but if a slave raped this same girl, he was castrated (Hibbert, 1963). According to these laws, the compensation (fine) to be paid was carefully stipulated and calculated, as were alternatives to fines, namely, mutilations. Every part of the body had a value. An eye or a foot was worth fifty shillings, and a toenail only sixpence. A disabled shoulder was worth thirty shillings, a broken thigh twelve shillings, and a lacerated ear only six shillings. A mutilation or injury that hindered the power of speech warranted a higher form of compensation. Three broken ribs provided one such appropriate equivalent. Injuries that hindered the ability to work were compensated more than disfiguring injuries.

Mediating Vengeance and Seeking Truth

A system of fact-finding in ancient society relied on a process known as "trial by ordeal." Trials by ordeal were physically painful tests administered on the body as a way to provoke the judgment of God. It was believed that the accused's performance or reaction to the ordeal demonstrated innocence or guilt. If the accused could endure the ordeal of being doused with a boiling pot of water without scalding, it was considered an act of grace by God. This, in effect, was a pronouncement of innocence. If the accused drowned when thrown into a large body of water, it was viewed as a pronouncement of guilt.

The ordeals were later replaced by mechanisms of torture. While the ordeals were torturous, there was a distinct difference between "trial by ordeal" and torture. The ordeals relied on signs from God to determine the accused's guilt or innocence. Torture, on the other hand, relied upon pain to extract admissions of guilt from the accused.

Another method of fact-finding was known as "compurgation." Compurgation involved a process whereby the accused was judged according to the presentation of references and witnesses. If the accused was able to produce a certain number of individuals to testify on his behalf, he would be absolved of guilt. This method of fact-finding was typically reserved for the free/elite members of society. Though compurgation was available to the slave/lower class, a greater number of witnesses were required to substantiate innocence and character. Most often, the upper class resorted to private means of resolving disputes (e.g., dueling) to avoid trials of any sort. As a result, it has been suggested that the original court system was reserved for dispute settlements between members of the lower class, which consisted primarily of slaves.

EARLY MIDDLE AGES (700–1000)

In the early Middle Ages, religion pervaded all aspects of society. Under the reign of Charlemagne and his successors, religion united the previously numerous and fragmented territories. The legal system was centralized and, therefore, applied to all inhabitants of the Holy Roman Empire. Laws were no longer to be prescribed locally, but rather a single system of rule would govern all Christians in all territories, regardless of political origin.

During this period, the Church and its ecclesiastical courts operated with unprecedented levels of power in religious and public matters. Bishops assumed judicial responsibility for all matters concerning the clergy, church property, and immoral behavior within their communities. The Church maintained its own system of laws and punishment, which became known as the "benefit of the clergy." The benefit of the clergy provided protection from prosecution in the secular courts for church officials and leniency or immunity from punishment for other protected groups. The privileges granted by the benefit of the clergy also extended to those who could read, a luxury available to only a small and wealthy fraction of the population.

The Church punished its own through confinement and isolation in monasteries. At this time, the Church rejected any form of punishment that resulted in death, mutilation, or the shedding of blood. The belief was that such punishment would inevitably lead to the offender's despair, which impeded the ability to repent. Punishment was to be a devoutly cathartic experience, and an overwhelming sense of despair would disrupt the process of "getting right with God."

Brutal forms of punishment, often referred to as "blood sanctions," were reserved for secular courts. By the middle of the tenth century, death and mutilation were imposed for a broad range of offenses. The type of mutilation corresponded with the type of offense. In an exaggerated attempt to match the sanction with the offense, liars could have their tongues cut out, female gossips could have a hole bored into their tongues, rapists could be castrated, and spies could have their eyes removed. Exile and compensation (fines) remained as core punishments.

LATE MIDDLE AGES (1100–1300s)

Numerous historians have interpreted the emerging and changing historical context of the twelfth century as a turning point in European history. Economic development, in particular, accelerated in the late eleventh century and appeared limitless. Land tenure was becoming less important and money payment more important. The Church's preeminence in intellectual and administrative life was also waning (Gorringe, 1996). Other changes included dynamic growth in the number of towns and cities and the rediscovery of Roman law. In fact, students throughout western Europe flocked to Bologna, Italy, to study law. So prevalent was the interest in law that clerics feared the death of theology was near and that men would learn law and nothing but law (ibid.). It was from this historical context that changes in punishment emerged.

During the eleventh and twelfth centuries, the state as a governing entity took hold. The growth and content of criminal laws and procedures set the stage for a stronger state presence in society. In England, the Assize of

Clarendon in 1166 A.D. established a jury system (i.e., a grand jury and a pe-
tit jury), which led to the abolishment of trials by ordeal by 1215. The con-
stitutions of Clarendon also provided for the classification of offenses as
"offenses against the king's peace." These offenses were subsequently categorized as either felonies or misdemeanors.

To further consolidate the power of the state (the monarchy), the Assizes
of Clarendon mandated the construction of gaols (jails) in every locality.
These were often makeshift facilities that were extensions of existing houses,
monasteries, castles, or mills. However, at this time, imprisonment had a limited use for debtors, for pretrial detention, or as a place where other punishments (e.g., flogging and other forms of torture) could be administered.
Though incarceration was certainly punitive, it was not utilized as a punishment in and of itself. Most dominant were the public punishments of the pillory, mutilation, branding, stocks, ducking stools, and capital punishment via
hanging, drowning, burning, live burial, or decapitation. Less dominant, and
disappearing altogether as the power of the state increased, were private
forms of vengeance.

During the late Middle Ages, fining persisted, and often the monetary
gains from fining became a major source of corruption. What began as a
method of compensating offended parties became a method of enriching
judges. By imposing more and larger fines, judges could easily supplement
their salaries. Corruptive practices also took the form of bribing juries. It has
been argued that throughout the fourteenth century, justice in the courts was
difficult, if not impossible, to obtain. Jurors could not be induced to convict
criminals without some form of bribery or intimidation. Acquittals as well
could be bought and sold. Juries had little difficulty siding with the accused,
believing their behavior to be no less reprehensible than the extortion practiced by judges through the fining system. The justice system was considered
by the general public to be discriminatory, arbitrary, and uncertain.

Despite a growing state presence, the power of the ecclesiastical courts
did not subside until the thirteenth century. The Church broke from its tradition of nonviolence by permitting the types of punishment that were once
condemned. Though society appeared to be more humane, the Church grew
preoccupied with the idea of individual suffering as a prerequisite to repentance and conversion. Throughout the age of the Inquisition, punishment became increasingly brutal in the effort to weed out heretics. The crime of
heresy was broadly defined and could include acts of bigamy, prostitution,
astrology, magic healing, and scientific discovery. The Church imposed such
punishments as incarceration, condemnation to wearing crosses, death by
burning alive, branding, stoning, whipping, and hanging.

The punishment of heretics was later extended into secular law as the offense of treason. This shift signaled the ultimate demise of ecclesiastical power in matters of formal social control and public policy. By 1540, the Church

no longer served as a sanctuary for crimes of arson, burglary, rape, and murder. Lawyers were increasingly taking the lead role in the administration of society at large.

MERCANTILIST ERA (1400–1700s)

Fueling consolidation of new political power (the nation-state of lawyers) were deep changes in the economic structure. The sixteenth century witnessed the downfall of feudalism and the beginning of capitalism. Existing cities became more autonomous and powerful and new cities developed in relation to expansion in manufacturing, trade, and investment. This expansion in private commercial activity has been attributed to improvements in ship-building, new methods for credit and insurance, and the creation of joint stock companies such as the powerful East India Company in 1600 (ibid.). As a result of this transformation, power passed from soldiers to holders of private wealth, namely, the merchant class.

The economic transformations brought about displacement of agricultural laborers, the disbanding of feudal armies, and ultimately a growing nonproductive and displaced population. By the second half of the sixteenth century, Europe was densely populated and no longer riding a wave of economic prosperity. As the numbers of poor increased, their life condition deteriorated. Consequently, the "vagabond" poor became a new focal point in crime and punishment.

The problem of the vagabond had been growing for years as a result of the disintegration of the agricultural economy and the dissolution of monasteries that had often cared for the poor. The Statute of Vagabonds was just one of the laws enacted to address this growing problem. The statute prescribed strict punishments for runaway servants. The first offense carried a penalty of branding and enslavement for a period of two years. A second offense resulted in a different branding to signal the offender's enslavement for life. A third offense brought death by hanging.

The spread of a "criminal" vagabond class prompted questions of how individuals came to be vagabonds or beggars. It was considered important to know the circumstances surrounding their situation to properly classify the status of the vagabonds. Special attention was given to whether the vagabonds' plight was "deserving" or "undeserving" and/or whether or not they were "able-bodied." These questions reflected the importance of work and the view that the poor constituted a potential threat to the stability of society. Purposeful idleness and laziness were not only condemned, they were deemed sinful, evil, and disreputable behaviors. Overall, the notion of moral entrepreneurship, namely, hard work, discipline, and industriousness as moral criteria, underlay the laws and customs of the Mercantilist Era.

This attitude toward poverty and work and the overall political, economic, and cultural shifts of this era coincided with a revision of punishment priorities. Of particular significance was the prospect of exploiting offender labor through such punishments as the galleys, the workhouse, and transportation. These punishments were imposed on the serious and not so serious offenders and could be used with fines and as alternatives to fines and corporal and capital punishments.

The Galley

The galley sentence was used throughout Europe, but was particularly popular in France, Spain, and Italy. The galley sentence arose in response to specific labor needs associated with the naval fleets of the southern European naval powers. When the staffing of naval fleets became problematic, condemned criminals provided a ready and "reliable" workforce. Offenders were literally shackled to their oars and branded on the forehead to prevent their escape. Though sailing ships were coming into use, oarsmen continued to be an important shipping and military tool.

The galley was used primarily for offenders sentenced to death or bodily punishment. Servitude on galley ships was typically a life sentence and was often combined with mutilation. However, the more scarce labor became, the more this punishment was used. For less serious offenses, this sentence could be imposed for a specific number of years. Though the galley sentence appeared to be more humane and lenient than death, it was uniquely brutal in its own right. In fact, the galley was reputed to be worse than death and even more feared than execution, with harsh and unsanitary working conditions that often led to the offender's early death.

Given these conditions shaping the administration of this punishment, the galley sentence has been interpreted by contemporary scholars as an economic and administrative achievement rather than a humanitarian achievement. Galley ships required several hundred oarsmen rowing in unison under extremely strenuous, dangerous, and disciplined conditions. When they were not out to sea, offenders were closely monitored while employed in penal servitude ashore. This form of punishment did not disappear completely until approximately 1803, whereupon sailing ship advancements and slavery rendered galley punishment uneconomical.

The Workhouse

In the second half of the sixteenth century, the workhouse rose to prominence. The first workhouse, the Bridewell, began operation in 1557 in England. Unlike the galley, the workhouse directly addressed the problem of poverty and vagrancy. The aim of the workhouse was not simply to exploit the offender's labor, but to use labor as a vehicle for changing one's character. By introducing the offender to a regimen of honest labor, discipline, and moral instruction, it was believed the offender could be positively transformed. Following the transformation, the offender could then be released to society a productive citizen. So confident was the belief in the powers of discipline, labor, and moral instruction that King George III was sent to a workhouse to "cure" what were considered his erratic and inappropriate ranting and ravings (it has since been speculated that he suffered from a neurological disorder that results in various uncontrollable outbursts and mental lapses). Given the emphasis on behavioral transformation, the workhouse has been considered the predecessor to the modern prison. However, imprisonment and hard labor for serious offenders did not emerge until the mid–nineteenth century.

Once the rationale for the workhouse had been firmly established (i.e., reform through labor), its use quickly expanded. A wider range of offenses and offenders became qualified for the workhouse. In addition to idlers and vagabonds, the workhouse held prostitutes, juveniles, and other minor offenders for whom the blood sanctions were now considered too severe. The workhouse was considered an ideal sanction because it simultaneously punished and corrected and did not aggravate the problem of vagrancy, as had the practice of banishment. An additional advantage was its purported cost-effectiveness. Offender labor was contracted to the private sector, allowing offenders to use their wages to pay for their keep. By 1596, workhouses could be found throughout Europe.

Transportation

Beginning in the seventeenth century, transportation was introduced as a punishment throughout Europe. Unlike the workhouse and the galley, transportation accommodated the demands of European colonization. Transportation of criminals to other territories not only satisfied labor needs in various European colonies, but also alleviated the problem of vagrancy and overpopulation at home. England transported offenders to develop colonies in America, followed by Australia and New Zealand. Spain and France utilized transportation to develop colonies in Africa and South America. The practice of transportation began between 1615 and 1660 and, by 1717 it flourished. In the years prior to 1665, only two hundred offenders were transported to American colonies. Between 1661 and 1700, forty-five hundred offenders were sent to the colonies. This number rose to thirty thousand by 1717. By 1775, England was sending approximately two thousand convicts annually to American colonies, mostly in the form of indentured servitude (Barnes, 1972).

Like the galley, transportation originated as an alternative to death. In 1615, the English monarchy declared that some of the "lesser offenders adjudged by law to die" be punished in a manner that would correct them and "yield a profitable service to the Commonwealth in parts abroad." Eventually, transportation served as an alternative to sanctions other than death.

The transportation of convicts from Europe to various colonies was performed by private merchant contractors, which marks one of the earliest examples of private sector involvement in punishment. The contractors supervised offenders until they reached their colonial destination, whereupon the contractor would sell the offender as an indentured servant to the highest bidder for a profit. The treatment of servants varied, as working and living conditions were dictated entirely by the kindness or the cruelty of the master. As the American Revolution approached, England halted its practice of deportation of convicts to the American colonies to preserve manpower.

The galley, workhouse, and transportation represented attempts to reduce reliance upon blood sanctions and increase reliance upon offender labor. The galley and transportation exploited offender labor for reasons that had little to do with the offender's reform (e.g., manning naval fleets, developing colonies). With the workhouse, however, there was hope that the offender would embrace a work ethic and become a law-abiding and productive citizen. Altogether, these punishments marked the end of punishment as a relished public spectacle, involving the elaborate exhibition of the condemned's last moments, last words, and last breath before an electrified crowd of hundreds.

By the end of the eighteenth century, growing public distaste for the brutality of mutilations and exposure of corpses helped changed the way punishment and, more specifically, capital punishment was administered. Some scholars have argued that the public display of torture, mutilation, and death disappeared because it was no longer feasible politically. The political power of kings was threatened as the masses came to sympathize with the condemned, revering them as heroes and martyrs. It was also the case that the mere gathering of the masses to witness the ceremony of death and punishment itself was criminogenic, by inciting such behaviors as stealing, fighting, and drunkenness. It is often argued that the brutal displays were abolished simply because they offended the sensibilities of an increasingly civilized populace. Whether these practices were abandoned for cultural, political, economic, benevolent, or some combination of these factors, punishment was steadily removed from public view.

SUMMARY AND DISCUSSION

Much of punishment's history centers on violence, discrimination, public ceremony, vengeance, and repentance. The infliction of bodily pain served the purposes of fact-finding as well as punishment. Though such legally sanctioned violence is so different from today's standards, it has been noted that violent physical punishment was simply introduced into a world already accustomed to brutality and suffering in daily life. Private forms of retaliation had been violent so it is not surprising that the formal punishment system would reflect violence as well.

Punishment's history was also purposely discriminatory. Penal codes established an openly dual system of justice based on class. The social status of the offender and victim were as important as the severity of the offense in determining appropriate punishment. Fines were generally applied to the free/upper class, while corporal punishments were generally applied to the slave/lower class.

Punishment was expected to be visually "impressive" as well. The harsh theatrical elements of punishment were to serve as a reminder of the awesome and infinite power of God, who demanded satisfaction and retribution. Those same exhibits would later serve as a reminder of the awesome and infinite power of the state. The nature of punishment was also linked to the essential objectives of humiliation and degradation. The fulfillment of vengeance and repentance depended upon the display of humiliation and degradation. In ancient society, the reform or "correction" of offenders was of negligible importance.

It was not until the late sixteenth century that the human brutality that had long characterized punishment began to disappear. The galley, workhouse, and transportation to penal servitude represented examples of the shift in punishment's focus and purpose. Though punishment still targeted the body, the explicit aim was not the destruction of the body through torture and mutilation, though the physical demands of the galley and servitude were often unbearable. Rather, the aim was to involve the body in productive labor as society itself was now organized around the economically inspired notions of industriousness and utility.

Attempts to explain changes in punishment over the course of this early history and the history to be presented in forthcoming chapters have tended to focus upon either notions of progress or economics. The "march of progress" argument holds that throughout history mankind has been engaged in a cumulative and progressive march that results in a better and/or more humane way of life. In the case of punishment, the "march of progress" perspective assumes that a series of steps have been taken to reduce previously violent, inhumane, and brutal practices as evidenced by the use of the galley, transportation, and workhouse in place of brutal death and corporal punishment.

In contrast, the economic argument reduces all historical events to an economic-based class struggle between the "haves" and "have nots." From this historical perspective, changes in punishment do not reflect progress, but rather conscious and self-interested efforts by the "haves" to effectively exploit the "have nots" in accordance with the demands of the labor market. What might appear as progressive is better understood as planned strategies by the "haves" to maintain their power and privilege over the "have nots" by bolstering the economic and political order from which the power and privilege of the "haves" are derived.

While each of these historical explanations possesses some explanatory merit, this chapter and the chapters that follow argue that shifts in punishment forms have been motivated by a constellation of factors, some of which are more influential than others at different points in time. For example, the role of religion in shaping early punishment practices during the early middle ages and, in contrast, the role of economics in shaping the Mercantilist Era's punishments of the galley, workhouse, and transportation. However, these relevant factors cannot be viewed in isolation from one another, but rather as dynamic and related, and include intellectual, religious, political, and demographic changes. These changes shape a particular social context in which previous punishment ideas and practices emerge as outmoded, and new punishment ideas and practices emerge as more appropriate and functional. Explaining the rise of punishment practices is not unlike explaining criminal behavior: each defies a single-factor interpretation.

3

Punishment and Public Justice in Colonial America (1600–1790)

INTRODUCTION

THE AMERICAN COLONIAL PERIOD spanned nearly two hundred years, beginning with the establishment of Virginia in 1607, and ending after the American Revolution. Because most colonial Americans were of English descent, punishment ideas and practices in colonial America resembled those of England. Early colonial American settlers brought with them only a basic understanding of the English common law, which had just been formulated in England. The English common law system established the practice of oral testimony, a jury of peers, and the classification of offenses. However, because colonial Americans were geographically separated from England, they were required by England to only "establish laws not contrary to those of England." Consequently, colonists were free to discard those elements of English law they did not favor. Criminal codes were generally more lenient in the colonies, particularly with regard to capital punishment. As Friedman (1993) notes, the physical and social circumstances of colonial life (e.g., starvation, Indian hostility, and bouts of internal dissent) "bent the English patterns out of shape."

What emerged were not only differences between colonial and English law, but differences in the laws between colonies. Individual colonies developed their own ideas about crime and punishment that corresponded with their religious beliefs and immediate surroundings. The colonies were essentially "little worlds on their own" (ibid.). While each colony maintained its own character and laws, there was a general pattern to ideas about crime and punishment practices in colonial America. This chapter describes these crime and punishment ideas and practices, and, more generally, the historical contingencies that shaped and gave rise to these ideas and practices.

LIFE IN THE COLONIES

Those coming to the New World were well aware of the dangers that await-ed them. They were also aware that religious conviction alone might not be enough to ensure fidelity to the laws (Bonomi, 1986). There was a genuine fear that men and women might overindulge in the liberties of the New World and become "worse than brute beasts" (quoted in ibid.:18). For the Puritans, in particular, the only way to secure their mission as a "light unto the world" was to firmly fix the church and state into a mutually reinforcing relationship (ibid.).

Colonial life was ultimately governed by the institutions of family, com-munity, and church. Colonists maintained very rigid ideas about the role and importance of these institutions because the family, community, and church provided their only social safety net. The English believed that an orderly society required orderly families and even orderly gender relationships (Nor-ton, 1991). Colonial society was organized into small, closely knit commu-nities where every community member had a particular role to play. Obedience, whether to the highest authority of God or to the lesser authori-ties of parents, ministers, and masters, was an ever-present fact of life. It was, as Friedman (1993) describes, a "paternal society" built on the model of a patriarchal house. Colonial authorities were like stern fathers who sought to mend the ways of their undisciplined and wayward children. It was believed that as long as system and order were maintained, society would function smoothly and peacefully.

Community cohesion and order was facilitated by worshiping at the same church, marrying neighbors, and the necessary pooling and sharing of re-sources (Rothman, 1971). Colonists were not particularly tolerant, liberal, or pluralist in their views. They were, in a word, conformists. It was an excessively communal life, which meant that nothing escaped the watchful eye of the col-lective (Friedman, 1993). Consequently, colonial society was "well stocked with moral monitors who did not miss much in the goldfish bowl existence of daily life" (Thompson, 1986). Even as late as 1760, there were only seven cities in the colonies with more than three thousand people (Preyer, 1982).

As scrutinizing of one another as they were, colonists were loyal to mem-bers of their immediate community. Towns were responsible for their own, and permanent residence was fundamental to establishing a good reputation. Not surprisingly, outsiders were feared because they posed a potential threat to the stability of the community. In some colonies, laws were even enacted to exclude outsiders. Only after investigation or the offering of a certificate of good standing from the community of previous residence were outsiders welcomed into a new community. Colonial communities aspired to obtain perfect order, an order that was intimately related to survival as well as a divine existence.

American colonists' preoccupation with community order was linked, in part, to an intense preoccupation with obedience, namely, obedience to God. "Religion was the salt that flavored colonial life" ("Religion was 'salt,'" 1998). Although some settlers came to North America for economic opportunities (e.g., to "catch fish"), the majority came in search of religious freedom. Colonial Americans founded communities they sometimes called "religious experiments" or "plantations of religion" (ibid.). The Puritans, in particular, were looking for a way to serve God and so they built Godly cities that were to be ruled by the word of God (Friedman, 1993). For example, the Puritans of the Massachusetts Bay colony thought they were on an "errand into the wilderness." They sought to build, through their communities, a beacon of light that would serve as an example to the entire world. In fact, when John Winthrop, leader of the Massachusetts colony, arrived in Boston Harbor, he proclaimed in a sermon that "the eyes of the world will be upon us." If the colony and its Christian mandate failed, "we shall be a by-word (i.e., a laughing stock) among the nations" (Gomes, 1996:54).

Religion permeated every aspect of life, if for no other reason than religious institutions had to be rebuilt in the colonies (Bonomi, 1986). But even as colonists came to the New World under the banner of religious freedom, they did not tolerate religious diversity within their communities ("Religion was 'salt,'" 1998). The Puritans of New England and the Anglicans of Virginia demanded uniformity of religion (ibid.). What they did share in common, though, was belief in the notion of predestination.

The colonists held that there was no need to alter the existing social divisions as this represented God's ordained order. To interfere with this order was tantamount to interfering with God's will. Consequently, those born into poverty were to remain poor and those born into wealth were to remain wealthy. The ideal Christian community was one where the strong would bear the weak and the rich would relieve the burdens of the poor. In contrast to Europe, the poor of colonial America were not viewed as a threat to social order. Instead, the poor were viewed positively because they provided the wealthy an opportunity to do good deeds. It was only the willfully idle or able-bodied poor who were viewed with disfavor. Colonial American's adherence to predestination doctrine has, in retrospect, been termed "grim determinism." Man was to live out his lot in life, content in knowing that it was the will of God.

CRIME AS SIN

In eighteenth-century America, religion entered into all discourse, marked all observations, and gave meaning to every private and public crisis—crime included (Bonomi, 1986). An offense against God was a crime against society, and a crime against society was an offense against God. Yet, as with poverty, colonial Americans did not perceive crime as a social pathology or "problem" to be studied and solved. They were not consumed with discovering crime's causes and cures because they already knew why crime occurred and what to do about it. Crime, like any sin, was an expected consequence of the depraved human condition and the active forces of the devil. Like sin, crime was to be punished. Criminal behavior was blurred with sinful behavior; crime, sin, guilt, and punishment were understood as one.

In the absence of such distinctions, colonists judged a number of behaviors to be criminal, ranging from profanity and drunkenness to the more obvious crimes of theft and murder. Even trivial transgressions, such as flirting and gossiping (idle tongues), were considered criminal. More serious were crimes of idolatry, blasphemy, witchcraft, and other violations of the faith. For example, until the mid–eighteenth century, the Puritans called for strict punishment for violations of religious laws, such as failing to attend church or failing to pray on the sabbath. New York and Boston went so far as to forbid traffic through the city on the sabbath, unless one was traveling to church or to some other urgent lawful occasion (Bonomi, 1986). Drinking and gambling on the Lord's day were tolerated virtually nowhere. The importance of the sabbath in colonial Law is illustrated by the following charges recorded in historical court documents:

> In 1668 in Salem, the Kitchins were fined for "frequent absenting themselves from the public worship of God on the Lord's days."

> In 1682 in Maine, Andrew Searle paid a fine of five shillings for "not frequenting the publique worship of god" and instead "wandering from place to place upon the Lord's days."

> Virginia law in 1662 required everyone who had "no lawfull excuse" to resort "diligently to their parish church and chappell."

> In Plymouth, in 1758 a young boy was brought to court for "irreverently behaving himself by chalking the back of one young girl with Chalk."

> In 1656, a Boston man sat in the stocks for two hours because of "lewd and unseemly behavior" on the Sabbath. He kissed his wife having returned from three years at sea. (Friedman, 1993)

Colonists were also mindful of behaviors that would unduly burden the community. Consequently, criminal codes could "assist" parents in child-rearing. Incorrigible children could be severely punished, even executed, as respect for parental authority was considered a precursor to religious discipline and civic responsibility. A 1648 Massachusetts law prescribed capital punishment for any youth over the age of sixteen who "shall curse or smite their natural father or mother." Even sexual offenses were viewed in the context of responsibility to community. Contrary to popular belief, colonists were not preoccupied with sexual offenses solely because of their grave moral implications. They were concerned with the impact of illicit sexual activity on the well-being of the community. For example, it was feared that if a master impregnated a slave/servant, the community would have to bear the responsibility of supporting that child. In deference to community standards, criminal codes were also used to control prices and wages. It was unlawful for merchants to gain unreasonable profits through the sale of goods. A carpenter was in fact convicted of charging an excessive fee and sent to the very stocks he constructed and overpriced.

While some semblance of a criminal code existed, what constituted illegalities tended to be culturally determined (Norton, 1991). Legislators of the day often wrote purposely broad statutes, assuming that they and the community shared the same values (ibid.). Since they believed everyone, at least those of English descent, agreed on what constituted criminal behavior, there was no need to define crime precisely. In effect, the community defined what was acceptable behavior. A law might declare a certain behavior as criminal, but if the community viewed it as harmless, then it went unreported. Conversely, if no law existed for behavior the community found reprehensible (e.g., a severely beaten child), then members of the community would seek remedy together (ibid.).

Most crimes, then, whatever their nature, were brought to the attention of the courts by residents, not by sheriffs or constables. For example, Maryland relied almost exclusively on the reports of victims or witnesses. Broad wording as a basis for its criminal justice system is illustrated by the following Maryland statute:

"The Lawes of the Province and in defect of Lawe, then according to the sound discretion of the said Governor or other Chiefe Judge and such of the Councill as shall bee present in Court" (quoted in Norton, 1991:126). This did not mean that the colonies codified nothing. Specific statutes often existed for crimes considered to be most troublesome, such as runaway servants and servant women who bore bastard children (ibid.).

Though a wide range of behaviors was considered criminal in colonial America, the majority of crimes committed in colonial America were not, by today's standards, serious. Historical records show that fornication, lewd behavior, drunkenness, petty theft, assaults, and Lord's day violations were the most frequently prosecuted crimes (Powers, 1966). Historical records in New York show that men overwhelmingly made up the ranks of the accused and criminal, accounting for 94 percent of the violent crimes and 74 percent of

Table 3-1. Crimes Most Frequently Committed
by Women

Type	Percentage	Number
Bastardy	37.7	58
Running Away	10.4	16
Infanticide	7.1	11
Adultery	6.5	10
Theft	5.8	9
Fornication	5.2	8
Mistreating Servants	3.9	6
Assault	3.2	5
Murder	3.2	5
Other	16.9	27
TOTAL	99.9	155

Source: Norton (1991).

the thefts. In Massachusetts, between 1673 and 1774, women committed only 20 percent of serious crimes. Women were most often charged with the offenses of witchcraft, fornication, bastardy and infanticide. Tables 3-1 and 3-2 identify the crimes most frequently committed by men and women. Still, the crimes listed comprised only 2 percent of all offenses, which again speaks to the diversity of behaviors deemed criminal.

Table 3-2. Crimes Most Frequently Committed
by Men

Type	Percentage	Number
Contempt of authority, treason	14.5	80
Neglect of duty	12.8	70
Theft	10.0	55
Assault	7.5	41
Running away	7.5	41
Bastardy	5.5	30
Murder	5.3	29
Drunkenness	4.9	27
Killing animals	4.4	24
Aiding runaways	3.3	18
Mistreating servants	2.9	16
Profanity, blasphemy	2.7	15
Other and unknown	18.8	100
TOTAL	100.1	546

Source: Norton (1991).

PUNISHMENT FOR PUNISHMENT'S SAKE

In colonial America, the strong sense of community and religion lessened the need for formal law enforcement mechanisms except in times of mass disturbance or an outside enemy threat. The law enforcement that did exist tended to be unorganized, understaffed, and comprised of the most elderly members of the community. There was little need for day-to-day surveillance for detection of wrongdoing. In their unyielding observation of each day's activities, colonists were, in effect, self-policed. Strangers were few, and neighbors protected neighbors and reported wrongdoing. However, when the informal social control mechanisms of family, community, and church failed, colonists employed relatively harsh punishments. Given the importance of preserving a sense of community, it was not unusual that crimes committed by non–community members were treated more harshly than those from members within the community. An outsider who committed vagabonding or begging would be banished or shamed before the community, usually by whipping or stoning. However, a member of the community would be treated more leniently for the same offense. This often led to the distinction between responses as either welfare oriented (community members) or punishment oriented (outsiders).

Methods of punishment in colonial America consisted primarily of fines, whippings, mutilation, shaming techniques, banishment, and death. Because the colonists had no real expectation of eradicating crime, they did not develop preventive or rehabilitative programs. This did not mean colonists were indifferent or cynical about crime. They were just not consumed with identifying and treating the causes because of their strongly held religious beliefs that crime was ordained by God and beyond mankind's efforts.

Fines were by far the most frequently imposed alternative to corporal punishment and were used nearly three times as often. The amount of the fine was left to the discretion of the judge, though there was an attempt to tailor the fine amount to the particular offense and offender. There were fines for just about any offense, including unauthorized borrowing of horses and peddling quack medicines (O'Toole, 1998). For example, an ambitious servant who engaged in freelance trading without his master's permission was fined and flogged (ibid.).

Fines were primarily reserved for the propertied class. Those without property, namely, slaves, had their period of servitude extended or were whipped. A slave master and a slave could both be charged with the same offense, but the master could pay his fine in tobacco leaves, while the slave paid his fine in whippings.

Whippings were the second most frequently imposed punishment in colonial America. They were administered primarily for women found guilty of bastardy and insubordination by servants or slaves. In the latter case, the whippings could be carried out privately within the home. Servants, slaves, and women were particularly vulnerable to whippings because they lacked the money or property for paying fines. Fining a woman usually meant fining her husband. To ensure that the woman was the one punished, judges resorted to whipping when they deemed it appropriate. Officials were even reluctant to impose economic penalties on widows or single women, fearing their estates or dependent children would be harmed as a result (Norton, 1991).

Because whippings required what everyone had—a body—few people escaped some form of corporal punishment in colonial society. Whippings could be administered for such offenses as repeatedly failing to observe the Sabbath, sex offenses, lying, and idleness. Stealing a loaf of bread, a sheet, or a pair of shoes could also invite whippings. In Massachusetts, 46 percent of those sentenced to whippings had been convicted of sex offenses. As with fines, the number of whippings administered was left to the discretion of the judge. Generally, the number of whippings to be administered for a certain crime was vaguely articulated. Generalizations such as "to be whipped" or "to be severely whipped" provided the only guidelines. What constituted "severe," however, is unclear. Some colonies relied on biblical scripture for guidance. In Massachusetts, for instance, the maximum number of whippings was set at forty, as dictated in a verse from the Old Testament. In other colonies, the offense of immorality could result in forty lashes and false accusations by servants regarding their masters' chastity could warrant one hundred lashes. Bearing an illegitimate child could invite twelve lashes.

Whipping posts were located near the site of court sessions. Whippings were usually delivered on a court day when the colonists had gathered from miles around to attend the session (ibid.). Whippings not only inflicted physical pain, but they were intended to be intensely humiliating; men and women were required to strip to the waist during the ordeal (ibid.). They were moral degradation ceremonies in which the crowd played an important part.

Colonists also relied on banishment and various shaming techniques. Banishment was typically reserved for offenders viewed as a permanent danger, for recidivists, and for noncommunity members. Though banishment may not seem like a severe sanction, its harshness must be considered in the context of the importance of community. Recall that even outsiders of good standing were questioned and references could be required for admission into a new community. It was not likely then that a banished offender would be welcomed into a new community. He was more likely to encounter alienation and rejection and could even face incidental death, particularly if the punishment was executed during harsh winter months. If the offender attempted to return to the community from which he was banished, he could be charged with the offense of "defiance of a banishment order." This offense was punishable by death.

Shaming techniques assumed a variety of forms, including the stocks, pillory branding, letter wearing, mild mutilation, and the public cage. Though these types of punishment have become hallmarks of the Colonial Era, their reputation far exceeded their use. For example, various forms of branding, heavy locks on legs (runaway servant), cleft stick on forked tongue, involving the placement and wearing of a stick in the mouth for swearing and spreading rumors, and cutting off ears were rare sentences. Yet, when imposed, these highly public punishments did not go unnoticed: they subjected the offender to ridicule, and verbal and physical abuse (pelting with stones) by community passers-by.

Colonists employed harsh measures for recidivists, including death, and what can be termed "shock" death. In the case of shock death, an offender would receive the sentence of death by hanging but would later be granted a reprieve. The reprieve, however, came only after the offender had proceeded through each and every ritual leading up to the execution. To elaborate, the offender would be led from the jail out to the gallows, with the mask placed over his head and the noose placed around his neck, and then wait for the trap door to open, ending his life. The sentenced offender could remain at the gallows for more than three hours, fully expecting to be executed. Finally, the noose and mask were removed and the offender was informed that his life had been spared.

The actual sentence of death by hanging could apply to recidivists, murderers, arsonists, horse thieves, and incorrigible youth. The Body of Liberties of 1641 established twelve offenses as punishable by death. By 1654, twenty-five offenses were identified by this Massachusetts statute as punishable by death. Though the death penalty could apply to a wide range of offenses, it was, in fact, used sparingly. Between 1630 and 1692, fifty-six persons were executed in Massachusetts. The offenses for which they were executed included adultery, arson, treason, murder, witchcraft, bestiality, rape, and defiance of banishment. Pennsylvania had the mildest criminal code, permitting only the offense of murder to be punishable by death. Prior to the American Revolution, ninety-four offenders were executed in Pennsylvania, amounting to approximately one per year.

Though infrequent, execution was a "deeply spiritual experience for all those who witnessed" it (Friedman, 1993). Whether the sentence was death or shock death, the full impact of these punishments depended on the presence and participation of the judges and the community. Oratory and high drama were integral parts of the punishment. The process of condemnation required an "audience" that anxiously awaited satisfaction via confessions of guilt and visible expressions of remorse by the repentant sinner/offender.

Crowds of people gathered, many of whom even traveled long distances. At a hanging in 1827 in New York, it was estimated that between thirty and forty thousand attended.

LESS THAN PUNISHMENT

As in Europe, the benefit of clergy, jails, and workhouses also existed in colonial America. By 1600, eligibility for the benefit of clergy had become so relaxed that it protected not only church officials but anyone who could read. The criteria for qualification had eased considerably: the only requirement was the reading of a particular Bible passage, which was nearly always the same. The passage came to be termed the "neck verse" (ibid.) because it saved many offenders from death by hanging. It was not long before even women and slaves could claim benefit of clergy. By 1706, benefit of clergy was so diluted it was abolished.

In colonial America, jails were not instruments of punishment. They were places to hold offenders awaiting trial. Table 3-3, which identifies the use of

Table 3-3. Jail Sentences in Colonial America: The Case of Essex and Middlesex Counties

Date	Punishments	Percentage involving jail
Essex County		
1650–1659	471	3.3
1660–1669	742	7.9
1670–1679	719	1.1
1700–1709	244	<1.0
1710–1719	305	0
1720–1727	305	<1.0
1744–1749	127	0
1750–1759	180	1.1
1760–1769	285	<1.0
Middlesex County		
1650–1659	117	5.1
1671–1680	218	3.2
1700–1709	121	1.5
1710–1719	192	0
1720–1729	333	1.2
1730–1739	375	1.6
1740–1749	199	3.0
1750–1759	180	<1.0
1760–1769	188	<1.0

Source: Kuntz (1988).

jail in two Boston counties, illustrates how "insignificant" the jail was as a punishment in the Colonial Era.

In colonial America, jails resembled any other house in the community both externally and internally. Offenders were housed in rooms, not cells, and prison uniforms and lockstep marching were nonexistent. The keeper (warden) was expected to be married, and his family, along with the offenders, resided under one roof. Nevertheless, the conditions of the jail were not as pleasant as the family model would suggest. Offenders were required to pay for their keep, and there was no attempt to separate offenders by gender, age, or offense severity. Women and children were detained with men and others who had committed violent crimes. Jails were overcrowded, disorderly, and unsanitary, and there were few, if any, security measures to prevent escapes.

Workhouses, on the other hand, combined the functions of a poorhouse and a jail. As in Europe, workhouses were designed for keeping and setting the unproductive to work. The workhouse was used for training and caring for the poor as well as for idlers, beggars, prostitutes, and other minor offenders.

Overall, punishment in colonial America emphasized condemnation, repentance, and shaming. However, the idea of punishing in order to deter others was not completely lost on colonial officials. The public (e.g., whipping) or private (fine) nature of the punishment could depend on the crime itself. If authorities feared the offense might spawn imitators, or was a serious problem, punishment was more likely to be made public (Norton, 1991).

Punishment was also considered to be a moral obligation of the community. To neglect this obligation was a crime itself, equally subject to the wrath of God. While colonists did not expect to eliminate crime through punishment, they did hope to comply with God's wishes in their treatment of criminals.

SUMMARY AND DISCUSSION

The Colonial Era lasted just under two centuries. Colonial communities were small and close-knit and characterized by social cohesion. Everyone knew one another, and there existed a strong and necessary level of community solidarity. In a harsh and unfamiliar new world, community members depended upon one another for daily survival. Daily life was equally structured by the church and associated religious beliefs, as evidenced by the notion of grim determinism and colonists' views on crime and punishment. Family, community, economic necessity, religion, and related ideological forces (e.g., grim determinism) contributed to a social context in which specific punishment ideas and practices were viewed as necessary and appropriate to the colonial American way of life. It was not until 1790 that the foundations of family, a subsistence economy, community, and church began to weaken. The American Revolution marked the beginning of a new political age and much more. As the American landscape changed geographically, demographically, and economically, so too did ideas about crime and punishment. The onset of the Industrial Revolution, westward expansion, and social optimism ushered in the era of penal modernity.

4

Punishment and Deterrence in the Period of Transition (1790–1830)

INTRODUCTION

THE CLOSE OF THE EIGHTEENTH CENTURY constituted a period of transition in a number of respects. Between 1790 and 1830, the new republic experienced rapid and marked social changes that culminated in what is now referred to as modernity. The norms and social values consistent with capitalism, democracy, and egalitarianism were established during this period (Elkins and McKitrick, 1993). Nationhood also established a "centralizing presence" that was absent in Colonial America. For example, a federal government precipitated the development of federal laws—seventeen crimes against the national government were enacted in 1790—as well as the development of a postal system and a national road, lighthouse, and navigational system. Despite numerous developments that were establishing a new American way of life, the ultimate fate of the nation still hung in the balance. Fear, excitement, and internal dissent were simultaneously prevalent as Americans reminisced and longed for the perceived security and solidarity of the colonial way of life.

As colonial Americans' previous preoccupation with crimes of sin and morality faded, attention was turned to crimes of property and violence. The frequency and seriousness of crime was commonly considered to be on the rise and cries of alarm could be heard in both the developing cities and countryside. Citizens and civic leaders complained of drinking, gambling, prostitution, robbery, and a general sense of lawlessness. Crime was now believed to be a social "problem" in need of remedy, rather than as a predictable consequence of original sin. The family, church, and community could no longer absorb the rising numbers of poor, insane, and criminal. The informal mechanisms of control that prevailed in colonial America were ill-suited for the rapid transformations that were taking place. This chapter identifies selected historical contingencies that helped shape particular ideas and prac-

35

tices related to crimes and its punishments during this approximate forty-year period.

POSTREVOLUTIONARY AMERICA

The Demise of Community Cohesion
The parallels between postrevolutionary America and colonial America are difficult to discern. Demographic and economic shifts, in particular, had disrupted the order of the small, closely knit, and contained communities of colonial America. Between 1790 and 1830, the nation's population exploded as did the number and density of cities. In 1790, approximately two hundred thousand Americans lived in towns with more than twenty-five thousand residents, and no American city had more than fifty thousand residents. By 1830, the number of individuals living in a city with more than twenty-five thousand exceeded one million and approximately five hundred thousand lived in cities with more than fifty thousand residents (Rothman, 1971). In this forty-year period, the population of Massachusetts doubled, the population of Pennsylvania tripled, and the population of New York increased fivefold. More specifically, between 1790 and 1830, the populations of Boston increased by 84 percent, Philadelphia by 114 percent, Baltimore by 156 percent, and New York by 191 percent. Regions of the country that were once desolate, namely, the Midwest, now had over three million inhabitants.

Not only were communities becoming towns, and towns becoming cities, but factories began to dot the Eastern American landscape. Commercial activity boomed from $20.2 million in exports in 1790 to $108.3 million in exports by 1807. The number of corporations in colonial America totaled only seven, but in the first decade following the Revolutionary War, there were forty corporations. By the turn of the nineteenth century, five hundred such corporations existed.

In the new republic, social, economic, and geographic mobility had replaced social, economic, and geographic permanence. Westward expansion and the first wave of eastern seaboard immigration altered customary relationships. Lured by the intrigue of opportunity, numerous youth left home earlier. Patriarchal authority was eroding, as were colonial notions of the traditional family (Elkins and McKitrick, 1993). The communalism that had sustained the colonial lifestyle was giving way to a lifestyle of individualism. The new entrepreneurs made fun of "old fashioned farmers who could not bear to work alone, who were always having to call a neighbor." They charged that "while it may be very pleasant to have our neighbors work with us, it tends to encourage idleness and neglect of business" (Birdsall, 1970).

The impending transition was viewed with considerable trepidation. While the beginnings of commercialism brought new conveniences and luxuries, the nation was antiurban at its core. Still able to recall the pristine colonial American setting, citizens feared that American cities would become decaying metropolises. Americans regarded London and other large European cities as cesspools of greed, poverty, and material excess. The period of transition, then, was a period of searching for a national identity. How would America define itself? How should America present itself to the rest of the world? How should America's economic life be organized? The United States was stuck between two worlds: the world to be lost and the world to be gained.

The Enlightenment

A sense of the world to be gained was shaped in large part by *the Enlightenment,* also known as the secular rationalist movement. The Enlightenment movement originated in England and spread quickly throughout the European continent. Writers from England (Jeremy Bentham, David Hume, John Locke, Thomas Paine), France (Montesquieu, Voltaire), and Italy (Cesare Beccaria) radically transformed conventional beliefs about man, society, and the role of the state.

Secular rationalists exalted the principles of utilitarianism, liberalism, and equality over what had been viewed as savage, arbitrary, and irrational views of the world. They held that man was the supreme achievement of God's creativity and ingenuity and to devalue man's preeminence was an insult to God (Barnes, 1972). The fate of mankind was controllable, and not dependent on divine providence or the salvation of one's soul. Science, informed by human reasoning, would unravel the mysteries of life, and bring a measure of certainty to the future. Man was no longer viewed as a helpless and dependent sinner, and God was no longer viewed as a judgmental patriarch whose arbitrary demands must be met. God was a benevolent higher power that desired the general welfare and happiness of mankind. Therefore, the chief concern of the men of the Enlightenment was to procure the ideal relationship between man, society, and the state.

America was well situated to feel the effects of the intellectual forces from Europe. British rationalists and French philosophers had lived and traveled in the colonies, particularly Philadelphia. Their ideas shaped the content of the U.S. Constitution, the Bill of Rights, and the structure of the new system of government. With recollections of England's tyranny still fresh, power was viewed as a "thorn in liberty's side" (Elkins and McKitrick, 1993). The acquisition and concentration of power were not to be desired. The new nation sought virtuous leaders who would abolish any traces of the old parochial laws of English and colonial rule. Americans despised the patronage of British kingship and its "above the law" arrogance. They were equally opposed to the rigid theocracy of colonial America.

The common enemy of the new nation was the legal codes of the old regime. Colonial laws and customs were considered crude, backward, arbitrary, chaotic, irrational, and barbaric. Neither king nor God was to rule in the new republic. Instead, reasoned free men were to be the arbiters of their own fate and justice. This did not mean that religion and a revolutionary spirit were opposing forces. In the colonies, for example, many religious leaders were ardent supporters of independence. It was written that many a "fighting parson" would fire up the congregation for the cause of independence by tearing off his clerical robe to reveal the uniform of a rebel militiaman ("Religion was 'salt,'" 1998). Some (e.g., Hutson) even argue that without the clerics' approval, the revolution would not have been successful (quoted in ibid.). However, the broadly held ideology of grim determinism of colonialism was pushed aside in favor of a belief in the ability of mankind to manipulate destiny. However, the spirit of freedom did have its limits. In the new republic, freedom carried the expectation that all men would be diligent, hard-working, and sober.

CRIME AS FREE WILL

The impact of scientific developments on intellectual life was not limited to the disciplines of physics, math, and biology. The Enlightenment provided a scientific foundation to the study of human relationships as well. In stark contrast to colonial America, where sin and destiny explained the presence of crime, in the nineteenth century, archaic penal codes and free will explained the presence of crime. As indicated, the leaders of the new republic were greatly influenced by the Enlightenment and were familiar with the writings of Jeremy Bentham, John Howard, and Cesare Beccaria, to name a few. In *An Introduction to the Principles of Morals and Legislation* (1789), Jeremy Bentham challenged the assumption that life was predetermined by God and therefore was unalterable. His principal argument was that mankind was ruled by the two masters: pleasure and pain. Pleasure and pain, not God, dictated the words, thoughts, and actions of individuals. It was held that man was fundamentally "hedonistic"; he was driven by the desire to maximize pleasure and minimize pain. Bentham argued that despite all efforts, man could not free himself of the overriding subjection to seek that which afforded pleasure and to avoid that which afforded pain. He termed this law of human nature the "principle of utility."

According to Bentham, man, being bound by the principle of utility, would necessarily engage in behavior that was purposeful. Consequently, man weighed the anticipated intensity, duration, certainty, remoteness, fecundity, purity, and extent of the pleasure and pain derived from his actions. Fecundity referred to the chance that the initial pleasure or pain would be followed by sensations of the same kind (i.e., pleasure would be followed by pleasure, or pain by pain). Purity referred to the chance that the initial pleasure or pain would not be followed by sensations of the opposite kind (i.e., pleasure would not be followed by pain, or pain by pleasure). Extent referred to the number of persons affected by the pleasure or pain. While Bentham did not expect that every decision would involve this degree of mental scrutiny, he maintained that the process of making decisions would be approximate. These various considerations, he claimed, would "always be kept in view."

If it was true that man was not ruled by abstract forces of good and evil, then it was also true that whether or not man was a criminal was based on his own free will. The criminal of the nineteenth century was no longer a sinner to be punished in accordance with biblical principles for offenses against God and the moral order. The criminal of nineteenth century was a threat to property and social stability and was to be punished in accordance with legal principles for offenses against the state.

PUNISHMENT AND DETERRENCE

The Philosophy of Deterrence
The assumption that criminal behavior was a function of free will was reflected in the legal reforms of the day. In 1822, Edward Livingston (quoted in Friedman, 1993) reaffirmed that "laws to be obeyed and administered, must be known, to be known, they must be read, to be administered they must be stated and compared. To know them is the right of the people." The crime message being communicated to the new republic was clear. Penal codes needed to be plainly articulated, codified, uniform, and simple. Only then could a rational man calculate the costs of crime. Colonial penal codes, on the other hand, were so severe, inconsistent, and irrational as to encourage deviant behavior.

In *Essays on Crimes and Punishment* ([1764] 1963), Cesare Beccaria also alluded to the relationship between free will, criminal behavior, and archaic laws. Beccaria declared that "if we glance at the pages of history, we will find that the laws which surely ought to be the compacts of free men, have been, for the most part, a mere tool of the passions of some." Beccaria asserted that barbarism had no place in punishment for it was not the intensity of punishment that had the greatest effect on the human spirit, but its duration. He maintained that "our sensibility is more easily and more permanently affected by slight but repeated impressions than by a powerful but momentary action." This sentiment was also echoed by French philosophers; to impose suffering upon anyone because they have made another suffer is an act of cruelty, condemned by reason and humanity. It was generally believed that brutality in punishment only led to the arbitrary administration of punishment. For example, judges or juries often acquitted the accused or ignored the law rather than impose death for a minor offense.

Beccaria maintained that a punishment that was certain had a far greater impact than a severe punishment that might never occur. He further declared that the more closely the punishment followed the crime, the more just and useful it would be. Put simply, punishment had to be certain and prompt. Beyond the principle of certainty and promptness, Beccaria also advocated proportionality in punishment. The notion of proportionality referred to the now proverbial assertion that the punishment must fit the crime. Punishment should never be excessive, only severe enough to deter. The French philosopher Montesquieu similarly argued, "It is essential that there be a proportion between crime and punishment because it is essential that the restraint upon commission of a major crime be more powerful than the restraint upon commission of a less serious one" (Montesquieu, [1748] 1966). Altogether, the effectiveness of punishment depended on its duration, promptness, certainty, and proportionality. The key to eliminating criminal behavior was the establishment of a penal code that prohibited unbridled discretion, favoritism, and oppression.

These men of the Enlightenment did not denounce punishment, per se, but they did denounce the prevailing forms and functions of punishment. In their view, punishment was justified only if the harm it prevented was greater than the harm inflicted on the offender. It was reasoned that unless punishment could deter crime, it was only adding to human suffering. Punishment was to be justified on the grounds of serving a greater social good, namely, prevention. The philosophy of deterrence advocated a forward-looking justification of punishment. It was to prevent future criminal acts committed by the apprehended offender (specific deterrence) or potential offenders (general deterrence) by way of the former serving as an example to the latter. Consistent with the intellectual thinking of the day, punishment was intended to serve a function other than mere vengeance and moral condemnation for past misdeeds. It was now premised on the utilitarian function of crime prevention.

The writings of Bentham and Beccaria, in particular, formed what has since come to be termed "classicism." Classicists focused on the legal character of the offense, rather than the character of the offender. As Radzinowicz (1994) noted, "The classical school exhorts men to study justice," not criminals. It was the punishment of the offense that was of interest to these reformers, not the pathologies of the offender. The classical school of thought assumed that all men were of one rational mind and therefore subject to one rational system of laws.

To fully appreciate the "certain" and "swift" requirements of deterrence, the specific role of police must be acknowledged. During the first half of the nineteenth century, police forces were created. These police forces were to be full-time agencies whose functions were crime prevention, keeping the peace, and apprehending criminals. Before the establishment of full-time police, social order was maintained through watchmen who made rounds at night to deal with disturbances and constables who provided daytime law enforcement. They arrested vagrants and drunks and delivered offenders before the grand jury. Assisting the watchmen and constables were vigilance committees or yeomen, or volunteer part-time police. There were problems and limits to this part-time, haphazard approach to law enforcement, and, with the 1829 establishment of the London Metropolitan Police, change was inspired in the new republic. While a pattern of increasing law enforcement was already underway in the new republic, it was not until after 1830 that a fully deployed professional police force was formed. The belief was that if crime was to be successfully combated and punishment was to be ultimately effective, a more systematic and reliable method of detecting and apprehending criminals would be necessary. This is not to say, however, that this early version of a modern police force was organized, systematic, or reliable in its crime-fighting efforts.

Penal Code Reform and Penal Confinement
Consistent with the other transitions of the day, American penal thought moved away from biblically based arguments. By the 1820s, most states had amended their penal codes to reflect the various classical school principles. In 1793, William Bradford, justice of the Supreme Court of Pennsylvania and attorney general of the United States, expressed the mood of much of the nation toward the old penal codes:

> We perceive, by this detail, that the severity of our criminal law is an exotic plant, and not the native growth of Pennsylvania. It has been endured, but, I believe, has never been a favorite. The religious opinions of many of our citizens were in opposition to it; and as soon as the principles of Beccaria were disseminated, they found a soil that was prepared to receive them. During our connection with Great Britain no reform was attempted; but as soon as we separated from her, the public sentiment disclosed itself and this benevolent undertaking was enjoined by the constitution. This was one of the first fruits of liberty and confirms the remark of Montesquieu, "That, as freedom advances, the severity of the penal law decreases." (Bradford, [1793] 1972)

One of the first casualties of the new penal codes was the death sentence. After the American Revolution, an attack on the death penalty was intensified. The allure of the hangman had lost its luster, as illustrated by Quaker William Penn, who spoke of "the wickedness of exterminating, where it was possible to reform" (Gorringe, 1996:154). For example, in 1790, the Pennsylvania legislature abolished the death penalty for robbery, burglary, and sodomy. New York repealed the death penalty except for murder and first-degree arson. Virginians, as of 1796, utilized the death penalty only for murder and certain offenses committed by slaves. All other states followed by sharply curtailing their use of death as a punishment.

It should be acknowledged, however, that the widespread attacks on the death penalty were not motivated by benevolence alone. Rather, the abolishment of the death penalty was a pragmatic move aimed at fulfilling the goals of certainty, predictability, and, ultimately, deterrence. In fact, it has been argued that the reforms in capital punishment were driven by a desire to increase rather than decrease [the certainty of] the punishment of offenders (Kuntz, 1988). Juries often failed to convict many offenders, property offenders in particular, because death was considered too severe a penalty. Consequently, offenders were going free without penalty, though their guilt was not in question. This problem was articulated in a Philadelphia report entitled, "Considerations on the Penalty of Death." In that report, Benjamin Rush declared:

> Punishment of murder by death multiplies murder, from the difficulty it creates of convicting persons who are guilty of it. Humanity, revolting at the idea of the severity and certainty of a capital punishment, often steps in, and collects such evidence in favor of a murderer, as screens him from death altogether, or palliates his crime into manslaughter. If the punishment of murder consisted in long confinement, and hard labor, it would be proportioned to the measure of our feelings of justice, and every member of society would be a watchman, or a magistrate to apprehend a destroyer of human life, and to bring him to punishments. (quoted in Kuntz, 1988)

William Bradford's "An Enquiry How Far the Punishment of Death is Necessary in Pennsylvania" provided a similar sentiment. He stated:

> In my opinion the certainty of conviction of a crime punishable by imprisonment by death, and if juries were permitted, by law, to relieve themselves of the terrible responsibility which they now feel in capital cases, growing out of the existence of the death-penalty, convictions would be had where acquittals now take place. (quoted in ibid.)

Finally, in 1826 Roberts Vaux stated what had become conventional wisdom among many penal reformers:

> There is an aversion in Pennsylvania from inflicting death; and the difficulty of convicting when the crime is so great as to defeat in many instances the purpose of justice. The prisoner who has deliberately extinguished the life of a fellow creature may, for want of that clear evidence which our human judges and

juries rightfully require, receive, in place of the merited sentence, some very inadequate punishment or escape altogether. (quoted in ibid.)

Reducing the severity of the penal codes applied to bodily punishments as well. An enlightened system of punishment was to be predicated on moderation, dignity, and decorum, rather than bloodlust or raw animal-like instincts. Therefore, provisions for whippings and all other forms of corporal punishment soon disappeared from the penal codes. For example, the Act of 1791 in Pennsylvania ordered that there would be no more branding (Barnes, 1972). Moreover, in an age of rapid growth and social migration, shaming and banishment were no longer appropriate. Ultimately, the public aspects of punishment vanished.

The precise reasons for the new interest in privacy have been the subject of much debate. Some have argued that such displays repulsed the softening sensibilities of the middle and upper classes (Spierenburg, 1984). It has also been proposed that the spectacle of death and corporal punishments was inconsistent with the political requisites of the new republic. The vulgarity and drama of these bodily punishments were part of the old regime's attempt to demonstrate the infinite and awesome power of the king or God. A democracy, on the other hand, was premised on the idea that all men were created equal and deserving of an equally reasoned and rational system of punishment.

It can be reasonably assumed that the deprivation of liberty through incarceration provided an ideal and rational substitute to public shame and bodily torture. It imposed a punishment that conformed to the Beccarian principles of predictability, certainty, and proportionality of duration, while responding to the various needs and demands of the new republic. Incarceration concealed the strong arm of the state and deprived men of a revolutionary heritage of their most cherished value, liberty. Moreover, the severity of punishment (i.e., the degree of liberty denied) could be calibrated in direct relation to the seriousness of the offense through the duration of imprisonment. It also enabled American reformers to reduce the number of capital offenses while reassuring that meaningful punishment would be administered. The following sentences as prescribed by Pennsylvania law— which served as a model for the nation—illustrate the dramatic shift from the old way of punishing to the new.

According to Pennsylvania law, those convicted of robbery, burglary, sodomy should forfeit all property and be sentenced to not more than ten years at hard labor in the jail or house of corrections. Horse stealing was penalized by full restoration to the owner, the forfeiture of an equal amount to the state, and imprisonment at hard labor for not more than seven years. Simple larceny was punishable by full restitution, forfeiture of a like amount to the state, and imprisonment for a term of no more than three years. It was also stipulated in the Pennsylvania statutes that any other noncapital offenses that were previously punished by burning in the hand, cutting off ears, nailing the ears to the pillory, or whipping should now be punished by imprisonment at hard labor for two years or less. The offenses qualifying as capital offenses were also reduced. Consequently, second-degree murder drew a sentence of five to eighteen years in prison and manslaughter two to ten years (six to fourteen years for a second offense). Arson resulted in a sentence of five to twelve years. Rape was punished by ten to twenty-one years in prison, and counterfeiting was punished by four to fifteen years in prison and a fine of up to one thousand dollars (Barnes, 1972).

Radical penal code reform clearly necessitated the establishment of a comprehensive institutional system. However, in the rush to abandon old punishment practices, little thought was given to what this substitute of incarceration should look like and how it should operate. The old colonial jails and workhouses could hardly suffice, but they would have to. Consequently, the earliest American prisons were poorly conceived and operated. Essentially, they were makeshift facilities. For example, in 1773, in Connecticut, a prison was fashioned out of copper mines (Friedman, 1993). In 1790, under the new name of Newgate, it was deemed little more than a dungeon. Contemporary observers described it as "horrid gloom," where prisoners were heavily shackled and ate pickled pork thrown on the floor (ibid.). The Walnut Street Jail in Pennsylvania was also converted into a prison. The improvised facilities could hardly accommodate the increasing numbers of prisoners created by the new laws. Not surprisingly, overcrowding became a major problem for the various makeshift prison facilities.

In New York, hundreds of offenders were pardoned because there was no place to house them. In 1812, 740 inmates were pardoned. In 1813, 198 offenders were admitted and 134 of them were pardoned. In 1814, 213 offenders were admitted and 176 of them were pardoned. Between 1792 and 1822, 5,069 offenders were admitted and 2,819 were pardoned (Barnes, 1972). Prisoners typically completed no more than 50 percent of their sentence and often felt unduly wronged if no pardon was forthcoming (Kuntz, 1988). Semiannual clemency sessions resulted in the release of forty to fifty convicts simultaneously. Lawyers generated a circuslike atmosphere by swarming the prison gates to bargain with inmates. They often circulated petitions with forged signatures and presented faulty evidence of the offender's reformation to governors (ibid.). Without question, the move to incarceration was fraught with trial and error.

Regardless of the unintended consequences associated with this period of penal transition, incarceration was still considered a vast improvement over the punishments that had gone before. As one warden of the time stated: "When one studies the history of crime and its punishment up to the middle of the eighteenth century, he must be struck with the gruesome fact that the law of crime punishment and penal progress has made its way over dead bodies" (quoted in Rothman, 1980:29). Correcting the architectural defects of the early prison system was the focus of penal reformers in what would subsequently emerge as the age of the penitentiary.

SUMMARY AND DISCUSSION

The American period of transition involved forty years of rapid and unyielding change. These changes included adjusting to independence following the American Revolution, the scant beginnings of industrialization and urbanization, and, most importantly, the significant intellectual shifts associated with the Enlightenment. Together, these changes contributed to a social context in which colonial American versions of crime and punishment were quickly outmoded. The new republic was profoundly optimistic and viewed crime and punishment as problems that could be resolved through careful reasoning. Beccaria and Bentham were not necessarily championing the kind of humanitarian history that has been generally suggested. Rather, they were championing the values of rationality and efficiency. Punishments were to be severe enough to deter, but not so much so that the offender would become notorious, martyred, or economically imprudent (Miller, 1980).

By 1830, the promises of a reformed penal code and swift and sure adjudication and incarceration via the prison had not been fulfilled. Prison overcrowding emerged as one of the foremost problems. The earliest institutions housed a mixture of offenders that included the young, old, men, women, feeble-minded, debtors, witnesses, pretrial felons, and sentenced felons. The perils of such arrangements were quickly discovered and acknowledged, contributing to much needed modifications in the external and internal design of the prison that began in earnest during the decade of the 1830s.

5

Punishment and Reform in
Nineteenth-Century America
(1830–1880s)

INTRODUCTION

REVOLUTIONARY IDEAS do not come fully formed, though it would seem that reformers hold the contrary to be true. Therefore, it is not surprising that America's incarceration system was flawed from the outset. Still, rather than abandon the idea and practice of incarceration altogether, Americans embraced and revised the invention they believed stood between barbarism and enlightenment. Americans maintained an unbroken confidence in their ability to eliminate crime and perfect the prison accordingly.

The penal reform ideas that followed were, in a word, grand. America was a nation of achievers, with a string of economic and political successes behind them that were the envy of the world. So curious were Europeans about America's approach to punishment that emissaries were sent to witness the promise of the prison-turned-penitentiary firsthand. For much of the nineteenth century, U.S. penology centered on the process of reforming the prisons of the late eighteenth century. However, the ideal of reforming the prison so that men too might be reformed was eventually lost in the familiar realities of overcrowding and recidivism. By the Civil War, the hope of eradicating crime through confinement was subsiding both in the progressive-minded North and, most certainly, in the South, where high expectations scarcely existed. One need only to recall the different social contexts of this divided nation to understand the North's steadfast commitment to building a better prison, and the South's commitment to inmate leasing and plantations.

This chapter describes some of the historical contingencies that contributed to the particular social context from which various prison ideas, reforms, and practices emerged between 1830 and 1880. An underlying argument is that beginning in 1830, America was no longer in transition from Colonial America's thoughts and practices nor were Jacksonian Americans content with the period of transition's alternatives to Colonial American practices. Rather, these Americans confronted still another social context, in which a sense of social optimism was blended with a growing sense of disenchantment with the fast-rising cities that together gave rise to new ideas and far-reaching prison reforms and practices. The fundamental thinking was that crime was not so much a product of free will but instead a consequence of a rampant moral and social disease associated with the disorganized and even evil environment of the city. The goal was that the prison would not only reform the criminal through well-organized regimens but serve as a model of proper social organization for the socially disorganized cities as well.

JACKSONIAN AMERICA AND BEYOND

Building a Nation

European observers of the day summed up the state of the nation well when they characterized Americans as "children of the frontier," "democratic men," "products of equality," and "entrepreneurial seekers" (Pessen, 1969). By the 1830s, Americans were enjoying participation in political life and the seemingly boundless opportunity and freedom that the western frontier offered. Democratic principles (as they knew them) were in full force and American patriotism was running high (Rossiter, 1971). Americans even believed they resided in a providential nation, singled out for the purpose of changing human affairs around the world (ibid.). In the words of one contemporary writer, S. A. Stephens (1820), America defined itself as an "exporter of the spirit," "a redeemer," and, interestingly enough, "an asylum" (quoted in ibid.).

By 1830, traces of the communal rural landscape of pre- and postrevolutionary America remained, but the landscape was decidedly more populated, mobile, and commercial. The population shifts that occurred between 1830 and 1880 changed the way Americans lived. These shifts took the forms of massive westward expansion and burgeoning cityscapes along the eastern seaboard. By 1860, 50 percent of the population (i.e., 15.6 million) lived in territories beyond the original thirteen colonies (ibid.). The nation grew from 3.9 million inhabitants in 1790, to 12.9 million in 1830, to 31.5 million in 1860, and to over 50 million by 1880. While an urban revolution had not fully transpired, cities were becoming more important to the vitality of the nation. The urban population increased to twice that of the rural population (Pessen, 1969). In 1790, 5 percent of the population lived in or around urban areas. There were only two cities with populations exceeding 25,000, and not one U.S. city had more than 100,000 residents. By 1860, nearly 30 percent of the population lived in or around urban areas. There were thirty-five cities with populations exceeding 25,000, and ten with populations exceeding 100,000. Between 1830 and 1860, New York grew from 197,000 to 806,000 residents. At the same time, Philadelphia's population grew from 80,000 to 566,000 and Boston's population grew from 61,000 to 178,000. The first wave of immigration (between 1820 and 1860) brought 5 million new immigrants to America. The second wave (between 1860 and 1890) brought an additional 13.5 million. In New York City alone, 3.5 million immigrants arrived between 1830 and 1860 and, by 1855, half of the population was foreign-born German and Irish (Kuntz, 1988). Densely populated cities, westward migration, and immigration furthered social instability and hastened the demise of community.

The Booming Economy
The population increases due to immigration were clearly linked to opportunities afforded by a thriving economy. America had just completed its initial phase of industrialization and was poised for economic independence. Though agriculture continued to be the most important economic activity, the push for innovation and diversity in economic affairs was strong, particularly in the North. By 1860, America was ready to challenge England's status as the world's economic leader. The major industries of the day, namely, cotton cultivation, textile manufacture, iron-building, and building railroads, represented the economies of old and new. New inventions, such as the cotton gin, the telegraph, the sewing machine, and vulcanized rubber, stimulated manufacturing productivity.

Despite all the economic prosperity, unsettling disruptions were bound to occur. The economic developments were just as jolting to traditional and communal living as were the population influxes. Fathers were losing their authority to discipline children, as they focused on their positions and future in a growing competitive market workforce (Rothman, 1995b). Driven by an entrepreneurial spirit, families were uprooted and marriage was delayed (ibid.). Consequently, a smaller nuclear household replaced the extended family household that had once prevailed. While many benefited from the changing socioeconomic structure, others did not. Many succumbed to the new temptations of the city, such as gambling, prostitution, taverns, and crime.

Charity, Crusades, and Religion
As the nation became more democratized (politically), so too did religion. Biblical interpretations were no longer the exclusive domain of elite eastern seaboard clerics. Some clerics were still preoccupied with the origins of sin and man's helplessness before God, but many new religious denominations challenged this belief. It was generally held that salvation was for everyone, and that the power to achieve it rested with each free-willed individual. Consistent with the optimistic spirit of the times, the new denominations stressed

God's humanity and goodness and the perfectability and responsibilities of man. However, this assumption also begged the uncomfortable question: If God is so good and omnipotent and man perfectable, why is there so much evil in our midst? All was not perfect in this free society. Freedom was revered, but it was also a nemesis. Racism peaked, communities became stratified, and crime and vice persisted (Pessen, 1969).

The response to this question of evil depended on a belief system that glorified man's power of mind and conscience (ibid.). The empowerment of man translated to the development of numerous charitable associations and social reforms. It was this religious and charitable zeal that prompted European observers to label Americans as "neurotic do-gooders" (ibid.). Travelers from abroad noted that America was a land of assorted benevolent associations, the leaders of which were not suffering from the abuses they sought to correct (e.g., alcoholism, gambling) (ibid.).

The temperance crusades served as a prime example of this reformist and religious zeal. Alcohol consumption was the first target of attack. As illustrated in Table 5-1, between 1710 and 1830, hard liquor consumption increased threefold. By 1830, annual consumption of hard liquor reached unprecedented levels, with each family consuming approximately 9.5 gallons per year. Not surprisingly, it was believed that an epidemic of alcoholism had stricken the nation. Americans were drinking more compulsively and in a variety of previously unheard of settings. Drinking now occurred at funerals, ministerial ordinations, elections, corn huskings, and house raisings. Neighborhood socializing in general seemed to center on taverns. It was reputed that every family, even prominent ones, had a resident alcoholic. The fear that America was becoming a nation of drunkards prompted the development of the American Society for the Promotion of Temperance, which boldly declared that all temperate people should remain so and that the others should kill themselves off. The temperance movement provoked a collective repression so powerful that consumption ultimately fell by 75 percent in the fifteen years following 1830. Temperance crusaders were endlessly en-

Table 5-1. U.S. Alcohol Consumption, 1710–1845[a]

Year	Hard Liquor	Cider	Absolute Alcohol (All Beverages)
1710	3.8	34	5.1
1790	5.1	34	5.8
1830	9.5	27	7.1
1840	5.5	4	3.1
1845	3.7	0	1.8

[a]Consumption in gallons for individuals over 14 years of age.

gaged in calculating the costs associated with alcohol, among them pauperism, lost labor, and crime.

CRIME AS A MORAL DISEASE

Alcoholism was not the only problem of the day. Psychic disorders and opium addictions surfaced alongside drunkenness. Accordingly, social and public disorder crimes were becoming more common, and moral panic ensued. Contemporary reformers viewed the prevalence of "houses of ill-fame" as nearly impossible to suppress. Crimes of violence were becoming more commonplace as well. Street gangs, such as the Plug Uglies, Forty Thieves, Swamp Angels, and the Slaughterhouse Boys, overwhelmed the still loosely structured and understaffed police forces. In poor sections of town, officers often left the gangs alone, as long as their fighting and associated activities did not spill over into the wealthier sections of town (Friedman, 1993). The problem of crime centered on property offenses, such as theft and burglary. Friedman notes that if one asks what the criminal justice system did in the early nineteenth century, the answer would be that it protected property and punished stealing.

As reported in Table 5-2, in Boston, larceny cases were much more likely to receive prison terms than the seemingly more serious cases of assault and battery. In Boston as well as New York, 58 percent of all the cases adjudicated were for larceny. In Philadelphia, 71 percent of all adjudicated cases were for larceny. Crimes of theft were also highly specified. For example, the punishment varied depending on whether the stolen object(s) was cattle, mules, or horses. The penal codes were further specialized by reflecting the needs of local economies. In the 1850s, in Mississippi, it was illegal to pack or bale cotton fraudulently. In Minnesota, laws targeted lumbering and logging practices (ibid.).

Table 5-2. Sentences for Larceny versus
Assault/Battery, Boston, 1830–1840

	Fines	Probation	Prison Terms (%)
		Larceny	
1830	0	1	9
1835	15	5	80
1840	8	0	92
		Assault and Battery	
1830	30	0	70
1835	76	0	24
1840	62	8	30

Source: Kuntz (1988).

Overall, the perception was that "safety everywhere was precarious" (Pessen, 1969). Crime was often attributed to the lower class and the immigrant newcomers, as criminal activity was more likely to be observed in urban areas with larger concentrations of people and economic activity. For those who could recall the harmonious existence of Colonial America and the excitement of the period of transition, Jacksonian America was, by comparison, a society in seeming disarray.

It is from the context of perceived social chaos and failed deterrence policy that yet another crime ideology emerged. Crime as a product of sin was an outdated ideology for enlightened times, and crime as a product of free will proved to be an ideological miscue, given the inconsequential effects of the new rational penal code. Through biographical interviews with offenders, early penologists discovered what they now believed to be the sources of crime. One of these sources was a broken family. The other was a corrupted community filled with temptation and vice (Rothman, 1971). Morally weakened environments (both familial and social) contributed to morally weakened individuals who were unable to defend against social vice. Influenced by the medical advances of the time, the idea of crime as a moral disease was popularized.

The notion of crime as a spreading disease was advanced by then prominent physician Dr. Benjamin Rush. Medical doctors of the day sought to make their mission one of reclaiming mankind from the grip of vice. Medicalizing all behavior, Rush taught that disease was a habit of wrong action and all habits of injurious tendency were diseases. Under this disease model, crime could ultimately be cured. In fact, Rush claimed that alcoholism and masturbation could both be cured through constant employment in bodily labor. For the insane and disobedient, he designed what he called an immobilizing tranquilizer chair. He held that two days of solitary confinement would internalize self-control through a guilt-driven conscience. He continued to promote this approach, despite being rumored to have driven his own son to insanity as a result of such experimentation.

Though doctors were still ignorant about the sources and treatments of bacterial or viral infections—bloodletting was still practiced, often killing more people than it cured—this did not stop doctors and others from portraying crime as a curable disease. The "inoculation" against vice, deviance, and crime was simply a strong dose of discipline and the closing of establishments of ill repute. As with surgery, the corrupting influences needed only to be removed, while the corrupted were nursed back to good moral health in a sanitary environment. Armed with the confidence of global economic leadership, new technological and medical innovations, and an optimistic outlook, Americans were certain their new assessment of crime's causes was accurate. They were equally certain that the penitentiary could not only transform the "disease" that had stricken, but society as well, by serving as a model of decency and order.

THE PROMISE OF THE PENITENTIARY

The initial defects of the prison did not dampen the optimism of penal reformers. The prison too could be "corrected." By 1830, penitentiaries had replaced the makeshift prisons that emerged in the late eighteenth century. Following the lead of New York, Pennsylvania, and Massachusetts, the states of New Jersey, Ohio, and Michigan constructed their facilities in the 1830s. Other states, such as Indiana, Wisconsin, and Minnesota, followed suit in the 1840s (Barnes, 1972).

Penitentiaries were markedly different from the earliest prisons. The first prisons were small and hastily assembled in accordance with deterrence-driven penal codes. They served as an alternative to death and other corporal punishments. The penitentiaries of the nineteenth century were architectural testaments to American pride and ingenuity. Awesome in size and elaborate in design, inside and outside, the penitentiaries were to resolve newfound social ills and restore order and proper social organization (Rothman, 1971). In fact, one prison chaplain proclaimed that "could we all be put on prison fare for the space of two of three generations, the world ultimately would be the better for it" (Rothman, 1995b).

The lofty objectives of the penitentiary were to be achieved through strict rules of obedience, routine, silence, labor, separation, and surveillance. The physical design of the penitentiary was influenced not only by the medical rationales put forth by such physicians as Benjamin Rush, but by Jeremy Bentham's image of the perfect prison, namely, the "panopticon." Rules of separation and silence, in effect, quarantined the offender from society and, more importantly, from his fellow inmates. In fact, in the Eastern Penitentiary in Philadelphia, inmates were hooded during any kind of transport, so that they could not recognize or reinfect each other upon release. In institutions that followed the "panopticon" blueprint, surveillance and self-discipline were to be assured though the constant and invisible monitoring provided by the central guard tower. Altogether, the features of separation and surveillance divided time, space, and bodies in such a way as to purify the pathological, prevent the spread of "disease," and render each man the arbiter of his own monitoring and control (Foucault, 1977). The penitentiary intended to remove the afflicted from the excitement of the city and place them in a well-ordered asylum from which they would reenter society with a "spiritual coat of armor" capable of fending off the most virulent of social/moral diseases and temptations.

The details of internal structure and regimen were considered key in the reformative process. Even the clanging of the steel doors was intended to pierce the soul. Nowhere was the fervor over design and regimen more fiercely played out than in the bitter competition between the two penitentiary systems known as Auburn and Pennsylvania. On the surface, the two systems were similar enough. In the Pennsylvania system, offenders lived and worked in silence and isolation, and, in the Auburn system, prisoners worked in silence but together. Yet, this one distinguishing feature of continuous solitude ignited one of the most notorious penal debates of modern time. The controversy gained attention not only in France and England but also throughout Europe. Prussia became a convert to the Pennsylvania system in 1836, Belgium in 1838, Sweden in 1840, Denmark in 1846, and Norway and Holland in 1851 (Barnes, 1972).

Initially, many states followed the Pennsylvania model of total isolation, only to later abandon the practice. For example, Maryland introduced solitary confinement in 1809 and abolished it in 1838. Massachusetts authorized it in 1811 and did away with it in 1829. Maine experimented with solitary confinement between 1824 and 1827 and Virginia between 1824 and 1833. Rhode Island introduced it in 1838 and abolished it in 1844. New Jersey retained it the longest, finally abolishing it in 1858 (ibid.). Most states followed the Auburn system, fearing the reality of too many offenders going insane as a result of continuous isolation. Despite their differences, each system was, at a minimum, committed to rules of silence, a certain amount of isolation, and mandatory labor.

The disciplinary regime of the penitentiary was to revolve around routine and specificity. This was evident in the assignment of clothing, the scheduling of the day, and diet. During the term of confinement, all "convicts" dressed alike, ate the same food, and slept, moved, and dined in concert. Each convict was allocated a specific number of shoes (two pairs), pants (two pairs), shirts (three), and socks (two pairs). An average summer day at Auburn penitentiary began at 5:30 A.M. with the ringing of a bell. Cells were then unlocked and men came out and emptied, washed, and placed in a row their "night tubs." The convicts worked until breakfast (7 or 8 A.M.) and, at the ringing of a bell, formed a line and marched across the yard. Upon entering the dining area, convicts faced their plates until everyone had arrived. They sat down simultaneously and next to each other to prevent across the table glances between offenders (Friedman, 1993).

At Auburn, meals were equally specific and uniform. Convicts were given no more than 2 ounces of pepper for every 100 rations. At Sing Sing prison, the daily ration consisted of 6 pounds 9 ounces of food a day. This food included beef, pork, flour, mush, molasses, and potatoes (ibid.). In the Pennsylvania system, the following dietary schedule was mandated:

Sunday	1 lb of bread, 1 lb of coarse meal made into broth
Monday	1 lb of bread, 1 qt of potatoes
Tuesday	1 qt of Indian meal made into mush
Wednesday	1 lb of bread, 1 qt of potatoes
Thursday	1 qt of Indian meal made into mush
Friday	1 lb of bread, 1 qt of potatoes
Saturday	1 qt of Indian meal made into mush

A half-quart of molasses to every four prisoners was permitted on Tuesday, Thursday, and Saturday (Barnes, 1972).

Louis Dwight, the Auburn silent system's most ardent advocate, described in 1826, in *A Brief Account of the Construction, Management and Discipline of the New York State Prison at Auburn,* the type of discipline enforced as a testimony to its transforming powers:

At Auburn we have a more beautiful example still of what may be done by proper discipline, in a prison well constructed. It is not possible to describe the pleasure which we feel in contemplating this noble institution, after wading through the fraud, and the material and moral filth of many prisons. We regard it as a model worthy of the world's imitation. We do not mean that there is nothing in this institution which admits of improvement; for there have been a few cases of unjustifiable severity in punishments; but, upon the whole, the institution is immensely elevated above the old prisons. The whole establishment, from the gate to the sewer, is a specimen of neatness. The unremitted industry, the entire subordination and subdued feeling of the convicts, has probably no parallel among an equal number of criminals. In their solitary cells they spend the night, with no other book but the Bible, and at sunrise they proceed, in military order, under the eye of the turnkeys, in solid columns, with the lock march, to their workshops; thence, in the same order, at the hour of breakfast, to the common hall, where they partake of their wholesome and frugal meal in silence. Not even a whisper is heard; though the silence is such that a whisper might be heard through the whole apartment. The convicts are seated in single file, at narrow tables, with their backs towards the center, so that there can be no interchange of signs. If one has more food than he wants, he raises his left hand; and if another has less, he raises his right hand, and the waiter changes it. From one end of the shops to the other, it is the testimony of many witnesses, that they have passed more than 300 convicts, without seeing one leave his work, or turn his head to gaze at them. This is the most perfect attention to business from morning till night, interrupted only by the time necessary to dine, and never by the fact that the whole body of prisoners have done their tasks, and the time is now their own to do as they please. After supper, they can, if they choose, read Scripture undisturbed and then reflect in silence on the errors of their lives. They must not disturb their fellow prisoner by even a whisper. (quoted in Barnes, 1972)

In light of this painstaking regimen and discipline, one would assume the prison was the paragon of order and obedience. However, as Rothman (1995b) pointed out, these "scenes of order and routine masked a much harsher reality." The penitentiary, though heralded as a structure that would reform, deter, and punish all at once, failed dismally, at least as a vehicle of reform or deterrence.

THE PENITENTIARY IN PRACTICE

The penitentiary, if nothing else, was promoted as more humane than the corporal punishments of earlier generations. Yet, these institutions did not hesitate to employ harsh measures in the face of even the slightest acts of disobedience. Breaches of the codes of silence and other rules were met with severe punishments. In Pennsylvania, the iron gag was used against "talkers." New York, Massachusetts, and Ohio relied on whipping. Maine preferred the ball and chain (Rothman, 1995b). In many institutions, offenders were frequently suspended in the air by their toes or thumbs, for disciplinary purposes. The stretcher, similar in principle to the medieval rack, was also used as a way of inducing discipline and obedience. Sweat boxes, which consisted of unventilated cells located on either side of a fireplace, were frequently used. In 1878, a New Jersey investigating committee found that authorities had habitually poured alcohol on epileptics and then set fire to the alcohol in order to detect possible faking of an epileptic seizure. In a Pennsylvania prison investigation conducted during 1834 and 1835, it was discovered that inmates were frequently tied up in the winter, while buckets of cold water were thrown upon them from extreme heights, freezing on their head and body (Barnes, 1972). Dorothea L. Dix (the period's most ardent advocate for the humane treatment of prisoners) concluded that, at Auburn and Sing Sing prisons, "the lash may sometimes be the only mode by which an insurrectionist spirit can be conquered."

Even in the absence of corporal disciplinary action, the inhumanity of normal living conditions was apparent. Upon their visit to the United States, Frenchmen Gustave de Beaumont and Alexis de Toqueville described the total silence as the silence of death, as if someone had just entered catacombs. In Cincinnati, they found that half of the inmates were imprisoned with irons and the rest were thrown into disease-infected dungeons (de Beaumont and de Toqueville, [1833] 1997). Numerous other observers and charitable prisoner associations also commented on the atrocities that accompanied this "advanced" form of punishment. Charles Dickens, who visited the Philadelphia prison in the 1840s, was most harsh in his denunciations of the prison. Dickens equally abhorred what he termed the "depth of terrible endurance, which no man has a right to inflict upon his fellow creature" and declared:

Those who devised this system . . . and those benevolent gentlemen who carry it into execution, do not know what they are doing. I hold this slow and daily tampering with the mysteries of the brain to be immeasurably worse than any torture of the body. The wounds it inflicts are not upon the surface, and it exhorts few cries that human ears can hear. They are nothing more than men buried alive, to be dug out in the slow round of years, and in the meantime dead to everything but torturing anxieties and horrible despair. Those who have undergone this punishment must pass into society again morally unhealthy and diseased. (Dickens, [1842] 1972)

The "round of years" referenced by Dickens is illustrated by the average length of imprisonment in the United States at that time. As shown in Table 5-3, the average length of imprisonment in U.S. penitentiaries between 1844 and 1846 ranged between four and eight years.

By 1852, numerous legislative reports and commissions conceded that penitentiaries did little more than incapacitate and that conditions were actually worsening. It was concluded that the likelihood of recidivism was far greater than reform. The recommitment rates for Sing Sing prison, reported in Table 5-4, help illustrate this point, though no clear pattern emerged as to whether longer or shorter sentences were more likely to increase recidivism.

Table 5-3.   Average Length of Imprisonment in U.S. Penitentiaries, 1844–1846

| | | | Average Terms of Imprisonment | | |
State	Year	Life Terms	Years	Months	Days
Vermont	1844	2	4	2	15
	1845	2	4	0	21
Maine	1844	6	4	11	22
	1845	7	4	4	14
	1846	8	4	4	2
New Hampshire	1845	11	6	4	20
	1846	10	6	4	11
Michigan	1845	1	4	6	11
	1846	0	4	1	13
Ohio	1846	6	5	0	22
Rhode Island	1844	3	5	11	10
Connecticut	1844	17	6	6	1
	1846	19	6	10	8
Massachusetts	1844	12	5	1	2
	1845	14	4	11	9
Virginia	1845	12	7	3	2
	1846	13	7	11	3
Maryland	1845	0	4	0	3

Source: Kuntz (1988).

Table 5-4.   Recommitment Rates for Sing Sing, 1817–1842

Term of Incarceration (years)	Ratio Recommitted	Number of Recommitted
1	1/3	3
2	1/17	109
3	1/13	145
4	1/10	68
5	1/6	218
6	1/6	19
7	1/5	96
8	1/11	6
9	1/15	2
10	1/9	49
11	1/7	1
12	1/10	4
13	0	0
14	1/10	13
15	1/9	3
16	0	0
17	1/1	2
18	1/3	1
19	1/0	0
20	1/3	3
20–30	1/4	2
Over 30	0	0
Life Imprisonment	1/8	34

Source: Kuntz (1988).

By 1860, the rules of separation and isolation had long been abandoned as a result of overcrowding. For example, in Philadelphia, during 1861, 801 inmates occupied 489 cells. Total admissions numbered 20,801. Those inmates given early releases due to overcrowding totaled 7,674. Another 6,578 were released outright by the sentencing judge because of overcrowded prison conditions (Kuntz, 1988). An 1867 report by the New York legislature estimated that approximately one-third of all prisoners were double-celled. In New Jersey, in 1867, prisoners lived as many as four to a cell that measured 7 feet by 12 feet or less (Friedman, 1993). Everywhere, overcrowding was so problematic that pardons had become an integral part of securing the safety and order of prisons. Without them, it was feared that rule infractions would become too frequent and that the minds of convicts would become "soured and intractable" (quoted in Kuntz, 1988). A contemporary observer noted that in the absence of early release via pardons, inmates were "less sensible to the influences of kindly treatment," which in turn encouraged the need for harsher disciplinary measures (ibid.).

The certainty of reforming offenders soon became viewed as a remote possibility. This sense of resignation was fueled by concerns of overcrowding and admissions of more serious offenders. For example, in Connecticut, between 1828 and 1840, 343 of the state's total of 839 inmates were convicted of burglary and robbery, 78 for attempted murder, 42 for rape, and 45 for arson and escape. The increasing gravity of offenses made it easier to justify use of various corporal punishments within the institution. The fact that the majority of inmates were also immigrants made indifference to inhumane treatment easier as well. Between 1830 and 1835, 20 percent of the inmates at Auburn in New York were born outside the United States. By the 1850s, the percentage of foreign-born inmates increased to 32 percent. By 1860, 44 percent of the inmate population at Auburn was foreign-born. In 1860, immigrants comprised 40 percent of the Massachusetts prison populations and 46 percent of the Illinois prison population. Included in these groups were not just European immigrants, but also African Americans, Asians, and Native Americans.

Managerial concerns, rather than penal theory, soon dictated the operations of the penitentiary. The famed Auburn/Pennsylvania controversy was little more than a war of words on paper. Fiscal considerations ultimately determined the rules of separation at both the Pennsylvania and Auburn systems (Miller, 1980). Not only were cruel punishments being routinely administered within overcrowded prisons, but administrative corruption also was becoming rampant. Bribery of guards by inmates was not uncommon (Rothman, 1995b).

The high hopes of the northern reformers had collapsed under the weight of fiscal ruin, disorder, disobedience, and overcrowding. In the South, however, no such hopes had ever existed. Little attempt was ever made to implement the "progressive" ideas of the northern states. Few efforts to emulate either the Auburn or Pennsylvania systems were under way before the Civil War. For example, in New Orleans, men were housed with hogs and often chained up (de Beaumont and de Toqueville, [1833] 1997). Following the Civil War, penal conditions deteriorated into further chaos and corruption. The South adopted a fundamentally different punishment strategy, based on their impending economic needs. Historian McKelvey noted that "while the prisoner of the North may have grown pale and anemic gazing through the bars in a tower, the southern counterpart dragged his chains through long years of hard labor, driven by brutal torture, often times to his grave" (McKelvey, 1936).

The penal system of the South had no ambitions of reconstructing a "utopian" Colonial America or of applying behavioral theory to prison design. Their penal system followed a slavery model for the purpose of rebuilding the war-ravaged economy and infrastructure (e.g., railroads). The need to rebuild the South contributed to widespread use of the convict lease system. Under the lease system, offenders, 90 percent of whom were newly freed blacks, were leased to private companies. These companies, in turn, paid the state a sum of money for the cheap labor. For example, in Georgia, eleven hundred prisoners were leased to three companies on twenty-year contracts for the sum of twenty-five thousand dollars (ibid.). In 1867, Mississippi operated its penal system under a similar arrangement, as did Louisiana, Arkansas, Tennessee, and Florida.

With the leasing system, corruption in the penal system flourished. Companies often lagged behind in their payments to states. As states sought to maximize their gain through the best possible bargains, inmates were shuffled from one company to the next without permanent quarters. They lived in camplike facilities, and there was little in the way of order, rules, or surveillance. Consequently, states often lost track of how many offenders were under supervision. They resided in quarters where there was barely running water and no heat during the winter. Their clothes were typically tattered, and shoes were considered a privilege. To prevent escapes, shackles were used, as were the ball and chain (ibid.). They labored under sweltering conditions where they often "died like flies" (Friedman, 1993).

The lease convict system was gradually replaced with the plantation/farm model and the "good road and chain gangs project," which existed well into the twentieth century. While each of these approaches was touted as "quintessential southern progressive reform" and as an example of penal humanitarianism, the reality was far from humane (Lichtenstein, 1993). So gruesome was the treatment of "negro convicts" that one scholar was compelled to issue the following warning in advance of an exposé on southern prison camps: "Please reader, do not read this chapter unless you can steel your heart against pain" (Tannenbaum, 1924:74; quoted in Lichtenstein, 1993).

SUMMARY AND DISCUSSION

In the 1830s, America was brimming with hope, determination, and ingenuity. But with optimism, democracy, and commercialism came diversity and mobility. New freedoms threatened established norms and values, and society, as many Americans once knew it, was crumbling even as it was advancing. Criminal activity was attributed to human interaction with a morally depraved environment. Having conquered England on more than one occasion, and now edging out England as the economic leader of the world, Americans had little reason to believe they could not conquer a much weaker foe in crime. The imposing structure of the prison made Europeans and Americans alike curious about the preoccupation with the "reformation of the objects of punishment" (Pessen, 1969). The fascination was such that the Eastern penitentiary was the second largest tourist sight in the nation.

Repeating the pattern of early reformers, penitentiary advocates were blinded by their own enthusiasm. The silent system had little staying power because it was virtually unenforceable and solitary confinement was far too expensive (Friedman, 1993). Despite laws and policies to the contrary, inmates were not always treated with kindness and uniformity. With the exception of overt mutilation, nearly every form of corporal punishment known to the preprison days was transferred into the prison system as a way of enforcing prison regimen and rules. Nevertheless, the rise of the Pennsylvania and Auburn systems did mark a step in the way of progress, at least in terms of classification and differentiation. Unlike the previous prison practice that herded offenders of all kinds into one place, these systems separated felons by the seriousness of their crimes and assigned males and females separate living quarters. In the South, different and even more corrupt and brutal conditions prevailed under the convict lease system.

Prisons did not deter crime, nor did penitentiaries cure their socially diseased inhabitants. However, the will to reform the institution did not cease. Simply put, Americans were not willing to part with the idea of incarceration. At a minimum, as Rothman (1971) argues, it was convenient because it housed the "strange alien hordes" (i.e., immigrants and undesirables), and its very failure (i.e., recidivism) contributed to its persistence. Rather than abolish the penitentiary, a new kind of prison (the reformatory) emerged, but so too did alternative strategies to incarceration.

6

Progressive America and the Rise of Reformatories, Parole, and Probation (1880s–1930s)

INTRODUCTION

THE PROGRESSIVE ERA was noted for its sweeping social, political, and economic achievements. Because these achievements permeated many aspects of social life, to the benefit of some and to the detriment of others, the role of government in the affairs of citizens and business became a paramount concern. This concern reflected the sentiment that government should be responsive to and responsible for the quality of life of all citizens. The call for government activism was prompted by a heightened sense of urban disenchantment, stemming from unchecked industrialization, urbanization, and immigration. America's cities were afflicted with poverty, disease, overcrowded slums, and crime, and the developing biological and social sciences provided a fresh interpretation of crime's causes.

Out of this context of a growing urban disenchantment arose a resilient optimism about the ability of government and science to resolve the problems that seemed to plague city life. The sciences taught that the less fortunate and criminally wayward were not to be punished for presumed moral failings, but were to be socially and economically rehabilitated. Progressivism taught that government was to be the outstretched hand that would make this rehabilitation of society and individuals possible.

Accordingly, America proceeded to reform the penal system once again. The results of these reform activities were adult reformatories, indeterminate sentencing, parole, probation, and the juvenile court (discussed separately in the subsequent chapter). These reforms expanded the number and type of penal strategies available to the state, and allowed for further differentiation and individualization in the penal process. However, in this chapter's consideration of these various reform efforts, it is argued that like the prison and the penitentiary that had gone before, the promise and the reality of pro-

gressive penology were far apart. Rather than providing more individualized treatment alternatives to the penitentiary, these reforms become implemented as supplements serving various managerial and offender control
purposes.

PROGRESSIVE AMERICA

Progressivism referred to a collectivity of movements that combined various
aspects of social, political, and economic life. These movements were mo-
bilized by diverse ethnic groups and classes, for diverse ethnic groups and
classes. Stated differently, progressivism was the culmination of pervasive
anxiety and vulnerability related to the abuses of unbridled private power
and the excesses and dangers of corporate capitalism (Diner, 1998; Unger
and Unger, 1977). Efforts to curb these abuses and dangers began at the local and state levels in the 1890s and expanded to the national level by 1900,
resulting in what is known as progressivism.

An overriding question of the progressive agenda was, How far should
government go? or, How much should it intervene in the affairs of the economy? How much should it tax its citizens? How far should it go to extend
democracy? and How much should it intervene in the leisure time of citizens
(Cashman, 1988)? Woodrow Wilson answered these questions by maintaining that industry, science, and governmental authority should be used to
place "our businessmen and producers under the stimulation of a constant
necessity to be efficient, economic, and enterprising" (Luke, 1986). At the
same time, Herbert Croly argued, "The American state will make itself responsible for a morally and socially desirable distribution of wealth" (quoted in ibid.). The three rapidly emerging processes of industrialization,
immigration, and urbanization generated pressing problems that progressivism sought to correct.

Industrialization
The industrial revolution alluded to in previous chapters reached its peak
during the Progressive era. The United States outperformed the world in both
its agricultural and industrial output, even as its agricultural economy was on
the decline. The United States was the leading producer of coal and was rich
in natural resources, including iron, gold, silver, copper, lead, and petrole-
um. By 1919, the United States supplied two-thirds of the world's oil. This
was the beginning of monopoly capitalism, as just a few companies owned
the bulk of the nation's industry. The Rockefellers owned Standard Oil, James
B. Duke owned American Tobacco Company, the Carnegies owned U.S.
Steel, and J. P. Morgan owned the House of Morgan. Coca Cola, Levi Strauss,
Eastman Kodak, Sears Roebuck, and R. J. Reynolds were equally powerful
corporate players (Cashman, 1988).

The material progress of the United States was unmatched and could be attributed to the growth of industrial production. Productivity was continually improved through mechanization, and mechanization was continually improved through a number of inventions. In 1900, a columnist for the *Washington Post* remarked that "in every department of science and intellectual activity, we have gone beyond the wildest dreams of 1800" (Parshall, 1998). An Englishman writing about his visit to America in 1900 proclaimed that "life in the states is one perpetual whirl of telephones, telegrams, phonographs, electric bells, motors, lifts, and automatic instruments" (quoted in Diner, 1998). By 1910, Americans could buy any number of automatic and electrical devices including sewing machines, fans, irons, washing machines, vacuum cleaners, stoves, heaters, and automobiles. In 1900, eight thousand Americans owned cars. In 1920, eight million owned cars. Americans were no longer just producers, they were mass consumers (ibid.).

The inventions of Thomas Edison and Alexander Graham Bell, in particular, revolutionized the nation's consumption and production capacities. The following excerpt from a 1929 AT&T report (quoted in Cashman, 1988) illustrates the importance of efficient production levels:

In 1781 One Man Working One Day Produced:	In 1925 One Man Working One Day Produced:
500 lbs. of iron	5,000 lbs. of iron
100 ft. of lumber	750 ft. of lumber
5 lbs. of nails	500 lbs. of nails
1/4 pair of shoes	10 pairs of shoes
1/2 ton of coal	4 tons of coal
20 square feet of paper	200,000 square feet of paper

The industrial revolution could not have taken place through invention, ingenuity, and raw materials alone. It also depended on a plentiful supply of labor. Six million were employed in manufacturing in 1900, increasing to 8.25 million in 1910. In construction, 1.64 million were employed in 1900, increasing to 2.31 million in 1910. In transportation, 2 million were employed in 1900, increasing to 3.2 million in 1910. The number employed in trade increased from 2.87 million in 1900 to 3.62 million in 1910 (Cashman, 1988). Immigrants largely performed this labor. Immigrants accounted for only 14 percent of the population between 1900 and 1910, but comprised 25 percent of the labor force.

Immigration

The word "immigrant" was coined by Jedidiah Morse in 1789 to describe the foreigners who were settling in New York (Cashman, 1988). The period most associated with the "huddled masses," however, was the Progressive era. In

Table 6-1.   Immigration to the United States,
             1890–1917

Origins	Number	Percentage
Central Europe	4,879,000	27.1
Southern Europe	4,369,000	24.3
Northwest Europe	3,637,000	20.2
Eastern Europe	3,328,000	18.5
Canada and Newfoundland	744,000	4.14
Central and South America	473,000	2.63
Asia	468,000	0.13
Australia and New Zealand	23,500	0.08
Pacific Islands	3,500	0.02

Source: Cashman (1988).

the twenty-seven-year period between 1890 and 1917, a total of 17,991,486 immigrants came to the United States. Upon arriving in the United States, immigrants generally moved to the industrial Northeast and to four states in particular: New York, Massachusetts, Pennsylvania, and Illinois (ibid.) (see Table 6-1).

Over one million immigrants arrived in the United States in 1905, 1906, 1907, 1910, 1913, and then again in 1914. More than fourteen million arrived between 1896 and 1917. They came from Norway, Italy, Germany, Russia, the Mediterranean, Poland, Hungary, Ireland, Ukraine, and Canada, just to name a few. In 1910, almost 80 percent of New York's population consisted of the foreign-born and their children.

The reasons for their coming to America were no different from those of immigrants of earlier generations. They sought religious and political asylum as well as economic opportunity. The hysteria over coming to the United States was best captured by Russian immigrant Mary Antin in her memoirs entitled, *From Plotzk to Boston*:

America was in everybody's mouth. Businessmen talked of it over their accounts; the market women made up their quarrels that they might discuss it from stall to stall; people who had relatives in the famous land went around reading their letters for the enlightenment of less fortunate folk. . . . Children played at emigrating; old folks shook their sage heads over the evening fire and prophesied no good for those who braved the terrors of the sea and the foreign goal beyond it; all talked of it, but scarcely anyone knew one true fact about this magic land. (quoted in Cashman, 1988)

From the perspective of the Americans descended from the British colonists, the new immigrants came speaking "strange" languages, wearing "strange costumes," and engaging in "strange" customs (ibid.). The city was a crowded showcase of intermingling and diverse cultures that were feared by the established elite. For example, it was at this time that Andrew Carnegie began his project of building more than 1,650 public libraries across the country in a campaign to ensure the "education and improvement of the poorer classes." In his estimation, the immigrants thought little of moral and intellectual culture (Marcus, 1999).

Urbanization

The combination of industrialization and immigration produced a city life and degree of urbanization that was both imposing and menacing. Cities were the most dynamic part of the nation by the turn of the twentieth century (Unger and Unger, 1977). The tremendous growth in city life charted in previous chapters accelerated and became far more concentrated at the turn of the twentieth century. For example, between 1890 and 1920, Brooklyn grew from 2.5 million to 5.6 million residents. In this same time period, Chicago's population grew from 1 million to 2.7 million, and Philadelphia's population increased from 1 million to 1.8 million. Los Angeles and Detroit experienced even greater increases, as their populations swelled from 205,000 to 994,000 and 50,000 to 577,000, respectively.

The city was a powerful magnet for all Americans (ibid.). It offered jobs of all varieties, including typists, school teachers, accountants, lawyers, unskilled factory workers, and journalists. Yet, cities were also alienating and intimidating places. Despite all the activity and people, their vastness bred loneliness. The pervasive sense of isolation and detachment experienced by so many was described by sociologist Emile Durkheim as anomie. Crime, high suicide rates, broken homes, prostitution, and alcoholism were some of the manifestations of this anomie or normlessness.

Americans of the lower and growing middle class felt unprotected for other reasons as well. Americans were not only producers working in hazardous factories, but consumers of unregulated goods. The wonders of science allowed companies to "transform" rotten spoiled food and sell any number of medical concoctions, infused with opium and other toxic chemicals (ibid.). They were at the mercy of unrestricted capitalistic enterprising. For many, the city seemed almost inhumane and unlivable. The numerous charitable associations and volunteer organizations alone could not effectively combat these social ills.

The perilous conditions of the city prompted two developments that were at the heart of the progressive movement's insistence and success in mobilizing government intervention. Those developments were exposé journalism and settlement houses. The journalists of the day were determined to do more than just record the events of the big city. They also researched controversial, disturbing, and sensational topics that would attract and captivate readers. Soon, a group of editors, novelists, and essayists, known as muckrakers, spotlighted many wrongdoings and dark corners of social and political life. Beginning in 1903, irreverent journalistic attacks were launched at the corporate community. Under the direction of such publishing moguls as William Randolph Hearst, the muckrakers relentlessly documented, fact by fact, detail by detail, the grave misdeeds of those in power. Article after article appeared that told of the shady and harmful dealings of the patent medicine business, the stock market, Standard Oil, local government, and the beef industry (Cashman, 1988). Upton Sinclair's novel *The Jungle* was one example of this brash journalistic writing. In detail, he described the exploitation of workers and the deplorable conditions of the meat-packing industry. The exposé journalists paraded before the public the social injustice, economic dangers, and political corruption that affected everyone but the powerful (Unger and Unger, 1977). Other journalistic writings advocated remedies such as strong government that would implement programs to improve the quality of national life (ibid.).

While journalists employed the power of the pen, a group of college graduates employed the power of settlement houses. Settlement houses responded to the predicament of the inner city in an equally zealous fashion. These houses were located in the slum districts and were occupied by male and female college graduates of the new social sciences. In these service centers/ social laboratories, social scientists and other advocates of social justice sought to serve the urban poor in a close, interacting, and learning environment. They documented the ill effects of industrialization and urbanization, and used this data to affect public policy. They fought for worker's compensation, consumer protection, child labor laws, clean government, tenement regulation, equal opportunity for blacks and immigrants, and improved recreational and educational opportunities (ibid.). Inevitably, their fight included consideration of criminal behavior and penal policy.

POSITIVIST CRIMINOLOGY

It has been said that how we govern ourselves is related to how we govern crime (Garland, 1998). Perhaps nowhere is this relationship more evident than in the era of progressivism. One of the basic tenets of progressivism was that scientific knowledge enabled government to master what seemed to be untamable social forces (Diner, 1998). This belief extended not just to the hard sciences and industry, but to the social sciences and human behavior as well. Scientific knowledge produced several theories that were expected to tame the force of crime in society. Biological, psychological, and, to a lesser degree, sociological perspectives all enjoyed distinction. Under the influence of Italian criminologist Cesare Lombroso, directly, and naturalist Charles Darwin, indirectly, the notion of inferior or degenerative criminal classes was widely embraced. Biological explanations held that criminals were born, thus constituting a less evolved class of human species. Drawing upon such evidence as physical appearance (e.g., jawbone shape, head size) and the prevalence of criminal behavior across generations of families (Dugdale, [1877] 1979; Goddard, 1912, 1914, 1915), it was concluded that criminality was inherited. (For a modern discussion of anthropological and biological perspectives see Baron, 1977; Ellis and Hoffman, 1990; Fishbein, 1990; Mednick, 1987; Rowe and Osgood, 1984.) In fact, this belief led to what was known as the Eugenics movement.

So fervent was the belief in hereditary perspectives, that Vermont, for instance, established a plan entitled the Vermont Eugenics Survey. This twelve-year plan was designed by the social scientists of the day to identify and study "good" and "bad" families and then eliminate those listed as "bad" ("Vermont," 1999). The final report was circulated among policymakers, leading to the passage of Vermont's sterilization law in 1931. The law resulted in the sterilization of several hundred poor rural Vermonters, Abenaki Indians, and others deemed unfit to procreate.[1]

Given the prominence of Sigmund Freud, various psychological explanations of criminal behavior drew considerable support as well. Some of those attributed criminality to various mental conflicts (Healey, 1915). For example, William Healey argued that "all conduct is directly an expression of mental life." He asserted that behind every action is "the idea, the wish, or the impulse existing as mental content." Though nebulous and vague in their assertions, psychological interpretations won many enthusiastic supporters. The language of psychiatry merged well with the increasingly fashionable and respected language of science. It was perhaps also believed that the habits of mind were easier to fix than hardened slums or predetermined biological defects (Rothman, 1980).

Sociological explanations of crime were finding their formative beginnings as well. Journalists and other social observers were acutely aware of the conditions under which new immigrants lived and worked. Against the backdrop of a growing self-indulgent upper class, it was quite conceivable that poverty, low wages, disease, overcrowded living arrangements, and unemployment could drive anyone to crime. In 1900, 5 percent of the population owned nearly half of the property, while more than one-third of the nation's 76 million existed below the poverty level (Bok, 1992). Robert Hunter's observations of the inner city in the book *Poverty: Social Conscience in the Progressive Era* ([1904] 1965) brings this line of reasoning into focus. He argues that the poor were largely not immoral individuals who rebuked the virtues of work and thrift. They were simply the overworked and underpaid victims of capitalism's robber barons.

In investigating the causes of crime, these men of science and progressive philosophy sought to intervene rather than assign moral blame. They maintained that variously motivated offenders could be individually "treated" and that one needed only to *know* the offender to dispense the proper treatment. Just as medical doctors obtained the medical histories of their patients, "behavioral" doctors obtained the *life* histories of their "patients." Consequently, boundless information and discretion became the tools by which offenders were to be diagnosed and corrected. Though quite dissimilar in their assumptions, biological, psychological, and sociological perspectives comfortably coexisted because a penal system based on rehabilitating each offender according to his own circumstances demanded flexibility of thought. Flexibility was to be the central feature of this era's major reforms of the reformatory, indeterminate sentence, parole, and probation.

THE PROMISE OF PROGRESSIVE PENOLOGY

Between 1850 and 1880, prison facilities again became overcrowded as soon as they opened their doors for business. In response to the post–Civil War pessimism about the reformative powers of the prison-come-penitentiary, penal reform advocates Enoch Wines, Franklin Sanborn, and Zebulon Brockway committed to revise the penal system during the 1870 Cincinnati Conference (Rotman, 1995). At the National Congress on Penitentiary and Reformatory Discipline, they charged that the existing system was outright ineffective. In their estimation, isolation, lockstep marching, and striped uniforms debilitated one's manhood. Brockway argued that the existing system of pure punishment and retribution failed to reform, not only because of its reliance on the fixed sentence, but because it was founded on a "mystic morality." One could neither see nor measure motives or morality, and the philosophy of deterrence assumed that free will was based on (rational) motives that could be affected through certain, swift, and harsh punishment (Brockway, 1997). Brockway argued that criminals did not make the essential cause and effect linkage between crime and punishment, as most offenders did not believe themselves to be guilty of any crime. He further dismissed Classical School assumptions because of the brutalizing effects of increased penal severity, and for the capacity of society to correctly adjust their cost/benefit calculus to differing penal severities.

With these criticisms in mind, the conference leaders crafted what would become known as the Declaration of Principles. These thirty-seven principles were so highly regarded they took on the aura of a sacred creed for penologists for decades to come. The content of these principles centered on individualized care and the scientific treatment of offenders based on a medical model (Barnes, 1972). Whereas deterrence strategies focused on the nature of the offense, progressive strategies would focus on the nature of the offender. In accordance with these principles, the specific recommendations of the conference included the establishment of adult reformatories, in conjunction with (1) the indeterminate sentence, (2) a mark/classification system, (3) intensive academic and vocational instruction, (4) constructive labor, (5) humane disciplinary methods, and (6) parole (ibid.).

Reformatories
The Elmira Reformatory opened in 1876 in New York and was designed to embody the recommendations articulated in the Cincinnati Conference's Declaration of Principles. In the words of its superintendent, Zebulon Brockway, the American Reformatory Prison system would involve an altogether "different prison procedure." So important was the distinction between the prison and the reformatory that a Mrs. Gibbons, head of the Women's Prison Association of New York, in developing a women's facility, pleaded to her friend and successor before her death, to "Be sure, Alice, thee make it a reformatory and not a prison."

New York was not alone in embracing the concept of an adult reformatory. Other reformatories were constructed in Michigan in 1877, in Massachusetts in 1884, in Pennsylvania and Minnesota in 1889, in Colorado in 1890, in Illinois in 1891, and in Kansas in 1895. Ohio, Indiana, and Wisconsin implemented their systems in 1895, 1896, and 1899, respectively (Pisciotta, 1994). Though patterned after Elmira, not all of these states followed Elmira's example precisely. Across states, there were variations in eligibility criteria (i.e., age, offense) and internal regimen. Michigan proved to be the exception on all counts, adhering to an expressly punitive philosophy and a lease-for-profit labor system.

Reformatories were envisioned as laboratories for a new scientific method of punishing offenders. In these purported "prison science" laboratories, offenders generally between the ages of 16 and 26 were to be studied, classified, and treated. The "prison science" that was to govern the process of changing men was to depend on the knowledge of experts, not the charity of philanthropists or ministers. Staff employed a vocabulary that was part medical and part educational. Inmates were known as students or patients, and Elmira was often dubbed the "college on the hill" or the "reformatory hospital" (ibid.). This change in vernacular brought an air of legitimacy to the punishment trade and those who were its artisans (ibid.).

Because the reformatory was tied to the new biological, social, and psychological sciences, the regimen of the reformatory was to be organized around principles that were measurable. For example, the system would rely on an indeterminate sentence structure. This would instill in offenders a self-regulated discipline because release dates were to be based on visible proof of reformation. Once satisfactory progress had been made and demonstrated, the offender would then be released to a period of supervision, known as parole. Meanwhile, daily life and activities in the reformatory were to consist of paid work, job training, physical exercise, and a well-planned diet. This schedule reflected what was believed to be a physiological connection between the mind and body. Penologists of the day preached the adage that good habits of mind were best developed through good habits of the body.

A hallmark feature of the reformatory was its classification/grading system. This system was how one gauged whether an offender was on the road to reform. "Students" were to be graded according to participation and performance in work (vocational) and school (educational) and compliance with rules. Three grades existed, and all offenders (students) were to begin their term of confinement in the second grade. At Elmira, if the offender conformed to the rules for at least six months, he could move up to the first grade. This afforded such privileges as comfortable blue uniforms, spring mattresses, daily writing allowances, extended library and bedtime hours, and better food. Demotion to the third grade, however, brought coarse red uniforms, lockstep marching, and denial of mail, library, and visitation privileges (ibid.).

Work was consequently an integral component of the grading system. Though work had always been a part of the incarceration experience, the importance of work in the reformatory was different than in the penitentiary system. It included an economic incentive (payment for work), with an overriding purpose to instill a morality of industriousness, namely the formation of a new social habit. As Simon (1993:29) notes, "work was no longer aimed at facilitating an independent process of moral reformation, but an opportunity to subject offenders to the discipline of industrial labor." The following statement issued by Brockway illustrates this point plainly. He argued that the "purpose of imprisonment and of treatment is to prepare such for industry, to train and transfer them from economic worthlessness to worthfulness" (Brockway, 1997). A quotation from the Report of the Special Committee to the Prison Association of New York on Convict Labor by the California Penological Commission in 1887, further demonstrates the message regarding the value of work in prison, and society more broadly.

> Industrial labor is not only the most powerful agency of reformation; it is the indispensable instrument, without aid of which reformatory results are wholly unattainable. Industry is the essential prerequisite of healthy life and progress in all human society; and to such a degree that any community deprived of productive labor must quickly lapse into moral corruption and decay. (quoted in Simon, 1993:28)

Indeterminate Sentence and Parole
A second outgrowth of the Cincinnati Conference, and intimately related to the ideal of the reformatory, was the indeterminate sentence. The indeterminate sentence began in the Elmira Reformatory and was replicated throughout the United States in the last quarter of the nineteenth century. By 1910,

nearly every adult reformatory used an indeterminate sentence structure (Pisciotta, 1994; Barnes, 1972). By 1923, almost half of all offenders admitted to U.S. prisons were sentenced under the indeterminate sentence structure (Rothman, 1980).

Where the determinate sentence was based on the character of the offense, and thus treated all offenders as being of one rational mind swayed by the threat of punishment, the indeterminate sentence was based on the character of the individual offender. Courts were not to fix or limit the duration of the sentence as offenders [theoretically] held the keys to their own release. As Brockway argued, "captivity is always irksome," but "the indeterminateness of the sentence breeds discontent, purposefulness, and prompts to new exertion" (Brockway, 1997). It was in the offender's own best interest to improve his behavior, giving rise to the then popular maxim "be cured or be kept" (Miller, 1980).

The typical sentence minimum was one year without a maximum time indicated. At the conclusion of the minimum sentence, a prison board would determine an offender's release date. Readiness for release was to be determined by the number of credits gained or lost within the reformatory institution, but it did not depend on institutional conduct alone. The factors that could affect release also included the social influences relevant to the offender's "constitutional and acquired defects and tendencies" (quoted in Friedman, 1993). The parole board was to be furnished with information about the offender's habits, activities, associations, and reputation. Altogether, they considered the offense of conviction, offense history, institutional conduct, work record, academic progress, attitude, and future plans. These items of information were considered essential for determining the perceived risk of recidivism. It should be noted, however, that the notion of indeterminateness and demonstration of reform as a requisite of release was never taken to its absolute extreme. No offender remained in prison until his natural death simply because he failed to convince others of his reform.

Parole made the indeterminate sentence a more attractive feature; the promise of supervision helped officials rest more comfortably with their release decisions. Though these complementary strategies were introduced together in Elmira, they were not immediately paired together elsewhere. By 1900, every reformatory had parole, and 20 states had parole laws for institutions other than the reformatory, namely prisons and penitentiaries. By 1923, one-half of all prison releases in the United States were under a system of parole (Rothman, 1980).

The concept of parole was not wholly new as different versions of early release such as "gain time" or "good time," were already being practiced. Gain time laws were used as an incentive to work, rather than as corporal punishments. Twenty-two states had enacted gain time laws between 1860 and 1880. If no disciplinary infractions were accumulated, an inmate could expect to serve approximately one-half to one-third of his or her sentence (Miller, 1980).

What distinguished parole from gain time laws, however, was the expressed intent to extend the reformative disciplinary process into the community under a period of close supervision. That supervision would be exercised by parole officers, who were expected to be policeman, detectives, social workers, psychiatrists, work supervisors, and judges all at once. Parole officers, not unlike probation officers, were to be the students of the new social sciences and specially trained for the task of reforming offenders. The offenders were to be model citizens, capable of continuing the reform process begun in the institution.

Probation

Though probation emerged during the progressive penology era, its implementation was not linked to the reformatory, as were the indeterminate sentence and parole. Still, the rationale for probation was consistent with progressive penology's desire to differentiate and treat offenders. The practice of probation was inspired, in part, by the efforts of a Boston businessman named John Augustus. Between 1841 and 1859, this shoemaker personally posted bail and served as a guardian to approximately two thousand offenders. In 1878, Boston institutionalized the practice, by implementing a paid probation officer system. In 1891, a second Massachusetts statute authorized a statewide probation system (Friedman, 1993).

The mood and momentum of the Progressive Era prompted several other states to follow Massachusetts' example. These states were New York, New Jersey, Michigan, Illinois, and Pennsylvania. Other forerunners in the probation movement included Maryland in 1894, Vermont in 1898, Rhode Island in 1899, and California in 1903 (Barnes, 1972). By 1930, the federal government and approximately thirty-six states and Washington, D.C., had legislation that enabled the practice of probation (Rothman, 1980). However, only nineteen states actually used probation on a routine basis (Barnes, 1972). All major industrialized states and every major industrialized city used probation regularly. At the outset, probation was primarily an urban, not a rural, practice. Texas, Kentucky, Tennessee, the Dakotas, Nevada, and Wyoming (Rothman, 1980), in particular, rarely employed probation as a sanction.

Probation, unlike parole, was designed as a dispositional alternative to incarceration. It was to be a suspended sentence for those who did not need confinement to be reformed. In attempting to determine who did not need to be confined, probation officers were given the task of conducting pre-sentence investigations. These investigations were to assist judges in assessing an offender's suitability for probation. Pre-sentence investigations, much like the investigations of the parole board, were to uncover every detail of the offender's life. They were to examine the personal history (vital statistics, place of birth, residence, immigrant status), education, early life (truancy record, injuries, early associates, habits of indulgence, grudges, ambitions, parental control), family, neighborhood (grandparents and sibling information, including education and causes of death), home situation (economic status, number of boarders, moral condition) and personality of the offender (ibid.). Armed with this knowledge, probation officers were expected to identify the offender's problems and recommend a sentence and treatment that could remedy the identified problems.

In their supervisory capacity, probation officers, like parole officers, were to be all things at once, ranging from policeman, friend, and social worker to expert on the science of human behavior. Having been educated and trained in the social sciences, they were to be gatherers of facts, and capable of converting those facts into an individually tailored treatment plan. This plan was to include not only contacts with the offender, but contacts with the offender's family, community, and employer. The officer was to become immersed in the life of his charges so that he could mold the offender into a "normal" and productive citizen. Consequently, it was expected that officers would maintain a small caseload of approximately fifty offenders (ibid.). For detailed discussion of this multipronged supervision strategy see Mary Richmond's book, *Social Diagnosis*. Published in 1917, it was regarded as the quintessential probation officer's handbook of the time.

PROGRESSIVE PENOLOGY IN PRACTICE

Reformatories

While the intentions of the reformatory were admirable, for reasons part administrative, political, financial, or even human nature, the intentions were not carried out in practice. The best account, and perhaps the only thorough modern account, of just how far removed the practices were from the intentions, can be found in Alexander W. Pisciotta's book, *Benevolent Repression: Social Control and the American Reformatory Prison Movement*. In this book, the findings from external investigations conducted of Elmira in 1893, Colorado in 1895, and Pennsylvania in 1892 are detailed. Pisciotta concludes that the reformatory offered little more than scientific jargon and justification for practices that were neither new nor humane.

According to Pisciotta, at Elmira and various other "sister" reformatories, overcrowding, understaffing, and gross mismanagement were the rule rather than the exception. The offender population actually housed in reformatories was not as intended. Designed for youthful offenders just beginning their criminal careers, reformatories, in practice, housed the same seasoned criminals found in regular prisons and penitentiaries. Moreover, and perhaps consistent with reformer intentions, they housed the classified poor, "illiterate," or ethnically "inferior degenerates" feared by middle-class reformers, sociologists, eugenicists, and bio-statisticians (Miller, 1980). Enoch Wines himself reported that blacks went to prison more often than whites for similar offenses and for longer terms (Wines, 1888). The heralded classification and treatment schemes were also marred by many problems, including violence, revolts, smuggling, arson, and homosexuality. Inmate resistance was indeed a severe problem that incurred severe penalties. The nickname given to the godfather of the reformatory movement, "paddler Brockway," merely hints at the tactics employed in confronting this resistance.

Brockway's mastery of public relations masked the corporal punishments he administered on a routine basis. In effect, brutality was carried out in the name of rehabilitation (Pisciotta, 1994). Employing carefully crafted terms and phrases, his "spanking of patients" (i.e., beating of inmates) was justified as "positive extraneous assistance," or "harmless parental discipline" (ibid.). Beatings were administered in "interview" rooms, using a 22-inch by 3-inch wide leather strap that weighed more than one pound when it was wet. The strap beatings were applied to the bare buttocks; no part of the body, not kidneys, eyes, nor face, were spared from hands-on beatings. Inmates and chaplains alike testified that inmates would reemerge with missing teeth and purple bodies (ibid.). T. B. Patton, superintendent of the Pennsylvania reformatory, employed similar tactics. However, in describing the beatings as "punishment rituals" he was not as clever or discreet as Brockway.

Corporal punishments were not the only methods of disciplining inmates in the Elmira Reformatory. For those who were not reformed by the "spankings," there was solitary confinement. Solitary confinement, or what Brockway termed "rest cure," was as physically devastating as the direct beatings. For days and sometimes months at a time, inmates would survive on nothing more than bread and water. While in confinement, they could also be shackled to a sliding ring on a bar or floor, for hours at a time. Depending on which device they were shackled to, they were either prevented from standing upright or forced to keep their hands above their heads. With no window openings or illumination, and little ventilation, offenders were surrounded only by the stench of their urination and defecation (ibid.).

More subtle forms of intimidation were also exercised in the reformatory. Brockway, in particular, regularly engaged in verbal attacks, either personally or through threatening notes. For example, in one note, Brockway wrote:

Ide, are you either a lunatic or a jackass? If the former, you should be sent to an asylum, if the latter, you should be knocked on the head; and if you don't improve your record, whatever you may be, I will knock you on the other end. (quoted in ibid.:40)

On many occasions, Brockway warned inmates who could not endure the military drills or solitary confinement that he would either kill them or send them out in a box. Altogether, it was discovered that Brockway administered 19,497 blows to 2,578 inmates between October 1888 and September 1893. In 1889, the number of inmates paddled was 261, increasing incrementally to 681 by 1893. During this same period, inmates spent 7,609 days in "rest cure" cells and 18,681 notices and warnings were issued (Pisciotta, 1994).

The dissolution of humane treatment in the reformatory system was not the only example of progressive penology's failure. For the most part, the entire knowledge/classification/treatment nexus crumbled. In the Colorado Reformatory, inmates were neither classified nor separated. The sick were housed with the healthy and the young with the old. School programs were without essential supplies (books) and the praised economic incentive work program was flawed as well. For example, inmates may have earned forty cents a day, but paid thirty-two cents for room and board, in addition to paying to see the doctor and dentist. They could also be fined approximately sixty cents for rule infractions. Consequently, with no money to spare because of payment given to other necessities, offenders could accrue written reprimands for failure to pay fines. This resulted in the offender being demoted to the third grade (ibid.).

The obvious defects of the marking/merit system had rippling effects. A proper system of release was necessarily linked to the proper operation of a classification and rehabilitation system. If the latter did not work as intended, then neither could the system of release. Consequently, the indeterminate sentence and parole became little more than mechanisms to regulate prison populations.

Indeterminate Sentence and Parole

The ideas given for the justification of the indeterminate sentence and parole may have been rooted in the progressive ideas of reform, training, and second chances, but their implementation encountered a number of pressing problems. For instance, fixed sentences without guidelines, which was the general practice, led to considerable sentencing disparity. It was hoped that, through indeterminate sentences, the parole boards could release offenders in a way that would reduce disparity. Predictably, indeterminate sentences without guidelines led to further disparity with offenders of matched legal status still serving sentences of very different lengths. Yet, wardens used this disparity and uncertainty as a means of gaining control over potentially unruly inmates. In this regard, the threat of denied parole served the needs of institutional control. The indeterminate sentence and parole combined also served the added functions of relieving prison overcrowding and idleness (Miller, 1980; Simon, 1993). As private sector contracts (leasing systems) with prisons developed opposition from outside labor groups, occupying inmates with meaningful work became extremely difficult.

The process of release to parole was flawed in a number of other respects. The decision to release was not determined by a panel of behavioral experts. Parole board members consisted primarily of other state officials, friends of politicians, and/or individuals with no qualifications whatsoever (Rothman, 1980). Moreover, those charged with the task of making such decisions had little or no time to conduct proper inquiries into the offender's achievements or failures while incarcerated. The boards met a few times a year, during which time they were to determine the fates of several hundred offenders. Not surprisingly, little effort was spent investigating the offender's institutional record and progress. In fact, as Rothman (1980) and Pisciotta (1994) have noted, the process of determining release typically lasted no more than three to five minutes.

During those minutes, there were no formal parole guidelines to follow. Major facts of the case were typically recounted. Other questions simply elicited verbal assurances from the offender. Questions of this nature included: "What would you do if released?" "Are you through with drinking?" (Rothman, 1980). The physical appearance of the offender was also taken into consideration. Was the offender well built, neat, or unkempt? The threat of recidivism was also determined by whether the potential parolee had secured a job or a job sponsor (Simon, 1993) and a residence prior to being released (Pisciotta, 1994). However, the requirement of retaining a job or job sponsor was greatly relaxed, given the need to expedite releases due to overcrowding.

While such release practices resolved managerial and fiscal demands, they were hardly responsive to public demands. As a result, the idea of improving the reformation process via the community was born (Simon, 1993). It was now espoused that "the real work of normalization would fall to parole, not the prison." Still, the promise of reformation was not to be realized in the community either.

Parole supervision had little to offer the offender in the way of rehabilitation and little to offer the public in the way of safety. Writing in 1930, Barnes contended that the only good to come from parole was that it got men out of prison sooner (Barnes, 1972). Barnes claims that parole was nothing but a "palpable paper parole, which neither provided supervision nor encouragement to reform." Work was the primary element of the supervision process, and it was undoubtedly the most important one. This did not mean that community and family ties and reintegration were not important, they were merely supplemental to the emphasis upon work. For example, parolees were to adhere to four basic rules or conditions: (1) remain employed, (2) submit monthly reports signed by their employer, (3) do not quit or change jobs, and (4) in all respects, conduct themselves with honesty, sobriety, and decency, avoiding low or evil associations, and abstain from intoxicating drinks (Pisciotta, 1994). Hans von Hentig observed that "in complying strictly with every one of these conditions, the parolee would at once draw the attention of his neighbors to his being either a crank or a convict who has been released on parole" (Von Hentig, 1942:364; cited also in Simon, 1993:57). Stated differently, how did one who came from a lower class community, where the criminal element purportedly resided, not associate with those who were of low associations? Consequently, parole violations and revocations were easy to justify. Moreover, lawyers were not to be present at parole hearings. The inmate could only submit documents in his defense.

Probation

The practice of probation fared no better in meeting the ambitious objectives of the progressive agenda. Relative to its intentions, probation failed immediately. To begin, probation positions, like parole positions, were not occupied by those trained in the social sciences. Probation officers were to be selected from the ranks of the new college graduates, but were instead selected from the ranks of volunteers, political supporters of judges, state attorney and most often police personnel, and various other individuals lacking the credentials for changing the lives and habits of offenders. Nor were the working conditions of probation officers likely to attract college graduates. Salaries were pitifully low, ranging between $900 and $2,500 dollars per year (the average salary for the unskilled factory worker was $1,200) (Rothman, 1980). The work environment served as an added disincentive, as officers were thrown together in one room where noise and crowding served as constant distractions. Overwhelming caseloads only contributed to the certain frustration. For example, historical documents show that in Newark, New Jersey, 37 probation officers were responsible for 5,800 cases, amounting to approximately 150 cases per officer. In Milwaukee, 3 officers were charged with the supervision of 839 offenders (ibid.).

The ability of probation officers to provide informed decisions to judges and supervision to offenders was clearly undermined by these burdensome circumstances. Pre-sentence investigations were comprised of a few facts and much speculation. They were more often "dossiers of gossip" (ibid.) rather than carefully composed diagnostic reports. In "watching over the offender" (ibid.), the record was no better than it had been in parole. Personal contact with offenders was rare and in some jurisdictions amounted to no more than 10 minutes a year (ibid.). Probation officers did not have time to "know" their probationers, much less become familiar with their family, work, and community environment. Supervision regimens ultimately dissolved into the nominal ritual of collecting monthly reports.

Probation also failed in its most basic function as an alternative to prison. Though probation was conceived as an alternative to state imprisonment, this

locally funded program was generally implemented as an alternative to local jail sentences or nothing. This outcome is not surprising when one considers that states required local jurisdictions to absorb the costs of supervising
state-remanded offenders. In response, local jurisdictions simply complied
with the state mandate to use probation, but did so in a way that served their
fiscal needs (ibid.). Very importantly, it was with this misapplication of
probation that the pattern of implementing alternatives to incarceration as
supplements to incarceration began.

Overall, progressive penology failed in the eyes of its designers, even
though it succeeded in the eyes of the reforms' users. Prison wardens utilized
parole and the indeterminate sentence as a control tool. Judges used probation to enhance their sanctioning options and, in effect, their discretion. Prosecutors improved their conviction rates as the prospect of parole and
probation facilitated plea-bargaining. Finally, through parole, legislators won
favor with their constituents. They contained prison costs through parole releases, and were able to deflect blame for the release of dangerous offenders
to parole boards (ibid.).

SUMMARY AND DISCUSSION

In the midst of the chaos and excitement of massive immigration, industrialization, and urbanization, progressivism was born. Progressivism enlisted citizens from all walks of life, for the purpose of safeguarding the quality of
American life. It attracted maverick journalists, college student idealists, op-
portunists, men, women, and the middle class, in an all-out effort to expose
the deceit and corruption of politicians and corporate capitalism (Unger and
Unger, 1977). As a result of these efforts, government and science, hand in
hand, were given the task of improving and correcting society.

It was out of this context of social, economic, and government engineer-
ing that an ambitious penal reform agenda was conceived. Prompted by the
failures of the existing system, and shaped by a progressive social context
and theories of the scientific community, the reformatory, indeterminate sentence, parole, and probation came into being. What these reforms shared in
common was the formal intent to investigate, classify, and then treat the offender according to his biological, economical, psychological, and sociological circumstances. However, the promise and the reality of these
monumental reforms diverged considerably. The simple premise of the reformatory, indeterminate sentencing, and parole was that confinement ought
to continue until reformation was demonstrated, and that, for young offenders deemed salvageable, a second chance ought to be afforded. However,
the reformatory failed to provide more humane and effective methods of
social reeducation. Meanwhile, parole was rendered a mechanism to ease

prison overcrowding and to extend the control of the institution into the community. Probation was conceived as an alternative to incarceration, but acted as a supplement in practice, thereby expanding control over populations previously not subject to incarceration. This pattern of expanded control and failure to reform was witnessed in another of the progressive movement strategies, namely the juvenile court.

NOTE

1. A short-lived and limited-use punishment policy enacted during the Progressive era was the sterilization of offenders of mostly immigrant background. The biological knowledge of the day held that criminal genes were inherited, and so the expedient and humane way of eliminating the "idiotic and feeble-minded" (Barnes, 1972) was to sterilize all its members. Following the precedent of Indiana in 1907, twenty-three states legalized the sterilization of the "hopelessly defective and the habitually criminal groups" (Barnes, 1972). By 1930, thirteen of those states—California, Delaware, Idaho, Maine, Minnesota, Montana, Nebraska, New Hampshire, North Dakota, Oregon, Utah, Virginia, and Wisconsin—had formally active sterilization laws. Sterilizing over five thousand offenders, California was by far the most active in its use of such laws. No other state approached even five hundred. While sterilization laws were challenged as unconstitutional, they were ultimately upheld by the U.S. Supreme Court in the case of *Carrie Buck v. Virginia* (Barnes, 1972).

7

Progressive America and the Juvenile Court Movement (1900–1960s)

INTRODUCTION

BEFORE JUVENILE COURTS, children in trouble with the law were, in theory, handled according to the Common Law Principle of Responsibility. The Common Law Principle specified three categories of youth that were differentiated by age and an associated presumption of criminal intent. Specifically, children under the age of seven were presumed incapable of harboring criminal intent and were not to be subject to criminal sanctions. Children between the ages of seven and fourteen were presumed possibly capable of harboring criminal intent and could be subject to criminal sanctions. Youth aged fourteen and older were presumed definitely capable of harboring criminal intent and were to be subject to criminal sanctions. As a result of the possibility that children aged seven or older could be subject to adultlike criminal sanctions, including the death penalty, the development of the juvenile court was commonly considered as a major benevolent reform that spared children from the harsh punishments meted out to adult criminals (Mennel, 1973). However, historical evidence suggests that the juvenile court did far more than appease the conscience of society.

To illustrate, a review of fourteen leading cases involving determinations of criminal responsibility of children in America between 1801 and 1882 demonstrates that children were generally treated more leniently than were adults. In these particular cases, seven youths were charged with homicide, one with manslaughter, five with larceny, and one with trespass. Of the fourteen cases, the jury verdict was not guilty in ten of the cases; the child charged with malicious trespass was found guilty with the sentence not reported; two slave children aged eleven and twelve were executed; the remaining child was sentenced to three years in prison for grand larceny. While these cases were not necessarily typical, they do suggest that children were not held as responsible as adults were for their actions. Moreover, given this period's prevalent racism and discriminatory practices, it is unlikely that the two ex-

83

ecuted children would have received the death penalty had they been white (Platt, 1977:207–212). Nonetheless, and despite the fact that children in trouble with the law were generally handled differently from adult offenders, the popular interpretation of history held that countless troubled children were treated like adult offenders before juvenile courts.

In light of this interpretation, the development of juvenile courts at the turn of the twentieth century is considered one of the most ambitious and influential reforms of the Progressive era. Juvenile courts were envisioned as a means to save children from criminal prosecution through individualized treatment with exclusive attention provided on a case-by-case basis. Such a policy necessarily required expansive court discretion and control. In fact, late nineteenth- and early twentieth-century child labor laws and mandatory school attendance, coupled with the newly emerging juvenile court, embodied a growing treatment and rehabilitative ideology that came to be known as the *twentieth-century rehabilitative ideal*. This general rehabilitative ideology would later be applied not only to children but adult criminal offenders as well as the mentally ill.

This chapter examines the social context, ideas, practices, and selected consequences of the juvenile court movement. Consistent with the experiences of earlier penal reforms, the juvenile court's formally prescribed goal of individual treatment was not realized in its everyday practices. As characterized by Bortner (1984), the juvenile court's espoused mission of individualized treatment has been little more than a tarnished ideal.

JUVENILE COURT AS ACCELERATED PROGRESSIVE IDEOLOGY

Progressive ideology and its associated penal reforms emerged in the context of late nineteenth century's anxiety and perception of needs associated with America's fast-developing corporate capitalism. The juvenile court, reformatories, indeterminate sentencing, parole, and probation were all part of a continuing stream of progressive experimentation aimed at responding to various social problems wrought by rapid industrialization, immigration, and urbanization (Schlossman, 1977).

Beginning with the Haymarket Riot of 1886, America's industrial centers were experiencing repetitive strikes, worker-related violence, and numerous business failures. Organizations like the Socialist party and Industrial Workers of the World were increasing their demands for major changes in the social and economic conditions of workers. Emerging from this conflict was a corporate-sponsored plan to save capitalism. What was needed was a strategy that could simultaneously regulate and stabilize production, while mollifying popular protest and militancy among workers (Platt, 1977). The ultimate choice, according to Williams (1966), was between a reformed capitalist system and a revolutionary movement. Given these high stakes, the pressures for effective and far-reaching reform were intense.

If America's newly emerging capitalist system were to prosper, not only were changes in business and industry necessary, but so too were changes in the education and preparation of the young. Scientific management arose as a means to increase efficiency and effectiveness in business and industry. Intelligence testing, compulsory school attendance, and child labor laws ensured that children would receive the proper education and skills for the industrial economy's changing employment needs. The prevalent thinking was that whatever was best for the newly emerging economy was best for the general public (Center for Research on Criminal Justice, 1975).

Progressive reformers considered previously held values and institutional strategies to be ineffective in successfully overcoming the turmoil associated with mass immigration, industrialization, and urbanization. Integral to the overall progressive reform agenda was what Platt (1977) termed "the child-saving movement." Like reformatories, indeterminate sentencing, and parole and probation reforms, the child-saving movement developed in response to rapid social change and to a growing belief in positivistic explanations of delinquency and the benefits of scientific social casework for rehabilitating offenders (Mennel, 1973; Ryerson, 1978; Schlossman, 1977). The progressives believed that by conducting individualized inquiries into the lives of troubled youth, the antecedent causes of their misbehavior could be identified. Once these antecedent causes were identified, an individual treatment plan could be implemented that would overcome these antecedent causes, thereby correcting the youth's subsequent behavior. This was the goal and promise of scientific social casework.

While the child-saving movement attracted individuals from a variety of political and social class backgrounds, its most ardent supporters were the daughters and wives of the old landed gentry or the industrial nouveau riche. Platt (1977) contends that the overall impact of the child-saving movement was both forward-looking and conservative in that it combined concern for the needy in the new industrial order with an earlier held class bias. While the rank and file members of the child-saving movement were aligned with corporate America, they were also concerned with alleviating the misery and suffering of the immigrant poor. In particular, they had to educate and socialize their children in accordance with the needs of corporate capitalism.

Immigrant children were to be molded into citizens committed to the American way of life. Various reform efforts would ensure not only the status quo but also the realization of the American dream for immigrants and other children in distress. The task, as stated by Henderson in 1899, was one that combined welfare of the defective with the good of the community:

The supreme test of philanthropy is not found in the blind and instinctive sat-isfaction of a kind impulse, nor in the apparent comfort of dependent persons, but rather in the welfare of the community and of the future race. Deliberate-ly, rationally, and with widest possible knowledge, we must try our success by this standard. Not that we admit any real conflict between the welfare of the defective and the good of the community. We follow the logic of the doctrine of solidarity to its extreme limits, and admit that every human being, even crim-inals and idiots, are members of the social body. To wound them is to hurt all, and the loss of the least of them would be a loss of the whole human race. (Hen-derson, 1899:25)

Ultimately, one of the reform strategies that emerged to accomplish these in-terrelated goals was the juvenile court.

THE PROMISE OF INDIVIDUAL TREATMENT

Officially prescribed juvenile court goals and practices were grounded in the notion of individual treatment within a nonadversarial system. Juvenile courts were not to operate according to due process, adversarial proceed-ings, presumption of innocence, and rights to a jury trial and defense coun-sel, but rather upon the presumption that troubled children were in need of treatment and care. The juvenile court was to serve as a "surrogate parent" for these troubled youth by providing them the approximate care that would be provided by responsible and caring parents.

Given the purpose of individualized treatment, punishment was not in-cluded among the juvenile court's functions. In fact, juvenile court judges' robes, terminology, and the physical design of court facilities reflected the "new" treatment or "medicalized" approach. Juvenile court judges routinely employed medical metaphors such as disease, treatment, cure, and pathol-ogy during their handling of cases. Juvenile court facilities were designed like medical clinics rather than traditional courtrooms. Juvenile court judges wore white robes rather than black robes, consistent with their role model of doctor or clinician rather than jurist. Such characteristics and practices were in keeping with the juvenile courts' underlying concept of *parens patriae* and the goal of individual treatment through scientific social casework (Rothman, 1980; Schlossman, 1977).

The concept of *parens patriae* provided juvenile courts with broad dis-cretion in dealing with troubled youth. Since the court's purpose was to save and treat youth instead of determining guilt or innocence and administering punishment, the reasoning was that broad and largely unfettered discretion was necessary if juvenile courts were to be successful in fulfilling the court's individual treatment goals. As Schlossman illustrates, Denver, Colorado, juvenile court judge Ben Lindsey, who presided during the early 1900s, was by far one of the court's earliest and most famous boosters.

> Lindsey's engaging tales of delinquents who responded positively to his coun-
> sel, who confided intimate secrets to him, who after appearing in court obeyed
> parents they had previously scorned, and who attended school, worked steadi-
> ly, and reported regularly to probation officers provided a glowing commen-
> tary on the achievements of one early juvenile court. If one is to believe Lindsey
> (and there is little solid evidence to challenge his view) neglected, dependent,
> and delinquent children in Denver received more solicitous treatment than
> would have been possible in a city where stricter rules of evidence and proce-
> dure applied. Lindsey appears to have wielded his enormous power with dis-
> cretion, humanity, and shrewdness. By taking familial, social, and economic
> factors into account, and adding a dose of his remarkable intuition, Lindsey me-
> diated constructively between an impersonal criminal code and the distinctive
> problems of children. Despite the seeming contradiction, he ruled as a benev-
> olent judicial despot. (Schlossman, 1977:56)

Judge Lindsey became an early role model for juvenile court judges and a major spokesman for the juvenile court movement throughout the country. Lindsey authored numerous books and articles reflecting his Denver court experiences and made speeches across the nation. In the opinion of Schloss-man, while other judges, probation officers, and child welfare workers wrote and spoke about their juvenile court experiences, it was Lindsey who "came close to dictating the form and content of contemporary opinion on the sub-ject for at least two decades, especially through his artful renditions or di-dactic sentimental stories" (ibid.).

Since the vision of the juvenile court was that of surrogate for the child's parents, the handling by the court of numerous childhood-related difficulties and problems that extended beyond lawbreaking was assumed appropriate and necessary. Consequently, four categories of troubled children were es-tablished and subsumed under the jurisdiction of the juvenile court:

1. Delinquent Children. Children who had committed an act that if com-mitted by an adult would be a crime.

2. Status Offenders. Children who could not be handled by their parents or guardians, or were engaged in behavior felt harmful but not considered criminal if engaged in by an adult.

3. Neglected Children. Children whose parents or guardians were failing to provide them necessary care and guidance.

4. Dependent Children. Children whose parents or guardians, for what-ever reasons, are unable to provide and care for them. (Paulsen and White-bread, 1974:32)

Such broad juvenile court authority over children could be understood as part of a larger effort to enforce what Empey (1982) termed "the modern concept of childhood." To summarize Empey, the modern concept of childhood assumed (1) that children go through several developmental stages; (2) that throughout these stages children are fundamentally different from adults; and (3) until children develop full emotional capacities, they should be quarantined from adult habits, vices, and responsibilities (ibid.:334).

The juvenile court emerged then as a benevolent surrogate not only for nonfunctioning parents but also for ineffective schools. The first juvenile court act passed in Illinois in 1899 specified, "The care, custody, and discipline of a child shall approximate . . . that which should be given by its parents" (ibid.:334). Additionally, the Educational Commission of Chicago stated concern that its Compulsory School Attendance Act was not sufficient to counteract the culture conflict experienced by marginal children. The juvenile court was to be the solution to parental and school failures. As emphatically worded by Harpur in 1899, "We should rightfully have the power to arrest all the little beggars, loafers, and vagabonds that infest our city, take them from the streets, and place them in schools where they are compelled to receive education and learn moral principles" (pp. 163–164).

To accomplish individual treatment, juvenile courts were to implement a series of interrelated procedures. The first procedure was intake, where children were referred to the juvenile court. Parents, school authorities, or the police could make these referrals. At the point of intake, juvenile courts were to have a number of decision options. These options could include releasing the child with a warning, placing the child in detention while the case progressed, filing a petition for formal juvenile court disposition, or referring the child to another agency or criminal court for more serious offenses. Ideally, the procedures and decision alternatives were to enable juvenile courts to provide each troubled child with individualized and therapeutic treatment that was responsive to the particular needs and characteristics of the child in question.

The use of probation officers was (and continues to be) fundamental to juvenile court practice. Probation officers conducted the social casework histories and screening of children, made recommendations to the judge before court dispositions, and provided case supervision following court dispositions. The probation officer's social casework histories of youth were intended to capture a child's past, thereby enabling identification and description of specific antecedent events, problems, circumstances, experiences, associations, or family characteristics that contributed to or caused the child's behavior problems. Based upon the probation officer's determination of the contributors to or causes of the child's behavior problem, the probation officer could recommend dismissing the case, handling the case informally through counsel and release, or referring the case to court for formal disposition. Further, probation officers determined whether the youth should be held in detention until court proceedings and case disposition.

For children judged by investigating probation officers to be in need of formal juvenile court adjudication, a hearing was held involving the judge with the probation officer providing assistance. The primary function of juvenile court judges at the adjudication stage was to determine if the child was delinquent, predelinquent, or dependent and neglected. In theory, in the adjudication process, judges and probation officers attempted to do for the child what caring parents would do when confronted with a troubled child.

Ultimately, the juvenile court judge decided what was to be done with the child and this decision was referred to as a disposition. There were two general categories of juvenile court dispositions: (1) children were judged suitable for return to their home under the care of parents or guardians or (2) children were judged suitable for some form of out-of-home placement. If the child was returned to his or her home, the child was normally supervised by a probation officer who met regularly with the child and family and employed other appropriate community resources for assistance. Children judged suitable for out-of-home placements could be placed in a variety of public or private correctional or treatment facilities. Both a return-to-home or out-of-home disposition by the juvenile court involved the use of indeterminate sentencing. This meant that juvenile courts could maintain control over children until the age of majority (eighteen or twenty-one, depending upon state law) or until the child was judged no longer in need of court jurisdiction.

Overall, juvenile court intake, adjudication, and disposition were conceived as analogous to medical diagnosis and treatment. The stated intention of juvenile courts was to provide individual diagnosis and treatment of each child, thereby ensuring ultimate rehabilitation and full societal participation by these children.

JUVENILE COURT IMPLEMENTATION AND PRACTICE

During the past several decades, a number of researchers have examined the implementation and characteristic practices of juvenile courts. Then and now, a major focus of this research was what has been termed "goals versus practices" of juvenile courts. What has emerged consistently throughout these studies has been a finding of disparity between the juvenile court's official goal of individual treatment and the court's routine practices of youth control (Bortner, 1984; Platt, 1977; Rothman, 1980).

Between 1899 and 1925, juvenile courts proliferated across the United States. While the philosophy and goals of the courts reflected the progressive ideal of individualized treatment, the actual design, organization, and jurisdiction of the courts differed widely within and between states. Many of these differences were substantial and resulted in very different organizational structures, procedures, and practices. For example, Rothman (1980) specifies that some states designated juvenile courts as chancery courts, thereby empowering them to implement their individual rules and procedures to handle different youth problems. Several jurisdictions, including Massachusetts, New York, and Washington, D.C., viewed juvenile courts as essentially criminal courts and mandated very specific rules and procedures to govern their operations. Additionally, considerable local variation in court practices occurred, with some juvenile courts handling all crimes committed by youth and others only dealing with less serious offenses. Most juvenile courts handled neglect cases as well as adoption, truancy, adults contributing to the delinquency of minors, and commitments of youth to mental institutions (ibid.:205–220).

The juvenile court's ad hoc design and jurisdictional differences were the result of a tendency by early juvenile court supporters to view the court in very ideal and general terms. Consequently there was little guidance or specificity in statutes establishing the courts. Lemert (1970) attributes the failure of juvenile courts to implement a generic set of legal and operational procedures to five factors:

1. The line of continuity between traditional courts of law and the juvenile court proved to be very tenuous, owing to the use of lay judges and the low level of commitment and interest among legally trained judges assigned to it.

2. Relatively few appeals were taken from juvenile court decisions and when they were, higher court decisions sustained wide limits of discretion for the lower court; hence, an important source of clarification necessary for the creative growth of law was absent.

3. Early probation officers and welfare workers connected with the court were nonprofessional and had little conception of procedure or its importance.

4. Clients of the court tended to be powerless people, often ethnic minorities, who were poorly equipped to make articulate demands on the court.

5. Legal counsel was seldom present to initiate adversary or other action that might have generated continuity with criminal or other legal procedure. (ibid.:25–26)

However, while juvenile courts did not implement a generic set of operational procedures, they did develop individually distinct court procedures. According to Lindsey and Burrough (1931) and Hart (1910), juvenile courts implemented distinguishable operational features from their day-to-day interactions with a variety of individuals and groups. Among them were parents, police, probation officers, judges, welfare workers, and church representatives, who reflected primarily the interests and values of the local communities in which the courts operated. The associated organizational resources available to judges also dictated the structure and activities of the court.

As a result of ambiguous legislation and different community interests, values, and functional needs, juvenile court organization and procedures developed in an uneven and fragmented fashion. In 1925, when a majority of states had passed juvenile court legislation, the courts varied considerably in their respective levels of probation service, use of social case histories in dispositions, availability of detention facilities other than county jails, and the education and experience levels of judges (Belden, 1920). During the 1930s, with the advance of social work, psychiatry, and psychology, and the increasing professionalization of probation officers, an accelerated treatment focus was embraced by a number of juvenile courts, particularly the larger urban courts.

Following World War II, many juvenile courts experienced major increases in the volume of cases, which resulted in increased court bureaucratization. For example, California's population increased by 50 percent during the 1940s. During this decade, the state's juvenile courts responded to this rapid population growth with increased commitments to state reformatories. Specifically, the state's youth reformatory population increased from 1,300 in 1941 to 2,526 in 1953 (Blomberg, 1978).

Before World War II, California's response to increased juvenile court commitments to the state's reformatories was to build more reformatories. However, during World War II and into the early 1950s, there were lags in the construction of new state facilities. These construction lags resulted in excessively long local detention stays for those juveniles awaiting state reformatory placement. Consequently, many local jurisdictions were forced either to rely upon jails to hold these youth or to construct new and larger detention facilities.

However, confusion remained as to the explicit role and function of local juvenile courts and the associated role and function of the state. In 1941, California's response to this general confusion was to establish the California Youth Authority to treat state-committed youth. In 1943, the California legislature expanded the Youth Authority's duties to include development of uniform juvenile court and probation standards and practices throughout the state. The Youth Authority's specific juvenile court and probation duties included inspecting local detention facilities and camps that received state funds and requiring each county to submit annual probation reports. Penalties for noncompliance were never specified and the Youth Authority never exerted formal authority over any county for noncompliance. Consequently, and despite the Youth Authority's efforts, California juvenile courts continued to develop in an uneven and divergent manner.

What characterized California's juvenile court experiences from the 1930s to the 1960s, as well as other juvenile courts across the country, were primarily locally determined court functions and associated services and practices. Local juvenile court functions, services, and practices reflected particular community values, group interests, and functional necessities. In rural counties throughout the country, children tended to be grouped into one of two dispositional categories: (1) those good enough to remain in their homes subject to probation supervision or (2) those who had committed serious enough crimes to be held in a state reformatory. In larger urban counties, local juvenile court services were more numerous and differentiated. They included detention facilities that separated delinquent from dependent and neglected youth, local institutions, camps, ranches, group or residential homes, and specialized probation services with varying caseload sizes and treatment modalities resulting in multiple types of court dispositions.

Ultimately, the philosophical preferences held by individual juvenile court judges for handling troubled youth were blurred with the dispositional alternatives available to the judges. As a result, juvenile court decisions can be understood not so much as individualistic but rather as typical and routine. Youth coming before judges were categorized as appropriate for an available juvenile court disposition and routinely processed into that dispositional alternative. Generally, as the numbers and types of youth problems changed, so too did the number and types of dispositional alternatives. In effect, the type of justice received by individual youth was substantially determined by when and where the justice was administered.

Pezman (1963) describes several cases in depression era Los Angeles that demonstrate the time and place association of juvenile court decision practices:

In 1932, depression-ridden, transient boys were coming to Los Angeles in great numbers. Available detention facilities were filled to maximum capacities. Continuing arrivals necessitated the returning of the boys to their "point of origin" at county expense. Transients throughout the nation learned: "If you ride the rods out to California, they will send you home on the cushions." Several amusing incidents illustrate the not-so-amusing problem: One small boy, it is recalled, promised the judge to return and stay home in Indiana if he would be allowed to see his favorite motion-picture star in person. The judge, in an indulgent mood, made arrangements and the boy not only met his favorite "cowboy" but also was allowed to ride the actor's famous horse. A month later the boy returned to California and appeared again before the judge, this time with three other transient companions. The boy explained to the judge: "You see, judge, my friends didn't believe I met him (the cowboy). They want to ride on his horse, too." Another boy, from the Deep South, listened to the judge remark: "This is the third and last time I am going to see you in this court." "What's the matter, judge," the boy responded questionably, "you going to quit?" To discourage the arrival of these transient children, the Los Angeles Board of Supervisors met in special session and approved a plan to establish temporary work camps to help them earn passage home. The plan carried the endorsement of the judge of the juvenile court, the probation officer, and the county forester and fire warden. (pp. 1–2)

Friedman (1993) concludes that the evidence on early juvenile courts demonstrates that they were viewed as popular courts among immigrant and working-class parents. He argues that these parents employed the courts as a means to control their troublesome children. Essentially, the courts were used as a weapon in the clash of cultures between Old World parents and children in a new American world and culture. Most delinquent cases handled by the courts involved boys; however, when girls were brought before the courts, a different standard often prevailed. Girls were regularly brought before the courts by their parents for sexual misbehavior, which did not trouble the parents of boys.

The following case summaries taken from Schlossman (1977) illustrate the often minor nature of cases referred to juvenile court probation officers and the haphazard types of resolutions reached:

In July, 1914, a probation officer received word that sixteen-year-old Gerald Muldower refused to work, stayed out late at night, and smoked cigarettes. Upon investigation it was learned that Gerald's parents were dead, and he was living with his grandparents who had filed the complaint. Further inquiry revealed that Gerald had been unemployed for nearly two years, refusing to work ever since he lost a finger on his last factory job. Confronted with these "charges," Gerald promised the probation officer that he would seek employment and pay board to his grandparents. Whether Gerald was threatened with a court appearance is impossible to determine. But he quickly corrected his errant ways and obtained a job in a hardware store, after which the officer closed the case as a successful settlement. Was Gerald "on the road to delinquency"? No one knew, of course, but at least for the moment the intervention of the officer seemed to improve the intrafamily relations.

Three weeks earlier a similar case had required more affirmative action. Mr. Pildowski complained about his two teen-age boys who refused to work or attend school and who spent their days "bumming around" railroad tracks or frolicking in outlying woods. The probation officer advised the boys to find work, but to no avail. After two unsuccessful visits to their home, he called them into his office and employed scare tactics, threatening to bring formal charges (probably for truancy or incorrigibility) against them. The ultimate fate of these boys remains unclear; presumably they found the officer's threat frightening enough to find employment. At any rate, this case was also listed as a successful settlement.

The complaints parents brought against their own children were often extreme, leaving the court with few dispositional options. It was a pleasurable, if
rare, achievement to resolve one of these cases out of court.

An example was the case of Mrs. Sherman, who accused her son Israel of
staying out late at night and stealing. At first Mrs. Sherman insisted that Israel
be locked up for at least a year, but a probation officer convinced her to see
whether the three of them might be able to talk out their problems. Israel, perhaps realizing that unless he agreed to the talk he would be taken into court
and possibly committed, volunteered to place himself on probation. The officer approved and also forced Israel to plead for forgiveness while on his knees.
Were it not for the probation officer's early intervention, Israel would surely
have been brought into court on a charge of incorrigibility and would have
been subject to the vagaries and uncertainties of the judicial decision-making
process.

Other cases similarly highlighted ambiguity in probation officers' attempts
to "prevent" delinquency. Overt criminal acts rarely entered into complaints.

Consider the accusation of Mrs. Elvehrer, who alleged that a neighbor's
child was molesting her children. Upon investigation, the probation officer realized the complaint had no basis in fact; the children were being used as
pawns in a quarrel between two adults. The officer sternly warned both parents to stop their fighting; once they agreed he closed the case as a successful
resolution. Similar to the Elvehrer case was a neighbor's complaint charging a
young girl with truancy. Investigation revealed the girl had a valid work permit
and that the neighbor was simply trying to upset the girl's mother.

This type of complaint frequently backfired. For instance, Mrs. Wolenski
charged in April 1915, that Peter Czerzak, who lived in a nearby rear basement
apartment, was neglecting his four-year-old daughter. Unable to locate
Czerzak, the probation officer decided to investigate Mrs. Wolenski's house.
Finding it in a "very filthy condition," she warned Mrs. Wolenski to clean up or
she would bring her family into court and charge her with neglect. Similarly,
Mr. Padrewski complained that three neighborhood youths had attacked his
son Lewis. The investigating officer learned, however, that Lewis had actually
instigated the quarrel and moreover, that the boy surreptitiously smoked cigarettes. The officer concluded that Lewis was "to all appearances a bad boy and
will need watching." From accusers, Mr. Padrewski and his son had become
the accused.

However ambiguous the relation of out-of-court settlements to delinquency "prevention," such settlements were often accompanied with extrajudicial
punishments. Two cases in August 1916 demonstrated this practice.

In the first case, Mr. and Mrs. Esk complained that their thirteen-year-old
daughter, Denise, was incorrigible. When they brought her to the probation office, she was "very saucy" to her mother, accusing her of immorality, among
other things. Thereupon the probation officer, on her own initiative and against
the parents' remonstrations, placed Denise in detention for four days. Realizing that they had no control over the proceedings, the Esks dropped the charges
against Denise after her release. In the second case Mrs. Debrink complained
about her daughter Ellen's "sauciness" and brought her to the probation office

to discuss their problems. Ellen, however, refused to pay any attention to the probation officer, whereupon he placed her in detention for several days and then put her on probation. (Schlossman, 1977:149–153)

The cases described thus far all originated with parents or neighbors. While charitable agencies and school authorities initiated fewer cases, the cases they did initiate required more immediate and affirmative action:

For example, in November 1916, a public school teacher alleged that every day all the Mordinski children arrived at school hungry. Upon investigation the probation officer uncovered a rather bizarre situation. Mr. and Mrs. Mordinski had been having a bitter dispute over the latter's refusal to transfer half of her property rights to her husband. In the interim Mr. Mordinski had refused to provide money for food and had not eaten at home in six months. When the probation officer arrived at the house the cupboards were indeed empty. Somehow the probation officer was able to effect a quick reconciliation between husband and wife; Mrs. Mordinski agreed to her husband's demands and Mr. Mordinski promised to give her money for food. The officer's early intervention may not have prevented delinquency, but it certainly prevented malnutrition.

Compared to their representation in cases brought to court, girls appeared disproportionately in out-of-court settlements. About half of the cases in the logbook involved girls of varying ages. Moreover, in stark contrast to their response in cases brought to court, the probation officers generally responded pragmatically to female moral improprieties. Seemingly comparable offenses could be found before the court as well as in out-of-court settlements, thus highlighting the centrality of discretion in the court's modus operandi. One never knew quite what to expect from the probation officers.

Consider the investigation of a complaint (origin uncertain) that sixteen-year-old Eloise was pregnant and was bragging about her condition to young girls in her neighborhood. Eloise's mother had died seven years earlier, her father worked half days, and three of her five siblings still lived at home. Eloise cooked and kept house for them and her father, thus helping to keep the family intact. Although she admitted to being pregnant, Eloise denied having told anyone but relatives. Furthermore, she was to be married to the child's father in less than a month. The reaction of the probation officer—nearly always a woman in cases like this—was temperate. After due consideration of alternatives, the officer decided to wait out the month and let the marriage take place. Thus the probation officer, who was clearly shocked at Eloise's condition, held her moralism in check. One may conjecture, based on other cases involving young unwed mothers, that had Eloise not been engaged she would have been allowed to have the baby and then would have been sent to the House of Good Shepherd. But in this instance, quite reasonable, the officer left well enough alone.

Another sex-related case further demonstrated the use of noninstitutional remedies for female sexual promiscuity. This time a group of boys and girls— schoolmates—were involved equally, but the boys, as usual, escaped with little more than a stern warning. The boys had formed a club devoted to group masturbation and the enticement of young girls into intercourse. The probation officer was content to break up the club and did not insist that its members be tried in court. For the boys' indiscretions she urged an educational solution. "I advised the parents that, as each of these boys had now arrived at the age of understanding, that it would be well if, instead of administering corporal punishment, they would take their boy and advise and educate him along the lines of sex hygiene and point out the danger they were putting themselves in by their acts."

Though the girls received harsher treatment, none was institutionalized. Jamie, age ten, whose immorality was confined to necking in nickel shows with the most amorous of the boys, was confined indefinitely to home under parental supervision. Nancy, age eleven, who had played kissing games regularly with boys and masturbated with female partners was, similarly, confined. Even Irma, age fourteen, who admitted to frequent casual intercourse with numerous paramours, was merely forced to transfer schools. (ibid.:149–153)

These case summaries demonstrate several juvenile court trends. Much of the intervention by juvenile court probation officers involved individual youth and family problem-solving rather than delinquency prevention. In their problem-solving efforts, juvenile court probation officers operated with substantial power over youth and their families. Further, while these cases document the practice of handling cases unofficially and without formal court involvement, what is remarkable is that some of these cases received court attention in the first place. Whatever the court's treatment or rehabilitative impact, these types of cases and unofficial handling practices enabled the court to exert new mechanisms of moral authority and control in the form of a surrogate parent. Further, these expansive court powers were not questioned until the 1960s.

During the 1960s, a series of legal changes were ushered into the juvenile court by the Warren Court in the landmark *In re Gault* case of 1967. Specifically, the Warren Court directly confronted and challenged the notion of juvenile courts as caring, supportive, substitute parents with the notion of the courts as legal entities meting out punishment. Juvenile courts were viewed to be more like adult criminal courts in which various legal safeguards and due process were necessary and fundamental. The Warren Court's reasoning was that since the courts could commit youth to reformatories where they were deprived of their liberty for years at a time, it was necessary to recognize the rights of these youth to due process procedures and safeguards.

Since the inception of juvenile courts, criticism has been centered upon the lack of services available to the courts to accomplish their individualized treatment goals. Underlying this criticism has been the assumption that expansion of court services through various reform efforts would result in more individualized and effective youth treatment, thereby reducing delinquency.

While studies have documented the movement of numerous juvenile courts from limited youth supervision agencies to local level correctional establishments complete with diagnostic, institutional, probation, and various community-based youth and family services, the reported results of these various court service reforms have been quite opposite to expectations. Specifically, it has been shown that the court's expansion of services has related less to the explicit treatment needs of youth than to the perceived maintenance and growth requirements of the court's organizational bureaucracy (Blomberg, 1978; Platt, 1977; Schlossman, 1977).

For example, Schlossman (1995) illustrates the juvenile court's pattern of organizational and client growth through consideration of the court's reliance upon state reform schools. Between 1950 and 1970, the total youth population placed in the country's reform schools by juvenile courts increased 75 percent from thirty-five thousand to sixty-two thousand. The number of public reform schools increased to almost two hundred, excluding several hundred additional local ranches, camps, group homes, and private institutions for the court's placement of less serious youth receiving out-of-home dispositions.

SUMMARY AND DISCUSSION

The juvenile court emerged at the turn of the twentieth century as part of the progressive strategy to confront societal turmoil. Juvenile courts were to serve the twofold purpose of individually treating, educating, and morally developing problem youth, and thereby providing for the continued welfare of the larger society. Between 1900 and the 1960s, juvenile courts proliferated throughout the country and substantially expanded their scope, services, and youth population subject to their control.

As discussed earlier in this book, different historical models have been applied to explain the origins of penal reforms, leading to different explanations. As applied to the juvenile court, was the rise primarily the result of a conspiracy by the "haves" over the children of the "have nots," whereby this movement was a planned system of control over the indigent, powerless, and dangerous classes, and juvenile court reformers were merely tools acting on behalf of the entrenched powerful class (Austin and Krisberg, 1981; Platt, 1977)? Or were juvenile court reformers unselfish humanitarians whose only purpose was to rescue helpless children from brutal and seedy jails as well as the gallows (Henderson, 1899; Mack, 1909; Mennel, 1973)? As argued throughout this book in relation to the origins of previous penal reforms, the juvenile court's origins were at once determined by a combination of economic interest, fear, optimism, and, to employ Schlossman (1977), "love of the American delinquent."

Efforts to explain the patterned disparity between juvenile court goals and practices have been centered increasingly upon the juvenile court's organizational and bureaucratic character. (See Blomberg, 1978, for a review of this literature.) These organizational studies of the juvenile court focus upon actual working conditions, available dispositional alternatives, and the larger environmental effects upon the court organization. The juvenile court's formally prescribed goals of individual treatment are considered in conjunction with other important factors in ultimately shaping and determining the court's everyday youth handling practices. These factors include the ambiguity and multiplicity of goals, relationships with other juvenile justice agencies, conflict between quality of individual youth treatment and routine production requirements, and everyday operation within an environment characterized by ever-present conditions of resource scarcity and uncertainty.

No matter how the origins and operations of the juvenile court are understood or interpreted, it is necessary to recognize the important role of the juvenile court's medicalized philosophy and associated methods of individual treatment and rehabilitation in stimulating a broadly embraced ideological ethos in early twentieth-century America. The court's individual treatment and rehabilitation functions were accelerated by the criminal justice system's handling of adult criminal offenders and by the mental health system in its handling of the mentally ill. This ideological ethos became known as the *twentieth-century rehabilitative ideal*. The next chapter considers the emergence and influence of the twentieth-century rehabilitative ideal on the search for the causes of crime and on the development of American penology from 1900 to the 1960s.

8

The Twentieth-Century Rehabilitative Ideal and the Proliferation of Penal Services (1900–1960s)

INTRODUCTION

THE DEVELOPMENTS of the juvenile court, probation, indeterminate sentencing, parole, and reformatories were all part of the progressive reform agenda aimed at combating explosive social change and the associated problem of crime that were occurring at the turn of the twentieth century. The belief underlying this reform agenda was that through the employment of scientific social casework, the causes of crime could be identified and individual treatment could be provided that would result in offender rehabilitation. This belief and reform agenda was termed by Francis Allen (1964) as the *twentieth-century rehabilitative ideal.* From 1900 to the 1960s, the twentieth-century rehabilitative ideal fueled a search for the causes of crime and an associated proliferation of penal reforms.

Beginning in 1900, at the newly created University of Chicago, the search for the causes of crime was a major undertaking. The Chicago school, as the university's department of sociology became known, dominated American thought about crime's causes until the late 1930s. In fact, many subsequent efforts to explain crime from the late 1930s to the 1960s largely involved attempts to refine, modify, or integrate previous Chicago school theories. While numerous theories emerged during this sixty-year period, the primary explanatory focus was upon the characteristics of individual criminal offenders, their group associations, and/or their immediate area of residence.

Coupled with the proliferation of theories of crime, "more is better" became the guiding rationale for various penal reform efforts during this sixty-year period. Federal, state, and local penal systems experienced substantial organizational expansion and offender service differentiation. The articulated reasoning underlying this expansion was that with the availability of additional penal services, the greater would be the capacity to provide more individualized treatment and offender rehabilitation.

This chapter traces the development of theories of crime and the penal reform from 1900 to the 1960s. While the causes of crime remained illusive, the penal system continued to expand. Once again, like previous nineteenth-century penal reforms, the ideas and practices of twentieth-century penal reform efforts were disparate. Rather than resulting in more individualized and effective treatment and rehabilitation, the resulting practices included increased caseload management and routinized control of a substantially increasing penal population.

THE REHABILITATIVE IDEAL

While attempts to explain and correct criminal behavior occurred early in the nineteenth century, the broad optimism, scope, and development of scientific disciplines associated with the twentieth-century rehabilitative ideal were unique and unprecedented. Underlying the twentieth-century rehabilitative ideal were four assumptions.

1. Human behavior was a product of antecedent causes. This assumption established the fundamental principle of the rehabilitative ideal. The reasoning was that all individuals were products of a particular past. Individual personal histories shaped who and what people were and how they thought and acted. For example, individuals who grew up in poverty or in affluence, individuals who dropped out of school or excelled in school, children of divorced or two-parent families, children with many siblings or no siblings, children raised in abusive homes or nurturing and supportive homes—these were the kinds of antecedent causes that were believed to shape and determine individual behavior, whether criminal or law abiding.

2. The antecedent causes of human behavior could be identified, and it was the obligation of behavior scientists to discover and describe the antecedent causes with all possible exactness. It was believed that individual case histories could be developed in which particular antecedent event(s) would emerge as more significant than others in causing an individual's behavior patterns. For example, through the construction of individual case histories, such events or circumstances as group associations, childhood sexual or physical abuse, chronic school truancy or failure, and living in dilapidated slum areas where crime was rampant and a way of life, emerged as particularly salient in causing particular problem behavior.

3. Knowledge of the antecedent causes of problem behavior enabled scientific treatment of human behavior problems. Once the contributing causes of an individual's problem behavior were identified, individual treatment

plans could be designed and implemented that targeted the contributing causes of behavior problems, thereby correcting these causes and changing the individual's subsequent behavior. For example, if an offender's behavior was judged to be caused by previous physical or sexual abuse, specific counseling and other related therapy could be designed and administered to counteract or overcome the identified negative antecedent causes of the offender's previous criminal behavior patterns.

4. Measures employed to treat criminal behavior served a therapeutic function: they were thought to be in the best interest of the offender and society by making those treated full contributing members of society. For example, once an offender received successful treatment, it was believed there would be not only a reduction in recidivism, but also an actual contribution to society as the offender successfully reintegrated into society by holding a job, paying taxes, and raising a family.

SEARCH FOR THE CAUSES OF CRIME

Beginning in the late 1890s, Rockefeller grants totaling several million dollars transformed a small Baptist College in Chicago into one of America's foremost universities—the University of Chicago. In 1900, the president of the University of Chicago, William Rainey Harper, searched the nation for prominent professors to establish the university's academic foundation (Schwendinger and Schwendinger, 1974:490).

In awarding grants to the university, Rockefeller was particularly interested in establishing an urban social-work purpose. Rockefeller, like other Chicago industrialists, was concerned about what he perceived to be instability among the workforce. Most of the industrial workforce in Chicago lived in the slums, which were believed to be a breeding ground for unrest and related social problems among the workforce and their children (ibid.:491).

The university's department of sociology, or the Chicago school, began with the purpose of improving the slums. In fact, much of the initial academic work involved charitable social service to Chicago's ethnic slums. Often, the university scholar's role was to speak out publicly in defense of ethnic groups and to call for various corrective actions aimed at improving the inferior living, working, and educational services in the slums. The early research was focused upon describing the difficult living conditions and associated feelings of slum residents through journalistic accounts framed within a social work orientation. Burgess and Bogue (1967) describe the community activist role of early Chicago school researchers:

> Quite often they defended the foreign groups publicly and spoke out for tolerance, sympathy and understanding. Much of the earliest "social research" was

little more than the discovery and reporting to the public that the feeling and sentiments of those living in the ethnic slums were, in reality, quite different from those imputed to them by the public. (ibid.:5)

Beginning in the 1920s, the journalistic and social work orientation began to give way to an ambition to explain the social and economic forces at work in the slums and their role in shaping the way slum residents thought and behaved. The early theme that emerged from these efforts was variously referred to as "social pathology" or "social disorganization." The social disorganization approach became one of the Chicago school's fundamental contributions to the explanation of crime. The theoretical imagery underlying the social disorganization theme was that there are characteristic processes and interactions whereby individuals are socialized and social control and community social organization are maintained. When these characteristic processes and interactions are disrupted, however, social control is weakened and social problems emerge in relation to the violation of morals, customs, or the law.

Yet, and as theorized by early Chicago school spokesmen Robert Park and Ernest Burgess (1924), while there are breakdowns in the socialization and social control processes that result in such problems as crime, there is an inherent capacity within American society to confront and overcome these breakdowns. Park and Burgess's assumptions can be summarized as follows:

1. American society is characterized by ever-present conditions of competition.

2. It is these ever-present conditions of competition that cause conflict that can be manifested in such social problems as crime.

3. American society possesses the inherent capacity to accommodate and/or correct both the conditions leading to conflict and the resulting social problems, such as crime.

4. Ultimately, American society's accommodation and/or correction efforts will result in assimilation of all society's members into a common culture and identity.

Together, these four assumptions reflected the image of American society as an ongoing social system that becomes disrupted by social change. Social change results in social disorganization and conflict, which precipitates social problems like crime. But as social reorganization progresses through accommodations and corrections resulting in assimilation, social problems disappear. The analogy is one of nonterminal disease, treatment, and cure.

The trend that followed in Chicago school studies of crime was to identify and describe various social correlates of crime that, taken together, could provide a grounded explanation of crime. For example, Shaw (1930, 1931,

1938) and Shaw and McKay (1972) contributed to a series of comprehensive ethnographic studies reflecting the conditions and circumstances of life in Chicago's slums. These researchers depicted crime and delinquency as inevitable reactions to the overwhelming environmental forces at work in the slum neighborhoods of Chicago. Specifically, Shaw and McKay (1972) documented that, in high-crime and -delinquency neighborhoods, there existed such pathological conditions as high numbers of foreigners, bad housing, poor sanitation, rapid population increases, and turnover. Moreover, the researchers found that despite rapid population increases and turnover, crime and delinquency rates in particular geographic neighborhoods remained constant. As a result, crime and delinquency became viewed more as a function of geographic locality rather than individual psychology. Shaw and McKay explained:

It appears to be established, then, that each racial, nativity, and nationality group in Chicago displays widely varying rates of delinquents; that rates for immigrant groups in particular show a wide historical fluctuation; that diverse racial, nativity, and national groups possess relatively similar rates of delinquents in similar social area; and that each of these groups displays the effect of disproportionate concentration in its respective areas at a given time. In the face of these facts it is difficult to sustain the contention that, by themselves, the factors of race, nativity, and nationality are vitally related to the problem of juvenile delinquency. It seems necessary to conclude, rather, that the significantly higher rates of delinquents found among the children of Negroes, the foreign born, and more recent immigrants are closely related to existing differences in their respective patterns of geographical distribution within the city. (p. 162)

The general theory of crime and delinquency that evolved from the social pathology or social disorganization research of the University of Chicago became known as culture conflict. The thinking was that the culture of slum neighborhoods was in conflict with the larger and more dominant culture of middle-class America. As these slum neighborhoods became subject to ameliorative reform efforts such as improved housing, better sanitation, improved schools, and health care, the communities and residents would become reorganized according to a middle-class measuring rod and such social problems as crime and delinquency would decline or disappear.

A shift from the theoretical reasoning of culture conflict occurred in 1938. In attempting to account for his role in this theoretical shift, Sutherland (1947) identified several incidents that played pivotal roles in his attempts to move criminological theory beyond culture conflict. First, Michael and Adler's (1933) critical appraisal of American criminology as essentially atheoretical, which antagonized Sutherland, turned his attention to the need for theoretical abstraction. Second, Professor Dean Ruml of the University of Chicago once asked a group, of which Sutherland was a part, "What do you know about criminal behavior?" Sutherland indicated that he could only summarize certain research findings on high-incidence crimes and refer to certain propositions that had been proven false. Sutherland recalled that he was unable to state any verified propositions and recognized the need for such. Third, Sutherland stated that, in the examination of a doctoral candidate, Professor Louis Wirth asked, "What is the closest approach to a general theory of criminal behavior?" The only possible answer was culture conflict, and Sutherland indicated he found this quite lacking. A final influence moving Sutherland toward an alternative theory of crime was his 1930s research with Thorsten Sellin in organizing national crime data and the problems they encountered when attempting to employ the culture conflict proposition to explain their data (Cohen, Lindesmith, and Schuessler, 1956:16–17).

Sutherland's "differential association theory" contended that people become delinquent or criminal through learning that is structured by the individual being subject to an excess of definitions favorable to the violation of law over definitions unfavorable to the violation of law. Surprisingly, Sutherland concluded that the Chicago school's research findings on the city's slums actually demonstrated differential social organization rather than social disorganization. He argued that the slum neighborhoods were characterized by specific community sentiments and ongoing activities that were directly connected to the creation, transmission, and, most importantly, learning of delinquent and criminal behavior (ibid.:13–18). According to differential association theory, delinquency and crime are learned through the same processes that law-abiding behaviors are learned.

Sutherland's theory of differential association comprised the following nine propositions:

1. Criminal behavior is learned.

2. Criminal behavior is learned with other persons in a process of communication.

3. The principal part of the learning of criminal behavior occurs within intimate personal groups.

4. When criminal behavior is learned, the learning includes (a) techniques of committing the crime, which are sometimes very complicated, sometimes very simple; (b) the specific direction of motives, drives, rationalizations, and attitudes.

5. The specific direction of motives and drives is learned from definitions of legal codes as favorable and unfavorable.

6. A person becomes delinquent because of an excess of definitions favorable to violation of law over definitions unfavorable to violation of law.

7. Differential associations may vary in frequency, duration, priority, and intensity.

8. The process of learning criminal behavior by association with criminal and anticriminal patterns involves all of the mechanisms that are involved in any other learning.

9. Though criminal behavior is an expression of general needs and values, it is not explained by those general needs and values since noncriminal behavior is an expression of the same needs and values. (ibid.:8–10)

Sutherland was very familiar with numerous crime and delinquency statistics and related research findings in criminology and believed that differential association theory could be usefully applied to explain these various statistics and studies. Sutherland recounted that, upon returning from a seminar with professors Lindesmith and Sweetser, Sweetser questioned why "the explanation of juvenile delinquency in the slum area [doesn't] apply, in principle, to murders in the South" (ibid.:18). That question was the specific occasion for the formulation of differential association theory. Sutherland explained:

> The hypothesis of differential association seemed to me to be consistent with the principal gross findings in criminology. It explained why the Molocean children became progressively delinquent with the length of residence in the deteriorated area of Los Angeles, why the city crime rate is higher than the rural crime rate, why males are more delinquent than females, why the crime rate remains consistently high in deteriorated areas of cities, why the juvenile delinquency rate in a foreign nativity is high while the group lives in a deteriorated area and drops when the group moves out of that area, why second generation Italians do not have the high murder rate that their fathers had, why Japanese children in a deteriorated area of Seattle had a low delinquency rate even though in poverty, why crimes do not increase greatly in a period of depression. All of the general statistical facts seem to fit this hypothesis. (ibid.:19–20)

During this same year, Robert K. Merton (1938) published an article entitled, "Social Structure and Anomie." In this article, Merton presented another general theory of criminal behavior that came to epitomize structural functional explanations of crime. Merton was particularly interested in explaining why the incidence of crime in America was considerably higher than in other Western industrial nations such as England, France, and Germany. While Sutherland was interested in explaining specific distributions of crime within American society, Merton was interested in explaining the overall high incidence of crime throughout America.

Merton argued that all Americans, regardless of social status, are subject to a common socialization process that stresses high aspirations and open access to the means for achieving these high aspirations. Merton claimed that everyone raised in American society is taught to believe that through hard work and postponed gratification they can achieve whatever they are willing to work and sacrifice for. This belief is known as the American Dream! However, as Merton elaborated, the American Dream is more myth than reality. Because Americans do not have equal access to the means for achieving high aspirations, many end up suffering relative deprivation (i.e., deprivation relative to their high aspirations), which can result in anomie. Those suffering from anomie, or normlessness, experience disappointment and frustration that, in turn, facilitates drift into various nonconformist behaviors, including crime. Merton further proposed that such drift into crime is particularly understandable because, in America, emphasis is not on how one succeeds but rather on the material possessions that are automatically assumed to be indicative of success.

Merton concluded that American society has a much higher incidence of crime than other Western industrial countries because of its uniformly high aspirations and failure to provide equal access to the means necessary to achieve these commonly held high aspirations. In other Western industrial countries, a highly stratified and well-defined socialization system exists. In effect, in these countries you are born into a particular place or social status, and your social status determines your socialization and levels of aspirations. Consequently, there is much less likelihood of major disparities in aspirations and achievement and, as a result, there is less relative deprivation, anomie, and crime in these other Western countries (Merton, 1938, 1949).

Sutherland's and Merton's theories of crime dominated criminological thought for the next several decades and were not subject to serious challenge until the 1960s. Moreover, in the 1950s, Sutherland's and Merton's theories individually, as well as collectively, shaped various theoretical accounts of crime and delinquency.

For example, Cohen (1955) contended that lower-class boys are driven into delinquent gangs through a process he termed "reaction-formation." Cohen, employing Merton's theory of relative deprivation and anomie, argued that lower-class boys are largely unable to succeed in middle-class structured public schools. These lower-class boys react to their public school failure by forming an alternative delinquent subculture. This subculture takes the middle-class norms and behaviors of the larger society and turns them upside-down. Cohen argued that the delinquent boy's subcultural norms and behavior patterns, when measured against middle-class norms and behaviors, emerge as malicious, hedonistic, nonutilitarian, and generally free of adultlike restraint (ibid.).

Another delinquent subculture theory was offered in 1958 by Miller, who argued for a more cultural-centered theory of crime that is distinct and disconnected from middle-class culture and associated behavior. Miller contended that while middle-class culture focuses upon achievement, hard work, and postponed gratification, lower-class culture's "focal concerns" are centered upon toughness, masculinity, and capabilities for such things as imaginative profanity. Borrowing from Sutherland's emphasis on learning and differential association, Miller concluded that these lower-class focal concerns are learned and result in culturally institutionalized delinquent behavior and associated lifestyles (Miller, 1958).

In 1960, Cloward and Ohlin provided an integration of elements of the delinquency and opportunity theories of the Chicago school, Merton, and Sutherland. Cloward and Ohlin contended that delinquents could pursue different and independent delinquent lifestyles. They argued that lower-class youth who experience relative deprivation and turn to delinquency will learn and pursue those delinquent opportunities that are readily available to them, be it drugs, alcohol, violence, prostitution, or gambling (Cloward and Ohlin, 1960).

Overall, what emerged in the development of theories of crime and delinquency from 1900 to the 1960s was a focus upon the individual offender. Various offender-based theories assessed the role of the offenders' residence, or their group associations, their socialization, their learning of behavior, or some combination. Guided by the rehabilitative ideal, the concern was to identify the key factors that cause crime, thereby enabling the development of correctional strategies that could successfully treat these causes. This was the goal and promise guiding crime and delinquency theories for the first sixty years of the twentieth century.

PENAL ASPIRATIONS, GROWTH, AND PRACTICES

During the first sixty years of the twentieth century, American penology experienced major organizational growth and bureaucratization. The prevailing rehabilitative thinking guiding this growth was that successful criminal and delinquent rehabilitation could only be accomplished through more individualized treatment. Moreover, individualized offender treatment required a range of prison, parole, probation, and juvenile court programs that could be matched to the particular needs of individual offenders. As a result, the bywords for penal reform became "more is better," based upon the underlying belief that the causes of crime were multiple and required multiple penal program responses if offender treatment was to be effective.

At the beginning of this period, the penal system was comprised of prisons, with parole, probation, and juvenile courts just beginning their respective implementations. What occurred over the subsequent sixty-year period were efforts to rationalize, professionalize, expand, and refine these major components of the penal system. The overriding goal was to be able to determine the cause(s) of an individual's criminal behavior and the associated treatment needs and then provide treatment that was responsive to these individual needs. To respond to this overriding goal, major organizational growth and bureaucratization occurred at the federal, state, and local levels of the penal system.

In prisons, what developed was an increasingly complex array of mini-mum-, medium-, and maximum-security facilities at the state and federal lev-els. The treatment process goal within these various prisons, as Irwin (1980) described it, was to implement a system in which a team of professionals— comprised of psychologists, caseworkers, sociologists, vocational coun-selors, and psychiatrists—would test, interview, and develop life history in-formation for each entering inmate. The classification team would then evaluate the tests and life history and plan the inmate's therapeutic regime. In the final classification stage, a team would periodically review the inmate's rehabilitation progress and recommend any necessary changes in treatment (ibid.:162–165).

Three fundamental types of treatment programs were generally available in the prison, including therapeutic, academic, and vocational (ibid.:64). The most heavily relied upon treatment approach was group counseling. Most prison systems established elementary and high school curricula for inmates by the 1950s, and a number of states had arrangements with colleges and universities for inmates to complete college-level correspondence courses while in prison. With regard to vocational training, during the 1950s inmates could receive training in cooking, baking, butchering, dry cleaning, shoe re-pairing, sewing machine repairing, sheet metal machining, printing, plumb-ing, painting, welding, and nursing (Irwin, 1980:165).

As an illustration of this pattern of prison development, until the late nine-teenth century, the federal government relied upon state prisons to house fed-eral prisoners and to provide leasing arrangements in which federal prisoners were leased to work for private employers. However, in 1887, Congress banned the leasing of federal prisoners, and, between 1885 and 1895, the number of federal prisoners increased from 1,027 to 2,516. These two events led Congress into the development of federal prisons, beginning in 1897 with the construction of the first federal prison in Leavenworth, Kansas. In 1902, Atlanta, Georgia, became the second site for a federal prison. In 1928, Alder-son, West Virginia, was chosen as the site for the first federal prison for women (Rotman, 1995:186–187).

The federal prisons constructed in the early 1900s were operated sepa-rately and without centralized administration. However, because of prob-lems related to overcrowding and the need for more efficient classification, differentiation, and segregation of prisoners, the Federal Bureau of Prisons was created in 1929. As Rotman summarized:

> Federal prisons erected in early 1900s were generally run as separate entities
> without any central organization. The problems caused by prison congestion,

and the need for a more efficient record-keeping system to facilitate the goal of proper classification and segregation of prisoners, led to the creation of the Federal Bureau of Prisons in 1929. The first Director of the Bureau was Sanford Bates, who was responsible for a number of important improvements. Bates altered the method of selecting wardens, substituting a merit system for political patronage. Wardens were trained at a special Bureau Facility and were promoted up the ranks within the Bureau. In 1937, the Bureau of Prisons placed all prison employees under the Federal Civil Service, throwing off the last vestiges of political patronage. Also, the Bureau began a system of staff rotation whereby any promotion was accompanied by a transfer to another facility. Prior to these changes, prison employees had moved up within the same prison and became entrenched in that prison, which had led to inflexibility and idiosyncrasies within the separate facilities. (Rotman, 1995:187)

The classification system for federal prisoners was based upon the bureau's criminological study of prisoners. Specifically, low-risk offenders were sent to noncustodial camps, while more serious offenders were sent to Leavenworth and Atlanta. Offenders judged to benefit from agricultural training were sent to McNeil Island, while the physically and mentally impaired were sent to the hospital prison in Springfield, Illinois. The most serious or hardcore federal prisoners were sent to Alcatraz, following its opening in 1934. While the bureau's classification system was far more comprehensive than the classification efforts of various states, some states were implementing similar prison classification methods and expanding their range of prisons (ibid.:187).

In 1929, the Federal Bureau of Prisons declared rehabilitation the fundamental goal and purpose and continued to develop an institutional network to enable offender classification and individualized decisions on custody and treatment needs. This rehabilitation purpose was so broadly shared that, in 1954, the American Prison Association changed its name to the American Correctional Association. This was the major professional organization for not only federal but also state and local correctional professionals throughout the country. The association proclaimed offender treatment to be its mandate and counseled its membership to redesignate their "prisons" as "correctional institutions" and to label their punishment blocks within prisons as "adjustment centers" (ibid.:190).

The California state prison system quickly embraced this call by renaming its prisons California Treatment Facilities. Soledad Prison was constructed just after World War II with a number of nonprisonlike facility characteristics, including fences as substitutes for granite walls, cell blocks with day rooms and outreach windows, inside walls painted with pastel colors, well-equipped libraries, gyms, educational facilities, better food, relaxed discipline, and a selection of counseling and education programs. Between World

War II and the 1960s, rehabilitation strategies were focused upon social learning and attempts to counteract the negative influences associated with institutional living.

Rotman pointed out that California's Chino Prison was an exemplary therapeutic community prison:

> Commissioner Richard McGee was the innovative administrator of the California Department of Corrections. According to the evaluative research units set up by McGee, the Chino experiment demonstrated the effectiveness of the therapeutic community method to change the antisocial behavior of offenders. The institution was decentralized into small units, with counselors housed in each of them. Convicts were used as therapists. The prison became a community center for special training, work release, and family contacts. Therapeutic communities focused on the transformation of the institutional environment, creating a network of compensatory social interactions, a network that was intended to replace the hierarchical structure of the institution with a horizontal association of mutually responsible human beings who would resolve their common problems through a process of intensive social interaction. The vehicles of this process were the frequent meetings and group discussions in which decisions were reached through the participation of both inmates and staff. The demand for active participation was intended to counteract such notorious negative effects of institutions as depersonalization, dependency, and loss of initiative. (pp. 191)

Parole, as previously discussed in Chapter 6, began as a component of the nineteenth-century reformatory and indeterminate sentencing movements. It soon developed independently, with its use becoming more widespread. By 1939 only the states of Virginia, Florida, and Mississippi were without parole systems (Cahalan, 1986:169–189). During the early implementation of parole, primary attention was given to selecting inmates for prison release with little parole supervision following release. Simon (1993) pointed out, for example, that in California more than ten years passed between the adoption of parole in 1893 and the actual implementation of a parole supervision apparatus. In this interim phase, "Parole was used, much as the pardon power had been, to select for relief a few worthy cases, or to mitigate apparently excessive sentences. Parolees were released with little more than a bona fide and approved job, a private sponsor, a list of rules, and a sheaf of monthly reports to be completed" (ibid.:45). Initially, community supervision was not needed, because parole was only to be dealing with a select few "low-risk" offenders with impeccable community ties.

Beginning in 1900, pressure was initiated by prison managers to expand parole in order to avoid new prison construction to deal with increasing prison populations. In 1910, California's parole agency began operations with a parole officer, an assistant parole officer, and a clerical worker. The state's early operations centered upon reviewing monthly reports and processing revocation orders for parole violations discovered by the police. The state parole officer was located in San Francisco and therefore made few personal contacts with parolees across the state (Berecochia, 1982:213).

At the end of World War I, many states revised their parole laws to enable the use of parole for a much broader array of offenders, including recidivists and murders. Rather than being used only for a select few low-risk offenders, parole fast became the method for releasing numerous inmates from prison. To illustrate, in California the percentage of prison releases by parole increased from 7 percent in 1907 to 35 percent in 1914 (Berecochia, 1982:218). Other states also adopted various indeterminate sentencing laws that made parole the presumptive release mechanism and provided parole authorities substantial discretion as to when to release inmates from prison. In 1936, for example, fifteen states, including California, employed parole in over 80 percent of their prison releases (Cahalan, 1986:170).

In summary, during the first half of the twentieth century, parole involved, primarily, a release-from-prison mechanism with such requirements as being employed and being a "good citizen." "Parole agents were given much discretion in enforcing parole's conditions, and the idea of supervision training seemed to hold little value. There was a shared understanding of what constituted normal behavior and the community itself provided much of the day-to-day monitoring. If the parolee refused to work, or was a troublemaker at home, the parole agent could respond to the complaints of the employer or family by threatening to reimprison the parolee. Parole agents could lean on the community, as the community imposed its own informal behavioral requirements. Therefore, control and normalization did not flow from the agent but through him. Parole was a three-sided structure—offender, community, and agent—with the most important factor being the community" (Simon, 1993:68).

Beginning in the 1950s, a new parole model emerged in response to a declining demand for unskilled workers and an increasing proportion of minorities in the prison populations. Actually, the new parole model exemplified many of the original progressive beliefs related to offender classification, training, and treatment. As Rothman (1980) elaborated, while the progressive penal agenda had subsided in the 1920s and 1930s, renewed interest emerged following World War II. In effect, a new optimism in government potential and capacity fueled the rebirth of the progressive-like approach in the 1940s and 1950s.

The progressive-like approach that emerged with parole as well as probation—and within prisons—was the "clinical model." The clinical model stressed the professional capacity of parole agents to craft treatment programs that were responsive to the individual needs of the parolee and that could operate independently of the community. The clinical model was conceptualized as a sequential process that began with an initial interview between the just-released-from-prison parolee and the parole officer. The purpose of this initial interview was twofold: first, to gather objective information about the parolee; and second, to begin the important process of influencing, guiding, treating, and motivating the parolee. Once established, the treatment and guidance relationship between the parolee and officer was to evolve over time.

Simon (1993) argues that the development of the clinical model in parole represented an institutional acknowledgement of an "underclass." He contended that in the 1950s and 1960s, policymakers believed there was a class of people who could not be absorbed into the labor force until they had been altered and prepared for the labor force. "Where once parole could satisfy its aim by reinforcing the disciplinary capacity of the community, parole in the 1950s and 1960s attempted to develop a model of supervision that could operate independently of the community" (ibid.:100).

Probation's aspirations, growth, and practices mirrored those of parole and prisons. Antecedent elements of probation, as described in Chapter 6, can be traced to fourteenth-century England, which used recognizance as a crime prevention measure. Recognizance was a sworn statement by a defendant to the court that he would conduct himself in a law-abiding manner if released. Frequently, in addition to this promise, financial surety or bail was required. As previously cited, John Augustus is generally considered the architect or father of probation. He was the first probation officer who worked as a volunteer. Augustus bailed his first case in August 1841 with a promise from the offender that he would not drink if released to Augustus's care. The courts charged Augustus thirty dollars bail for thirty days suspension of sentence and reduced the charge to one cent and court costs if the probationer did not reoffend. At the time of Augustus's death in 1859, he had bailed 1,152 men, 794 women, and about 3,000 girls (Duffee, 1989:188).

An issue that emerged immediately in the early implementation of probation was the use of law enforcement officers as the first probation officers. This practice signaled the theory of treatment versus the practice of control controversy that has plagued and continues to plague probation as well as parole and imprisonment. The tension between treatment and control in probation or parole takes on a particular character in the community. Because the probation or parole officer both provides treatment and has sentence enforcement responsibilities, the conflict is inherent in the officer's role. Moreover, given that probation and parole caseloads routinely exceeded one hundred, caseload management with routinized control necessarily came to characterize probation and parole practices.

The caseload dilemma for probation and parole is described in detail by Morris and Hawkins (1976). The authors reported that the best estimates

available from current research indicates that an average of 35 cases per offi-cer is about the highest ratio likely to permit effective supervision and assis-tance in either service. Of course, no caseload standard can be applied to all types of offenders. The optimum overall caseload of 35 is based on a determi-nation of what an average caseload would be when different types of offend-ers were given the appropriate types and degrees of supervision. Up to 20 persons in a caseload of 35 could receive close intensive supervision; if none required such supervision, the caseload could be larger. (ibid.:35)

In the 1950s and 1960s, average probation and parole caseloads greatly ex-ceeded such optimum levels. Over 76 percent of all misdemeanants and 67 percent of all felons on probation were in caseloads exceeding one hundred. Further, fewer than 4 percent of probation officers across the country oper-ated with caseloads of less than forty probationers. Nationally, adults on pa-role were supervised in caseloads of about seventy and the average parole caseload for juveniles was over sixty (ibid.:36).

In relation to these sorts of caseload statistics and other documented prac-tices, a number of studies have argued that during this sixty-year period, while the goal of prisons, parole, probation, and juvenile courts was indi-vidualized treatment and rehabilitation, the actual practices were largely characterized by offender punishment and control. For example, in the case of prison, parole, probation, and juvenile court decisions, it has been docu-mented that, instead of decisions based upon offender treatment needs, they were determined largely by such legal variables as seriousness of offense and prior record (Wellford, 1975). Controlling for legal variables, rather than of-fender characteristics and related treatment needs, was reported to be the best predictor of length of prison sentence, of when an offender was paroled from prison, and of whether or not an offender received probation, prison, or reformatory placements.

Regarding prison classification decisions and inmate receipt of counsel-ing, education, or vocational training, Irwin (1980) pointed out a number of goal versus practice disparities. To begin, multidisciplinary classification teams were seldom employed in prisons. Counseling centered upon groups and was generally employed to maintain control over offenders. The group counseling leaders tended to be correctional workers with little, if any, clin-ical background, and psychiatrists or psychologists were seldom used (ibid.:164–165).

Teachers with meager educational backgrounds and without teacher cer-tification credentials typically staffed prison education programs. Moreover, prison teachers were generally required to teach general education subjects rather than within an area of specialty. Teaching materials such as textbooks were typically outdated, and education technology and teacher training to deal with largely undereducated and illiterate offenders was nonexistent (Glaser, 1966). While numerous vocational training programs were available in prison, Irwin (1980) points out that these programs were largely oriented toward meeting specific maintenance-related needs within the prison rather than toward providing offenders with marketable employment skills.

Further, it has been argued in relation to caseload statistics and practices that probation and parole officers have little time to provide individualized counseling and treatment to their respective probationers and parolees. Often probation and parole officers can do little more than random checks, given their overwhelming caseloads (Carter and Wilkins, 1976). Lemert (1993) elaborated that only the probation or parole cases that are particularly difficult or problematic receive any level of individual care or control through a practice he termed "bank loading." In effect, probation and parole officers must attempt to "manage" and "control" their respective caseloads with little or no time for such lofty concerns as individualized treatment. Rather, the focus is upon the difficult or exceptional cases. As Lemert argued, the most common caseload management technique for probation and parole officers is bank loading. This is what parole and probation officers have always done—concentrate on serious cases and ignore the rest (ibid.:460).

Between 1880 and 1960, the rate per 100,000 population incarcerated in state and federal prisons almost doubled (see Figure 8-1). However, the actual extent of penal control expanded beyond this because of the increasing reliance on probation, parole, and the juvenile court during this eighty-year period. Unfortunately, other than at the federal level, no attempt was made to collect yearly state probation and parole data until the mid-1960s. Clearly, if state probation, parole, and juvenile court data were available, the extent of penal growth during this eighty-year period would be much more substantial. It is likely that the pattern of gradual imprisonment growth reflected during the post–World War II period reflected growing doubt about the effectiveness of prisons and growing enthusiasm for the use of community corrections. In fact, as interest in probation grew, it became common for many serious second- and third-time felons to receive sentences of probation instead of prison. Further, even selected violent felony offenders served their sentences in the community subject to special probation conditions (Clear and Cole, 2000:185–187). Consequently, if consideration was given to the steadily increasing numbers of adult and juvenile offenders subject to community sentences, the overall rate of penal control would increase substantially.

Another way to illustrate the proliferation of penal services and control is to consider the escalating costs of penology during this sixty-year period. For example, between 1902 and the 1960s, expenditures on state-run penal systems increased from $14 million to $1.51 billion. Moreover, from 1942 to

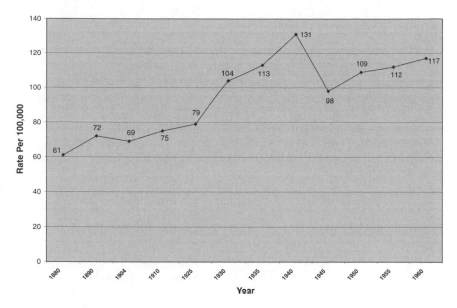

Figure 8-1. Federal and State Prison Incarceration Rates, 1880–1960.

the 1960s, state penal systems costs doubled every decade (U.S. Bureau of Census, 1975:416).

SUMMARY AND DISCUSSION

The twentieth-century rehabilitative ideal developed in relation to progressive America's effort to confront such social problems as crime through a combined effort involving government and emerging scientific approaches. Turn-of-the-century America faced many challenges that were viewed as consequences of social turmoil and change that could be corrected through scientifically grounded government efforts. The strategy was straightforward: determine the cause(s) of the social problem and develop policies and practices to correct it. As the search for crime's causes and associated theories proliferated, so too did penal services. The belief was that all individuals are products of a past that can be described and explained, and that this explanation, in turn, can be used to guide individualized treatment to change the problem behavior in question, provided a sufficient number of different penal service alternatives are at hand.

What occurred in penology, specifically prisons, parole, probation, and the juvenile court, was a pattern of service proliferation. The historical context and progressive ideology set in place an unquestioned purpose: to explain, treat, and correct. Ultimately, it was believed that these penal efforts would result in more individualized offender treatment, resulting in greater assimilation into and the perfection of American society. These were indeed the ideas and words of the twentieth-century rehabilitative ideal. But, like previous reform eras, the deeds or practices were far less than these ideas or words. The actual everyday practices of penology involved patterns of caseload management and routinized control. Offenders tended not to be treated as individuals but rather as categories or groups—for the purpose of management and control rather than individual treatment.

Several issues warrant consideration in relation to the words versus deeds of penology during this period. To begin, the anticipated discovery of the cause(s) of crime, while enthusiastically pursued, remained inconclusive. Was it culture conflict, learning, anomie, reaction formation, or differential opportunity? Moreover, how could a fast developing penal bureaucracy respond to inconclusive theory and related technology in fulfilling its offender treatment and rehabilitation goals? Were the goals to treat and to rehabilitate mere disguise for government efforts to control and punish? Or was this merely a case of good intentions gone awry in their implementation?

The development of various theories of crime and the simultaneous proliferation of penal services should not be interpreted as merely a cause/effect relationship between theories of crime and penal service development and expansion. Rather, the connection may be better understood as involving a recognition that there are potentially multiple causes of crime, thereby requiring multiple penal services. As various parole, probation, and juvenile court services were incorporated into the penal system, the services were promoted as alternatives to previous practices, thereby enabling more individualized offender treatment. However, as these various service expansions became implemented, they actually served a supplemental rather than alternative function. Among the salient consequences of this patterned implementation were increasing numbers of penal clients and escalating costs. This patterned growth of America's penal system and proportion of population subject to its control was unquestioned until the turbulent decades of the 1960s and 1970s.

9

Discovering Prison Subcultures
(1950s–1960s)

INTRODUCTION

THIS BOOK, thus far, has been about penal reform and the historical elements and ideas guiding these changes. Whether the change has involved the reforms of the prison, reformatory, probation, parole, or the juvenile court, the consistent focal point has been the historical context and origins of penal ideas and the various practice responses to those ideas and the resulting consequences of these practices. The feature actors then have been society, reformers, and the system. The objects of this penal change, namely offenders, have played a lesser part in this analytical scheme. While much has been said about the consequences of reform and the brutal conditions of confinement (i.e., what prisons are like inside and how inmates are treated), inmate responses to those conditions have not been considered. In particular, the psychological impact of confinement and the organization of life behind bars have not been examined from the perspective of the inmate. However, no story of American penology would be complete without consideration of how prisons shape those who inhabit them.

Prison life is discussed at this juncture in this book because the body of research that enabled understanding of prison life evolved from the theoretical developments of the twentieth-century rehabilitative ideal. Social-psychological, cultural transmission, and functionalist theories provided frameworks for describing and explaining the origins, structure, and function of the inmate social system. In the absence of these frameworks, investigations of the prison would have been limited to exposés of mismanagement and other forms of wrongdoing by prison officials (Sykes, 1995).

Because of these theoretical contributions, questions of how the prison's institutional life affects prisoners, how prisoners affect the prison's institutional life, and whether the prison's institutional operations are governed by relationships of power or exchange can be addressed. The purpose of this chapter, then, is to consider how inmates become assimilated into the prison community, the deprivations inmates experience, the adaptations prisoners make to those deprivations, why prison subcultures exist, whether prisons are "total systems of power," and whether prisons, that are so impervious to criticism, will fare any better in the future.

A SOCIOLOGICAL PERSPECTIVE OF PRISON LIFE

Sociological studies of prison life developed before World War II and were motivated by many of the same humanitarian and utilitarian concerns (i.e., effective means of rehabilitating) of earlier prison investigations. Where sociological studies differed from commissioned panel investigations, however, was in their focus. The research studies focused on the socialization patterns found in the prison, and the process by which inmates adopted the values and norms that constituted the inmate subculture (Sykes, 1995). These studies also presented the functional side of prison life. After World War II, a structural-functional perspective on imprisonment developed, which provided not only descriptions of the inmate subculture, but explanations of its origins and functions.

As already mentioned, a factor that gave rise to sociologically guided prison research was the direction of sociological inquiry in general. The previous chapter illustrated that sociology was evolving as a scientific discipline, with such objectives as to describe and explain the inner workings and origins of deviant subcultures. The prison, a minisociety in its own right, provided an excellent opportunity for exploring the requirements of social order and the transmission of deviant norms and values (ibid.). Moreover, the problem of order in prisons had become particularly strained in the 1950s. More than fifty riots broke out between 1950 and 1953, and beginning in 1952 there were approximately forty prison riots in a span of only eighteen months. By attempting to understand the exercise of power and the impact of confinement on the psyche, it is clear that these prison studies were not merely tales of how inmates "did their time." They were studies of small-scale societies in action.

THE PRISON COMMUNITY

The Prison Community, by Donald Clemmer (1940), was one of the first studies to consider how the prison community influenced and shaped the attitudes and behavior of prisoners. Writing in the aftermath of the twentieth-century wave of immigration and in the tradition of the culture conflict perspective, Clemmer employed the concept of assimilation as a framework for his analysis of the prison. Assimilation was defined as a person learning "enough of the culture of a social unit into which he is placed to make him characteristic of it" (ibid.). Borrowing from this general definition, Clemmer employed the term "prisonization" to describe the process of "taking on in greater or lesser degree the folkways, mores, customs and general culture of the prison."

Clemmer assumed that all inmates underwent certain experiences that made them part of the prison community. One such experience was that upon entering the prison community, the inmate was compelled to accept an inferior role. This inferior role was reinforced, in part, by one's anonymous status in the prison. The number that had replaced his or her name conferred this anonymity upon the inmate. The standard-issue uniforms that prevented individual expression further accentuated their anonymity and inferiority. In the eyes of the warden and prison staff, the inmate was to be without distinction and power. Goffman (1961) later referred to these initiation procedures as the "stripping and mortification process." Goffman claimed that this process was a practical and necessary feature of any "total institution" responsible for the care and/or control of large numbers of individuals.

A second experience that characterized entry into the prison community was learning the ways and means of the prison. An inmate had to learn the rules that governed the organization and operation of the prison, such as the appropriate "ranks, titles and authorities of the various prison officials" (Clemmer, 1940). Learning the new habits for daily existence constituted a third universal prison experience. This included altered patterns of sleeping, eating, and working, and the altered meanings given to these activities. For example, Clemmer noted that upon entering the prison, inmates were generally thankful and eager to begin work in any job. However, after some time had passed, inmates moved from being satisfied with anything to desiring a "good job." The same could be said of their preferences for food and shelter. This transition from being easily satisfied to articulating preferences reflected the fact that after a few months of incarceration, all activities and amenities assumed new meaning and importance. As one correctional officer recently indicated to one of this book's authors, even throat lozenges become a valued commodity. Inmates regularly come to the infirmary to eat a piece of this medicine-turned candy.

Clemmer's analysis of prison life did not end with identifying the universal features of prisonization. Having observed that not all inmates were indoctrinated to the same degree by these experiences, Clemmer sought to identify the factors that "bred or deepened criminality and antisociality and made the inmate characteristic of the criminalistic ideology in the prison community." In short, he sought to identify the factors that accelerated or delayed the prisonization process.

Toward this end, Clemmer identified five factors. These factors included the inmate's preprison personality, the type and extent of relationships main-

tained with persons outside and within the prison, and the inmate associations that were not of the inmate's choosing. For example, through no decision of their own, inmates are in constant contact with their cellmates and
workmates. A final factor affecting the degree of prisonization was whether
the inmate truly accepted the creeds and codes of the prison subculture or
merely followed them in order to survive. Clemmer acknowledged these factors were not the only determinants of prisonization, but they were the most
important. Though not as relevant as other determinants, he added that age,
race, and criminal record could not be separated from the prisonization
process (ibid.).

Clemmer's work highlighted that the prison experience necessarily disrupted the inmate's personality and that prospects for successful community
reintegration depended on how "prisonized" the inmate became. In testing
Clemmer's hypothesis that the longer the prison sentence, the greater the
likelihood for extreme forms of prisonization, Wheeler (1971) affirmed that
an inmate's conformity to socially prescribed norms varied with length of stay
and the number of close associations within the prison. He found this relationship to be generally U-shaped; prisonization effects were least evident at
the beginning and end of one's sentence and greatest midway into the sentence. Wheeler concluded that the inmate's apparent return to belief in
conventional norms toward the conclusion of the sentence occurred in anticipation of release and preparatory adjustment to life on the outside. He
also discovered that within the broader U-shaped pattern, the degree of prisonization varied by role types. For example, prisonization effects were greatest for "right guys" and "square johns" midway into the sentence, and for
"outlaws" effects were greatest toward the end of the sentence. Sykes and
Messinger (1960) and others (i.e., Irwin and Cressey, 1962; Wheeler, 1971)
expanded Clemmer's thesis, by finding that institutional structure also
affected the prisonization process. Prisonization was less pronounced in
treatment-oriented institutions than in custody/disciplinarian-oriented institutions.

Though Clemmer's contributions were many, he did not address the impact of prisonization upon release. How long did it take before conforming
attitudes resumed? How did prisonization affect adjustment on the outside
as measured by recidivism? Clemmer neglected the question of the origins
of the prison subculture. He described the process of prisonization, but took
for granted the fact that the prison subculture existed. Sykes (1958) and Irwin
and Cressey (1962) were among the first to address this question.

THE DEPRIVATION MODEL

In the book, *The Society of Captives* (1958), Gresham Sykes employed a
social-psychological perspective to study the inmate social system of the

New Jersey State Maximum Security Prison. Specifically, he examined the impact of the prison environment (i.e., the social) on the mentality and self-concept (i.e., the psychological) of the inmate. By adopting this perspective, Sykes brought attention to the fact that physical pains, namely, corporal punishments, were not the only pains inmates endured while incarcerated. In fact, Sykes contended that psychological attacks could be just as damaging as physical attacks. These psychological attacks had their roots in the extremely "depriving or frustrating" nature of the inmate's captivity. Recognition of these deprivations and frustrations—what Sykes termed the "pains of imprisonment—served as a starting point for moving beyond conventional perceptions of what constituted humane and inhumane treatment.

Pains of Imprisonment
Based upon participant observation in the New Jersey prison that included a series of interviews with inmates, Sykes classified five deprivations as the greatest pains of imprisonment. The deprivation of liberty constituted the first of these pains. Clearly, confinement to a secure institution necessarily required deprivation of liberty, but inmates were referring to the loss of liberty that existed *within* the institution. Inmates had to obtain permission to eat, sleep, shower, and interact, the last of which restricted the ability to maintain relations with family and friends. Personal visits and correspondence were regulated and monitored in ways that "frustrated" the ability to maintain close ties. Sykes found that 41 percent of the inmates in the New Jersey prison had no outside visits, which deepened the inmates' sense of isolation. As a result, inmates came to see themselves as others did, namely as social lepers to be kept apart from decent society. Sykes argued that to endure this psychological pain, inmates consoled themselves by rejecting their rejecters.

Closely related to the deprivation of liberty was the deprivation of autonomy, or the loss of self-determination. Subjected to all-encompassing regulations that prevented individual decision-making about the most basic of daily functions, inmates viewed these regulations as little more than "gestures of authoritarianism" (Sykes, 1958). Inmates did not perceive the detailed system of rules as a way of securing and managing large numbers of people in a small space with limited resources (Goffman, 1961), nor did officials feel obligated to explain their bureaucratic rationale for their system of rules. Though reasonable on its face, prolonged exposure to such an environment rendered inmates helpless and dependent. The diminished capacity to do for oneself is perhaps best illustrated by the story of one former inmate's struggle with doors upon release from prison. Even after several months of freedom, this former inmate stood at every door he encountered, waiting for someone else to open it. One can only imagine the impact of such conditioning in areas of the free society that call for not only greater individual responsibility but initiative as well.

A third pain identified by inmates was the deprivation of goods and services. While inmates had their basic necessities met (food, shelter, health care, recreation, and clothing), Sykes argued that a greater underlying material loss was being overlooked. To clarify the implications of this loss, Sykes posed the question "What was the psychological value of ownership and possession of necessities and amenities in a society that determined self-worth by the quantity and quality of individual possessions?" Sykes contended that inmates had difficulty rationalizing their material loss because it could not be justified. The deprivation of goods and services was not the result of "self-sacrifice in the interests of the community," nor the result of "present pleasures foregone for pleasures in the future." The impoverishment was his own fault and, so, self-worth was automatically equated with personal inadequacy (Sykes, 1958).

According to Sykes, the deprivation of heterosexual relationships had a particularly detrimental effect on the male psyche. He claimed that, with few exceptions, a man's self-concept was linked foremost to his feelings of masculinity. In the all-male prison environment, this masculinity was continually and variously challenged. Borrowing from Charles Cooley's concept of the "looking-glass self," Sykes noted that the portion of the inmate's self-image that was developed through simple interaction with women was gone. Added to this were the sexual frustration that resulted from the lack of heterosexual relationships and the surrendering to that frustration through homosexual encounters that further contradicted the male psyche and self-concept.

A final deprivation identified was the loss of security. As one inmate in Sykes's study declared, "The worst thing about prison is you have to live with other prisoners." While inmate solidarity existed to some degree, a number of "outlaws within this group of outlaws" made solidarity imperfect. Inmates described one another as "vicious" and "dangerous." However, one did not need to be routinely robbed, beaten, or raped to feel the loss of security, as the fear of eventually being "tested" was sufficiently overwhelming (ibid.). The inmate's manhood and self-concept, not to mention physical well-being, hinged on his reaction and ability to cope with this pervasive sense of insecurity.

Adaptations
Adaptations to the pains of imprisonment were varied and could include escaping physically or psychologically, mounting a violent insurrection, or seeking peaceful change though legal means. Sykes maintained that these were unlikely and risky recourses for the average inmate, and that the more realistic mode of surviving the pains of imprisonment was through the patterns of social interaction established by the inmates themselves. These patterns of interaction Sykes termed "adaptive endurance," and it was the key to understanding the origins of prison subcultures.

The patterned social interaction that constituted the inmate social system, or "society of captives," was not characterized by pure inmate solidarity, nor was it characterized by constant predatory behavior between inmates. Instead, adaptive endurance, or patterned social interaction, fluctuated between the two extremes of "collectivistic" and "individualistic" orientations. As one moved closer to the collectivist orientation, the greater the inmate solidarity and the less severe the pains of imprisonment (Sykes and Messinger, 1960). Moreover, the greater the inmate solidarity, the greater the adherence to the inmate code that governed daily life. According to this code, inmates were not to *interfere with other inmates' interests* (i.e., "don't be nosey," "don't have a loose lip," "keep off a man's back," "don't put a guy on the spot"), *lose their head* (i.e., "play it cool," "do your own time," and try to keep feuds and grudges to a minimum), *exploit fellow inmates* (i.e., "don't break your word," "don't welsh on debts"), *weaken* (i.e., "don't whine or cop out"), or *be a sucker* (i.e., guards were not to be trusted, and the inmate was always to side with the other inmates). The inmate who basically followed this code was known by inmates as a "real man" who "pulled his own time" and was viewed by other inmates as a man of integrity and autonomy.

As the term "individualistic orientation" implies, most inmates gave verbal rather than actual allegiance to the code. In the prison culture, there were other inmates who adopted "alienative" responses to the pains of imprisonment. The "rat" or "squealer" violated the codes on communication with guards on occasion, whereas the "center man" always sided with officials (Sykes, 1958). A "gorilla" violated the inmate code by forcefully taking from other weaker inmates, whereas the "merchant" used economic exploitation to manipulate other inmates. Sykes found that the merchant was among the most alienated because he was too willing to pursue his own well-being at the expense of others. Other inmates violated the code through their sexual conduct. "Wolves," "punks," and "fags" were so labeled because of their homosexual activity. Wolves were the aggressors, punks were sexually submissive, and fags were simply homosexual by nature. "Ball busters" were inmates who gave guards a hard time through constant and blatant disobedience. Because their behavior resulted in the potential punishment of all inmates, they were regarded by their fellow inmates as fools. Inmate roles also included "toughs" and "hipsters." Toughs were considered touchy and a threat because of their unpredictable outbursts. A hipster was a "wanna-be" who pretended to be tough by targeting inmates who were easily subdued.

The point in reviewing these various labels and roles is not to merely pique the interest of the reader with details about the various behaviors of inmates. The different labels ascribed to inmates by other inmates were not nicknames. They were, as Sykes termed them, "argot roles." These roles functioned within the broader context of the prison subculture. They reflected the principles of the inmate code and served as cues for interaction with other inmates and correctional officials.

Sykes's perspective on the origins and features of the inmate social system was not without its criticisms. For all its insights, his thesis did not allow for the possibility that the origins of prison subcultures or inmate behavior lay outside the prison environment. A counterperspective, known as the importation thesis, offered a different interpretation of the origins and features of inmate subcultures. This perspective was developed most thoroughly by Irwin and Cressey.

THE IMPORTATION MODEL

Irwin and Cressey (1962) argued that Sykes's deprivation model ignored the values and social standings that offenders brought into the prison. They contended that inmates were not "blank slates" upon entering the prison community and that the normative systems developed on the outside were inevitably imported into the prison. Many of the behaviors and attitudes that governed inmate interaction also governed group interaction outside the prison. Irwin and Cressey demonstrated their importation thesis by developing a typology of subcultures. This typology explained the origins of prison subcultures, and the impact of these subcultures on rehabilitative efforts in the prison and, ultimately, on recidivism.

Thief-Criminal Subculture

According to Irwin and Cressey, a discernible thief-criminal subculture existed in the prison. It was comprised of inmates known as "right guys" or "real men" and inmates who were generally regarded as trustworthy, cool-headed, and reliable. However, consistent with their thesis, Irwin and Cressey argued that the attributes of trustworthiness and dependability were not unique to the thief-criminal subculture found in the prison. They existed in the thief criminal subculture outside the prison as well, as illustrated by the proverbial adage "honor among thieves."

Those aligned with the thief-criminal subculture viewed this subculture as their primary "reference group" while incarcerated. Their self-image was derived from their connections to criminal subcultures inside and outside the prison and so remained committed to a thief-criminal life but not necessarily a prison life. Therefore, members of this subculture did not seek status and prestige within the institution, but sought things that made incarceration more bearable. Such things could include radios, contraband books, food, socks, and gadgets that enhanced leisure time. Those belonging to the thief-criminal subculture wanted to get out of prison and, until that time arrived, wanted a minimum of conflict.

Convict-Prison Subculture

Acknowledging the contribution of Sykes, Irwin and Cressey (1962) conceded that a convict-prison subculture did emerge in response to the deprivations of freedom, wealth, and goods and services. However, the distinguishing features of this particular subculture were not directly determined by these deprivations. To illustrate, inmates aligned with the convict-prison subculture consisted of gorillas, merchants, and toughs. Consequently, the central values of this subculture were utilitarianism and manipulation. However, Irwin and Cressey again argued that these values were not peculiar to the institutional setting, citing the work of Miller as evidence for their argument. In studying lower-class delinquent subcultures in free society, Miller (1958) found that autonomy, cunning, toughness, fatalism, and defiance of authority were the "focal concerns" of delinquent youth. In contrast to the thief-criminal subculture, members of the convict-prison subculture sought acceptance only from those within the prison. They sought positions of status by means only available in the prison and, unlike the thief, had a vested interest in the existing order of the prison.

Legitimate Subculture

Inmates aligned with this subculture shared none of the values of the previous two. These "accidental" criminals consisted of the drunk driver who hit a pedestrian, the manslaughter murderer, or middle-class embezzler. They subscribed to prosocial attitudes and behaviors on the outside and on the inside. These "accidentals" came to the prison with anticriminal and antiprison ties and looked to do their time in the most legitimate way possible. They ran for inmate councils, worked on the inmate newsletter, or spent time in religious study. They were what prison officials referred to as "good prisoners" who structured their behavior according to means considered legitimate on the outside of prison as well as the inside of prison.

Implicit in these typologies were indications of the nature and strength of inmate ties to inside and outside communities. These ties were identified by Clemmer (1940) as important in determining prisonization and, subsequently, reintegration success. Irwin and Cressey used this typology to understand the impact of rehabilitative efforts and the likelihood of recidivism upon release. For example, if deviant norms and values were indeed imported, and if thieves maintained their ties to the criminal subculture inside and outside, and if convicts maintained their ties to the prison subculture exclusively, then instilling new norms and values, or breaking old bad ones, would be extremely difficult. Predictably, Irwin and Cressey (1962) found that rehabilitative potential was highest for those aligned with the legitimate subculture and lowest for those in the convict-prison subculture. Accordingly, recidivism was most likely to occur in the convict-prison subculture because convicts remained the primary reference group. For these inmates, release was merely a short vacation from prison life. For those in the thief-criminal subculture, the prison was a "pitfall" or disruption to outside life. Their likelihood of recidivating was not as low as for those in the legitimate subculture, but it was not as high as for those in the convict-prison subculture.

Irwin's contribution to the understanding of the prison subculture and its impact of reintegration extended beyond his importation thesis. In *The Felon* (1970), Irwin addressed the more specific question that "theoretically every convict must ask himself: How shall I do my time? or What shall I do in prison?" (ibid.). He acknowledged that some inmates failed to cope entirely and slipped into suicide or psychosis, as Sykes, too, had suggested. Those who did cope chose one of three ways to do their time: "doing time," "jail-ing," and "gleaning." These three methods of coping corresponded closely with the subculture typology just presented. For example, "jailers" made the prison their world, while "gleaners" made the best of the situation through participation in education and other self-improvement programs.

An important point to emerge from *The Felon,* however, was that no mat-ter how inmates chose to do their time, they all acquired what Irwin termed the "convict identity." The convict identity, like prisonization, was acquired in degrees, but Irwin claimed it affected the future of all felons. Traces of the convict identity could be found no matter how much time had transpired. As a result, one's ability to make it on the outside was impeded, despite signif-icant positive lifestyle changes. For the "old cons" who served especially long sentences, the convict identity was particularly entrenched. These inmates succumbed to the identity completely and, in Irwin's words, were "suited for nothing more than dereliction on the outside or death in prison" (ibid.).

FEMALE INMATE SUBCULTURES

Giallombardo (1966) provided one of the first studies of life in female pris-ons, based on her observations at the Federal Reformatory for Women in West Virginia. She concluded that the pains of imprisonment did stimulate the formation of a subculture, but that the characteristics of female subcul-tures were best explained by factors external to the prison.

Giallombardo found that, in large part, the pains of imprisonment were just as intense for women as they were for men. Women too found the de-privations of liberty, autonomy, material goods, and heterosexual relation-ships "frustrating to the extreme." A major exception to this otherwise shared prison experience, however, was in the loss of security. Unlike men, women did not fear sexual and violent exploitation. Instead, their insecurity stemmed from the untrustworthy character of female inmates. Giallombardo claimed that, in the female inmate social system, distrust was so pervasive that inmate solidarity was little more than "calculated solidarity." Females determined their loyalties and actions on a situation-by-situation basis, in accordance with self-interest and preservation rather than moral obligation. Thus, while men feared being literally stabbed in the back, women feared a symbolic stab in the back.

To explain the phenomenon of calculated solidarity, Giallombardo relied upon the cultural norms of the day. In free society, women competed with one another in their attempts to secure a male partner. She argued that this rivalry was brought to the prison and manifested in the socialization patterns of female inmates.

The importation of culturally determined roles into the prison was also found in attempts to replicate family structures. It was in the context of creating pseudofamilies that homosexual roles and relationships were played out in the female subculture. As with male inmates, there were those who were homosexual regardless of incarcerated status (i.e., lesbians), and those who became so by virtue of their confinement (i.e., turnouts). But the pseudofamily roles were more intricately structured. They included the "femme" or "mommy," which was the most highly sought after role and paralleled the role of the wife in free society. They also included the "stud broad," which was patterned after the "daddy" or father role. This role also afforded much prestige in the female inmate subculture as it provided the only semblance of a male within the institution.

Giallombardo also observed that polygamy was a predominant feature of the pseudofamily. While finding and sustaining stable relationships were of utmost importance, there were often multiple wives in the family. The additional wives generally served a specific function. Some served an economic function by helping with material gains. Other wives refrained from homosexual activity and served only in an emotional capacity. However, the wives or family members who engaged in homosexual relationships achieved the greatest status.

Predictably, alienative roles were quite common in the female subculture as well. Most notably were the "chippie," "jive bitch," and the "snitcher." The chippie was the prison prostitute who engaged in sexual relations for material gain or purely sexual gratification. This label distinguished between those who were involved in promiscuous sex versus love/relational sex. The snitcher in the female subculture paralleled the rat or squealer in the male subculture. Similar to the members of the legitimate subculture identified by Irwin and Cressey, the "accidental criminals" of the female prison were known as "squares." They, too, possessed anticriminal loyalties and generally refrained from homosexual activity. They were viewed by their fellow inmates as naive, suckers, and even unwitting in their betrayals because they were so easily manipulated by prison officials. Consequently, squares were viewed as the pariahs of the female prison community. The "jive bitch" on the other hand was highly purposeful in her betrayals. Her sole intent was to create conflict and break up relationships between inmates. Her weapon was not violence, but lies and distortions or the previously mentioned symbolic stab in the back.

Though many of the argot roles identified in the female subculture involved self-interest and untrustworthy behavior, there were confidences that could be maintained in the female prison. "Rap buddies" and "homeys" were inmates who fostered a reasonable assumption of mutual trust. "Connects" worked in the prison economy and were respected for supplying needed goods and information. "Boosters" were the partial female equivalent of the merchant, except they garnered respect rather than scorn.

Giallombardo's study revealed obvious similarities between the female and male subcultures, but important differences as well. Absent were the argot roles of wolf, tough, gorilla, ball buster, hipster, and the right guy. The absence of the right guy role, in particular, reflected the diminished importance of the inmate code and the attendant notions of fair play and loyalty. A second important distinction was that male conflicts centered on the struggle for power, whereas female conflicts centered on the struggle for maintaining marriages; kinship ties constituted the principal factor of social integration. In light of these findings, Giallombardo concluded that the female inmate social system was not merely a functional response to the pains of imprisonment, as Sykes had proposed for the male inmate social system. While these pains provided the necessary conditions for the emergence of the social system, the pains alone did not explain the characteristics of the female subculture. The characteristics of the subculture were shaped by the same conditions that shaped the female existence in free society.

What is evident from these various depictions of prison life, whether based on the male or female experience, is that total power was neither a constant nor a mainstay of the prison setting. If total power was a de facto feature, one would not expect disobedience, fraud, rape, violence, murder, and other illegal activities of the ball busters, gorillas, or merchants to be "normal" features of the inmate social system. To explain the presence of generally orderly conditions, despite the absence of total power, the work of Sykes (1958) is again useful.

TOTAL POWER AND INSTITUTIONAL CONTROL

In *The Society of Captives,* Sykes (1958) challenged the conventional wisdom that prisons were institutions of total power. He contended that the exercise of total power within the institutional setting was more theoretical than real. In fact, maintaining order was a delicate balancing act that involved exchange and reciprocity. Officials were engaged in an ongoing struggle with their captives and enlisted the assistance of inmates to facilitate order (see also Cloward and Ohlin, 1960; Sykes and Messinger, 1960). Such arrangements were necessary at times to compensate for what Sykes termed "the defects of total power."

Sykes attributed these defects to a number of factors, the first of which was that the power of prison officials was not based on freely given authority. He reasoned that in order for power to be effectively exercised in any realm, the authority must be viewed as legitimate. If it was not, those who were subjected to it would feel no moral obligation to comply with the rules and regulations. Because many inmates profess their innocence, and view their convictions and incarceration as unfounded, there is no "just" cause to respect these agents of "unjust" authority.

The limited use of force also contributed to the defects. While force was not outlawed per se, Sykes proposed that repeated acts of force were limited in their effects. Physical force might temporarily subdue the inmate, but, on a repeated basis, it would have little impact in the long-term and in more complicated situations. For example, moving a mass of inmates in an orderly fashion or securing good work habits on a daily basis could not be ensured through repeated acts of force (Sykes, 1958).

In an environment where authority was not viewed legitimately and force was limited, a system of rewards and punishments might serve as a viable alternative for securing order and compliance. Yet, Sykes claimed even this strategy was destined for defeat. Many of the punishments administered in the prison had lost their "potency" because they did not constitute a discernible departure from the pains and deprivations already experienced. Inmates were already subjected to a steady diet of violence or threats of violence from other inmates and strict rules from officials. What form of punishment remained? Moreover, punishment often served as a status symbol to an offender, having the unintended effect of becoming a reward.

The system of rewards was equally flawed because the rewards were provided upon prison admission. Mail, visitation, recreation, and "gain time" privileges were given all at once immediately upon entering the institution. Consequently, they were viewed by inmates as rights or obligations, not as rewards to be gained separately and gradually. The rewards and punishments were ultimately blurred, as the only punishments available were the rights denied.

Lastly, Sykes claimed the defects of power could be attributed to guards who did not properly exercise their control and authority. Guards frequently ignored certain infractions and basic security requirements or even joined inmates in criticizing the higher prison officials to whom they were both held accountable. For a number of reasons, guards often took the path of least resistance when it came to the enforcement of rules. Sykes proposed that guards, like most anyone, wanted to be liked by those with whom they were in constant contact. The need to be liked clearly had a greater urgency in the prison setting. To be disliked was to expose oneself to violent retaliation in the event of a riot.

The guards' need to be liked applied to managerial considerations as well. Inmates could act out in a number of ways on a daily basis, which did not bode well for the guards in the eyes of their superiors. The guards' job performance was judged by how well they were able to "handle" those in their charge. Thus, a system of give and take served the end of "handling" inmates in a way that gave the appearance of order and good job performance. The guard-inmate relationship then was not one of complete dominance by the former over the latter. It was a relationship characterized by cooperation and exchange via bargaining, "deals," or "trades." In exchange for inmate co-operation and certain levels of order, staff overlooked certain infractions and permitted an underground economy. Here, inmates bartered for various and often illegal goods.

Sykes concluded that these defects in power were structurally induced. That is, the defects could not be eliminated by hiring more qualified, better paid, or better trained staff. The cooperative relationship was a functional feature of a social system beset with unavoidable pains and deprivations. However, it was this unofficial feature of cooperation and exchange that pre-vented the prison from spiraling into total and perpetual chaos. In light of this endemic feature, Sykes advised that any prison reform aimed at gaining more control that did not heed the culture of inmates was destined to fail.

SUMMARY AND DISCUSSION

Research on the social organization of prisons, both male and female, com-municates three major themes. The first theme deals with the process of ac-culturation or assimilation, as typified in the work of Clemmer. To varying degrees, all inmates are subject to prisonization—conformity to prison ex-pectations—and the degree of prisonization affects reintegration and recidi-vism potential. The second theme deals with the features, origins, and functions of inmate subcultures, as typified in the work of Sykes, and Irwin and Cressey. Sykes suggests the prison produces its own unique varieties of asocial behavior in response to various deprivations. Conversely, Irwin and Cressey assume the social organization of prison is a microcosm of broader society. The final theme articulated in this research deals with the question of whether prisons are "total systems of power." Sykes contends they are not. Nevertheless, order is still maintained because the inmate social system, with all its illegalities, is tolerated by officials in order to keep the peace.

The classic contributions of Clemmer, Sykes, Irwin and Cressey, and Gi-allombardo have provided the fundamental framework for the analysis of the features and origins of prison subcultures. While current research has mod-ified their ideas to accommodate changing times and inmate and prison char-acteristics, their collective insights about prison subcultures have not been overturned. For example, profound increases in African-American and His-panic inmate populations and the growth of prison gangs have *altered* the strength and structure of the inmate social system in male prisons. Moreover, while prisoner identities are still an integral part of adaptive endurance, they have become divided along ethnic and racial lines rather than criminal history, home affiliation, or any shared prison experience. For example, Chicanos view blacks and whites as more likely to "snitch," and place extreme importance on friendship and loyalty to their own ethnic group only.

A further illustration of modified patterns of interaction stems from the rise of inmate gangs and a younger "state-raised" generation of offenders. Violence, rather than "doing your own time," has become the more respected mode of adapting. Inmate gangs, such as the Texas Syndicate, the Mexican Mafia, and the Aryan Brotherhood, are highly militant and organized, and quite willing to impose death on those inmates who violate their codes. This increased proneness to violence renders the sanctions available to prison officials virtually meaningless (Ralph, 1997). The more gangs rule themselves and other inmates, the more the system of reciprocity and exchange between staff and inmates weakens. Certain hostilities and divisions have always existed between the staff and inmates, but the power balance was kept in check. Ralph contends that balance may be teetering in a dangerous direction, as gangs are at constant war with each other and are seeking to control not only the inmate subculture, but the institution altogether.

Since Sykes's articulation of the defects of total power, a counterperspective on power and prison governance has also emerged. In *Well-Governed Prisons,* Dilulio (1993) offers an alternative style of governance that he claims is better suited for this new and highly volatile prison climate. He argues that effective, well-ordered prisons are possible and that the prior literature has mistakenly created the impression that cons necessarily "run the joint." Indeed, at one time, administrators permitted some degree of inmate rule through inmate councils and the "building tender" system, which used inmates to discipline other inmates. Following the prisoner rights movement, such practices were declared illegal on the grounds that it contributed to an unsafe, insecure, and more violent environment.

Employing a public management approach, Dilulio assumes the effectiveness of any prison organization depends on a stable team of like-minded executives, structured in a paramilitary, security-driven, bureaucratic setting. The quality of management and prison life also depends on cooperative relationships with outside actors (i.e., legislators, judges, and community activists), not inside actors (i.e., inmates). The presence of order (i.e., rates of violence and other misconduct), good amenities (i.e., availability of clean cells, decent food), and good service (i.e., availability of various rehabilitative programs) is not contingent upon a "better class" of inmates, but rather upon effective prison administration (ibid.). Dilulio rejects the conclusions of most sociologists and penologists, namely, that "ineffective prisons" are a

foregone conclusion. He holds that responsibility for ineffective prisons ultimately rests with the failures of administration, but adds that these failures
are correctable.

Despite DiIulio's optimistic claims about the potential of more effective
prison administration, it does not appear likely that prisons will fare any better in the future. Rather, and quite the opposite, it appears that prisons will
worsen in their conditions and inmate consequences. Why then, after centuries of experiences with these crude, often brutal, costly, and ineffective instruments do they not only remain intact but also continue to flourish with
ever-exploding populations? What the future of imprisonment appears to
hold is that sentences will continue to be longer, more minorities and women
will be locked up, and the public and politicians may believe the streets are
safer despite the fact that rates of imprisonment do not correlate with crime.
What then is the answer? According to Rothman (1995a):

> We need an honest recognition of what criminal justice sanctions can and can-
> not accomplish and a frank acknowledgement that increasingly severe pun-
> ishments are no remedy for thwarted life circumstances. We require leadership
> that will help map out new directions and enable us to break out of the fixa-
> tion with prisons. But by every indication, we will go on marching lockstep
> along the same monotonous paths. (p. 43)

Given the current prison climate, Rothman's bleak speculation appears accurate. Prison riots, hostage taking, gang warfare, and inmate to inmate, inmate to staff, and staff to inmate violence are all increasingly routine aspects
of everyday prison operations. Nonetheless, and despite these deteriorating
conditions, prisons continue to be our penal strategy of choice.

10

Prisoner Rights in the Age of Discontent (1960s–1970s)

INTRODUCTION

SINCE ITS INCEPTION, the prison has been subject to numerous criticisms. Early state penological commissions, charitable associations, and other outside observers disparaged the brutality of prison conditions and the failure of different confinement strategies (e.g., rules of silence, separation, and the fixed sentence) to reform or deter offenders. In more recent years, sociologists assumed the role of critic by theoretically probing the reasons for prison's failings. Among their findings was the prison's capacity to foster deviant norms and values and inflict psychological damage on its inmates.

Despite these attacks over time, the legitimacy of the prison (and its alternatives) was never seriously challenged. While the attacks may have created controversy, the structures of the prison remain largely unchanged, in part because of an inherent popular belief in the benevolent intentions of the state and its "disinterested" professional agents. Stated differently, the government's ability to ultimately solve the problem of crime was not called into serious question.

By the 1960s, various formal and informal institutions that had been considered the guardians of social order came to be regarded as having taken on a life of their own that did not reflect their formal purposes. Blind faith in government—and crime control in particular—had run its course. Accordingly, many criminologists charged that conventional crime control practices were now doing more harm than good. The traditional response, more (control and intervention) is better, had become the problem rather than the solution to crime. Predictably, this major change in thinking led to a newer, Less (control and intervention) is best, approach to crime control.

As the activities of the justice system came under scrutiny, numerous reforms sought to temper and limit the powers of the state. The expansion of prisoner rights, a moratorium on capital punishment, and the growth of community-based correctional alternatives were among the major penal reforms.

The purpose of this chapter is to describe and assess the prisoner rights movement within the context of what Mannheim (1940) described as the fundamental democratization of post–World War II America.

RADICALISM AND SOCIAL REFORM

Between 1950 and 1960, the mechanisms of informal social control were working well. Few groups seriously disputed the legitimacy of existing social arrangements. In fact, social life was so conformist and lacking in diversity and individual expression that the student population was dubbed the "silent generation" (Skolnick, 1969). Art, science, learning, entertainment, and information were all mass-produced, leaving behind a narrow and singular vision of the norm. By all appearances, society was prosperous, orderly, and stable. Beneath the surface, however, was a stifled culture, marred by racism and sexism. Soon social and political revolt would bring this "pleasant" existence to a turbulent end.

The Hippie Generation
The beat poets of the late 1950s were among the first to malign the establishment. They did so by "dropping out," and retreating in silent protest to the world of intellectualism and poetry (Gross, 1986). It was the hippies who triggered the cultural revolution of the 1960s. Hippies, unlike beatniks, forcefully and openly communicated their dislike for the socially prescribed norm or convention. Hippies communicated their rejection of the establishment through drug use, rock music, language, dress, and communal living. The need for separation from the hypocrisy of the old culture drove many forms of opposition. But the hippies' cultural activism did not necessarily translate to political activism. Rather than organize and infiltrate the system they sought to overthrow, they contended that authenticity of lifestyle would alter politics and economics. Antisocial behavior and civil disobedience would tear down the "pig-power structure" (Gross, 1986). Consequently, hippie demonstrations were often festivals for radical and unconventional behavior. As one participant of these demonstrations stated:

> I support everything that puts people in motion, which creates disruption and controversy, which creates chaos and rebirth. (Rubin, 1971)

Another proclaimed:

> What's needed is a new generation of nuisances. A new generation of people who are freaky, crazy, irrational, sexy, angry, irreligious, childish, and mad. People who burn draft cards, and dollar bills . . . who burn M.A. and doctoral

degrees . . . who lure the youth with music, pot, and LSD . . . who redefine reality . . . who wear funny costumes. (ibid.)

Counterculturalist Gridley Wright wrote in 1969:

I don't believe that there is anything like rights and justice and to the degree I would see myself as hung up with concepts like that, I would be in a circular bag, because there never have been rights and justice. (quoted in Gross, 1986)

The nihilism of the counterculturalists was fueled by one disillusionment after another. American society was not all it professed to be. Poverty was not randomly distributed, but disproportionately concentrated among blacks and women (Bok, 1992). Politicians did, in fact, lie and mislead the American public. But the call, "Don't do it if it doesn't groove ya," was not the only rhetoric of the antiestablishment movement. Commitments to social good and justice ran high. Recognizing that full representation in the political and economic system could not be achieved by simply adopting the hippie lifestyle, others sought to change the system rather than to merely drop out altogether.

Government Protest and Civil Rights

The rumblings of social and political change began with *Brown v. Board of Education* in 1954, a black child being murdered in 1955, Rosa Parks's personal protest in 1955, and Martin Luther King's entry into the civil rights struggle. Under King's petition "to awaken a sense of moral shame in the opponent" (Skolnick, 1969), the civil rights movement gained momentum with the Mississippi freedom rides to register black voters in 1961 and the March on Washington for Jobs and Freedom in 1963. The cause of civil rights strengthened further with Freedom Summer of 1964, and the King-led march from Selma to Montgomery, Alabama, in 1965.

Despite seeking peaceful means to racial integration, violent forms of retaliation ensued. Southern judges, prosecutors, and local bar associations routinely suppressed civil rights and worked to maintain terrorist racism instead of prosecuting and punishing it (Skolnick, 1969). In the summer of 1964, when nine hundred summer college students volunteered to register black voters and teach the concepts of freedom in Mississippi schools, the result was three student deaths; one thousand arrests; thirty-five shooting incidents; thirty bombings of homes, churches and meeting houses; and eighty beatings (Graham, 1992). In the following year, during marches in Alabama, a young black boy and a Unitarian minister died at the hands of state troopers. More bloodshed followed on March 7, 1965, which was later dubbed Bloody Sunday. In the South, and during peaceful protest, blacks died for the cause of gaining respect and legitimacy in American society.

Impatient and frustrated, the civil rights movement in the North took a more aggressive and independent stance. The federal government was no longer regarded as a protector of rights or as a promoter of general welfare. Government promises to deal with urban decay and decline, racial tensions, and poverty had gone unfulfilled for too long. In response, leaders of the northern movement, such as Malcolm X, preached a message of increasing militancy and separatism instead of peaceful protest.

By linking racism in America to the history of "white" colonialism, Malcolm X portrayed black racism as a global Third World issue. His imperialist perspective on racism was not inconceivable. After all, many black Americans were being asked to kill and die in wars for free market capitalism abroad, though they could not achieve economic independence and political freedom at home. Malcolm X's objectives for civil rights were unequivocal: "complete freedom, complete justice, complete equality, by any means necessary." His passion was equally undeniable: "You show me a black man who isn't an extremist, and I'll show you one who needs psychiatric attention" (quoted in Skolnick, 1969:99).

The call to action by "any means necessary" contributed to the creation of the Black Panthers in 1966, in Oakland, California. The Black Panthers established the Party for Self-Defense to move black power into the electoral arena and to defend against the actions of the police. Stripped of faith in the criminal justice system, the Black Panthers policed the actions of police with the following motto: "The Panther never attacks first, but when he is backed into a corner, he will strike back viciously" (Skolnick, 1969).

On these and other provocative calls to action, ghetto violence erupted in the Watts neighborhood of Los Angeles and in Chicago, Cleveland, Dayton, San Francisco, Atlanta, Omaha, and numerous other communities throughout the country. The Watts riots of August 1965 resulted in 4,000 arrests, while the Chicago riots resulted in 3,000 arrests in 3 days. The Detroit Riot of 1967 produced 43 deaths, 7,200 arrests in 9 days, hundreds of injured, 1,300 destroyed buildings, 5,000 new homeless, and approximately $50 million dollars in damages (Graham, 1992). Less destructive riots erupted in the ghettos of Boston, Cincinnati, Milwaukee, and Newark. In Newark, 1,500 were arrested after 5 days of rioting in April 1968. In the week immediately following the death of Martin Luther King, protests in Washington, D.C., and Baltimore resulted in 7,444 and 5,500 arrests, respectively (Skolnick, 1969).

The residents of poor rural and urban black communities were not alone in their civil disobedience. Teachers, doctors, nurses, ministers, and priests from white America decried the hypocrisy of the government's foreign policy particularly in Vietnam, and timid response to racial and economic inequality. Students at Berkeley, the University of Chicago, Columbia, and the University of Wisconsin were prime instigators of antiwar and civil rights demonstrations. Between January and June 1968, a total of 38,911 students produced 221 demonstrations at 101 colleges (Skolnick, 1969). In the 1967–1968 academic year, 71 separate demonstrations occurred on 62 campuses. In 1965, 25,000 students protested the Vietnam war, and, by 1968, the protests involved 300,000 students (ibid.). Far from being the silent generation, the students of the sixties sought to affect social change and invigorate the democratic process.

Advancing with the antiwar demonstrations and black civil rights movement, albeit at a slower pace, was the women's movement. While the black and women's movements remained largely separated in their struggle, both shared a history of oppression by white males, and both were demanding equal treatment. Betty Friedan's 1963 book, *The Feminine Mystique,* was an often-cited reference source for the movement. According to Rhode (1989), Friedan chided the popular culture and the social structure that chained women to the kitchen, the bedroom, and the nursery, and the drudgery and tedium of a full-time suburban home existence. What was then referred to as "this problem that had no name" (ibid.) was perhaps best illustrated in the 1955 Smith College commencement address given by liberal democratic presidential nominee Adlai Stevenson. His topic: "How women can influence men and boys:"

> This assignment for you, as wives and mothers, you can do in the living room with a baby on your lap or in the kitchen with a can opener in your hand. If you're clever, maybe you can even practice your saving arts on the unsuspecting man while he's watching T.V. I think there is much you can do about our crisis in the humble role of housewife. I could wish you no better vocation than that. (quoted in Wilson, 1987; see also Graham, 1992)

Sexual discrimination was further illustrated in a number of state criminal and civil laws. Texas law charged women with murder for killing their husband's mistress, but charged men with justifiable homicide for killing their wife's boyfriend. Nebraska laws kept women off juries unless a judge approved of their restroom. Civil laws in seven southern states made fathers the presumptive guardians of their minor children. Washington law prevented married women from filing suit in a state court unless their husbands joined in the suit. Ohio union laws prevented women from holding nineteen different jobs (Graham, 1992).

The corrective action of civil rights legislation was far from immediate. Segregated classified ads were still prevalent in 1966. The Equal Employment Opportunities Commission (EEOC) found persistent violations by race, origin, and religion in twenty-one newspapers and eighteen thousand ads. Employers placed ads calling for "white attendants," "Anglo carhops," "executive sales positions for men," "lady in charge in shop," and "insurance trainees, men age 22–25." In 1969, women accounted for only 7 percent of all physicians, 1 percent of all engineers, 3 percent of all lawyers, and 8 percent of all scientists. Law and medical schools typically held female admissions to a 7 percent quota, despite higher scores by women on entrance exams (Graham, 1992). Sandra Day O'Connor, though a top graduate of Stanford law school, was refused employment in law firms for any position other than a legal secretary. College-student female activists were even excluded from leadership positions and ridiculed by male activists who rallied against discrimination of Native Americans, African Americans, and other ethnic groups (Rhode, 1989).

The demand for civil rights did not end with blacks and women. It was instead the beginning of a mass group rights movement that applied to Hispanics, American Indians, college students, welfare recipients, soldiers, gays, lesbians, consumer advocates, and a variety of environmental groups (Feenberg, 1986). One disenfranchised group after another—the poor, welfare mothers, mentally ill, handicapped—stepped forward to take their rightful place in mainstream America. All considered themselves oppressed by the contradictions of American society, both in the public and private arena. Each group had its own history of exclusion, its own leaders and methods, but all were seeking inclusion and the full promise of citizenship rights by way of group grievance (Jacobs, 1997).

It is from this context that prisoners launched their own fight against inhumane and unfair treatment. In fact, the prisoner rights movement and the civil rights movement shared much in common. Both met with violent resistance and both were about integrating or, in the case of prisoners, reintegrating alienated groups (Pallas and Barber, 1980). At times, the movements involved the same people; those who were politically active on the outside often found themselves on the inside (Wald, 1980). The prison world had become a microcosm of society.

PRISONER RIGHTS

Riots and Revolution

Pallas and Barber (1980) view the prisoner rights movement as involving three stages. The first stage was the riots of the 1950s, which erupted over demands for decent food, shelter, and health care, and the promises of early parole and good treatment. More spontaneous and disorganized, the riots had little impact on bettering prison conditions. Once the rioting had concluded, prison administrators largely ignored prisoner demands. To maintain future control, officials simply resorted to more restrictive conditions and corporal disciplinary measures.

The second stage of the prisoner rights movement involved the organization of the Nation of Islam by black prisoners (ibid.). Muslim leaders, once incarcerated, sought to educate black inmates spiritually and politically. Their efforts at education, however, were resisted. Prison administrators viewed the Black Muslim faith as threatening an already volatile prison atmosphere. Consequently, Muslim ministers were transferred, prisoners were thrown into isolation, meetings were broken up, and outside communication was cut off. Muslim inmates responded to these measures with peaceful strikes and lawsuits to obtain the right to hold religious meetings, purchase the Koran, and receive Muslim visitors (Vogelman, 1971).

To quell years of mounting disorder, prison officials continued to employ tactics that generated further agitation. Privileges (e.g., out-of-cell work or study activities), along with the basic amenities of daily living (e.g., showers, canteen, mail, television), became rewards for passivity and obedience. Activism, on the other hand, invited isolation, denial of rewards, denied parole, unofficial beatings, gassings, destruction of personal property during cell searches, or killing of prisoners (Wald, 1980). Inmate killings could occur through purposeful neglect of medical care, staged suicides, bribing other inmates to kill other inmates, or outright shooting under the pretext of an escape attempt (ibid.).

The third stage, the revolutionary stage, grew out of these worsening conditions (Pallas and Barber, 1980). What differentiated this stage was its politically charged nature. The politicization of the prisoner rights' movement owed much to the Black Panthers, whose impact was most profound in the California prison system between 1968 and 1971. However, support for prisoner rights came from outside the black community as well. White college students were sympathetic to the cause, as they too had been incarcerated for drug busts, war protests, and free speech rallies. Vietnam veterans also understood the plight of the prisoner, as many veterans were incarcerated in federal prisons. Feminists arrested for their acts of civil disobedience took their message to the women's prisons. Directly or indirectly, but by way of a shared antiestablishment rhetoric, each of these groups contributed to the groundswell of political support for prisoner rights. At times, various activists compared American prisoners to the "political prisoners" of the Third World (Wald, 1980).

During the politicized stage of the movement, prisoners of all races united. The inmate code assumed greater meaning and importance, particularly the part that emphasized inmate solidarity against guards. Prisoners were to regard themselves as a single, unified "class" and, at all costs, avenge the injustice committed against even one inmate (ibid.). For example, the San Quentin race riot of 1967 involved nearly one-half of the prison's four thousand inmates (Pallas and Barber, 1980). In 1968, prisoners united again in a strike that shut down the prison's industries. In October 1970, inmate strikes took over the Long Island branch of the Queens House of Detention, sparking minirevolts throughout a number of New York City jails.

Inmate revolts continued at Soledad, Folsom, and San Luis Obispo prisons in California. The work stoppage at Folsom in November 1971 was recorded as the longest, most nonviolent prison strike in history. Nearly all 2,400 inmates remained in their cells for nineteen days without food, while enduring constant physical and emotional intimidation. Their demands, articulated in a 31-Point Manifesto, called for an end to injustice and discrimination, the denial of political and legal rights to prisoners, and exploitation in work programs (ibid.).

In May 1971, at New York's Attica prison, the Attica Liberation Front employed the political language of amnesty. Among their twenty-nine demands was the right to organize economically and politically, to participate in choosing the officials who ruled them, and to rebel without repercussions. They also demanded better working and living conditions, that the current warden be fired, and that transportation to a nonimperialist country be provided for those desiring to the leave the United States (ibid.). In Massachusetts, in 1973, inmates organized with the help of numerous outside leftist groups, journalists, and liberal legislators (Martin, 1980). The end result of this act of defiance, as with the other inmate revolts, was generally dismal. More repressive measures again followed. In some instances, state police were called in to govern prisons; in other cases, the killings, gassings, and beatings of prisoners accelerated.

In 1970, the American Bar Association placed the prisoner rights movement at the center of the legal community by founding the Commission on Correctional Facilities and Services. As advocates of correctional reform, they operated a Resource Center for Correctional Law and Legal Services. By 1974, twenty-four state bar associations had special committees devoted to prison reform (Jacobs, 1997). The totality of their activity was far too vast to record here, but the use and impact of the constitutional amendments in the prisoner rights struggle are summarized in the following section.

Petitioning the Courts

It is widely assumed that prior to the 1960s no prisoner was ever given his or her day in court. The literature has generally suggested that this hands-off posture of the state was a function of a "slaves of the state" (*Ruffin v. Commonwealth,* 1871) interpretation of inmate rights. However, throughout the nineteenth and early twentieth centuries, the court frequently heard prisoner grievances and found conditions of institutions and actions of custodians to be in violation of legal norms (see, e.g., *Neal v. Ute,* 1881; *Avery v. Everett,* 1888; *McElvaine v. Brush,* 1891; *Westbrook v. Georgia,* 1909; *Anderson v. Salant,* 1916; and *Kusah v. McCorkle,* 1918). Wallace (1992) has argued that the statutory remedies available to the courts in those cases may have been limited, but that the courts were not entirely inactive or indifferent.

Wallace contends the hands-off doctrine more accurately describes the decades just preceding the sixties. The observed indifference of the courts in the 1940s and 1950s reflected the belief that courts lacked expertise about the affairs of correctional administration. It was held that intercession by the courts would only undermine prison discipline and generate litigation overload (Wallace, 1994). Therefore, courts should not interfere or encroach on the rights of states in the matters of prison rules and regulations (*Banning v. Looney,* 1954) (DiIulio, 1990). This deferential position by the courts was invoked, then, not because inmates were truly considered "slaves of the state." Rather, courts were upholding what they believed to be an appropriate separation of powers between the executive and judicial branch.

Wallace's interpretation of the history of court involvement in corrections may be unique, but his point is well taken. It is reasonable to assume that judicial involvement goes through periods of activism and retrenchment. The period commonly understood as the prisoner rights movement was undoubtedly a period of high activism by the Supreme Court, and federal and state courts.

The Warren Supreme Court (1953–1969) set the tone for judicial activism. Prone to broad interpretations of the Constitution, the Court was committed to extending constitutional protections to minorities (Branham and Krantz, 1994), many of which were confined in institutions. During this period of high judicial activism, the extent of involvement by the federal judiciary in jails and prisons was second only to the dismantling of segregation in public schools (Feeley and Hanson, 1990). Litigation brought by Black Muslims was among the most instrumental in mobilizing the prisoner rights movement. Between 1961 and 1978, an estimated sixty-six federal court decisions were issued relating to Muslim prisoners alone (Jacobs, 1997).

Jacobs has argued that religious persecution may have brought the courts into the prison, but it was deplorable conditions that kept them there. The number of lawsuits filed overall provides some indication of the courts' receptivity to inmate claims of any kind. In 1960, 1,305 federal and 872 state prisoner lawsuits were filed. By 1969, 3,612 federal and 9,312 state lawsuits were filed. This constituted a 177 percent increase in federal filings and a 968 percent increase in state filings, despite the fact that prison populations were slightly declining in both systems (Thomas, 1988). By 1974, federal and state lawsuits filed reached a high of 18,410.

Freedom of Religion

The right of inmates to freely exercise their religion has been fought on two constitutional grounds, namely, violations of the First and Fourteenth Amendments. For example, following the ruling in *Fullwood v. Clemmer* (1962), the

Washington, D.C., Department of Corrections was forced to permit Muslim religious activities within the prison. In denying Muslims the opportunity to practice their religious beliefs, correctional administrators were denying their First Amendment right of freedom of expression. The legal question at hand, in this case, was whether the Muslim faith constituted a religion or just a personal philosophy. The grounds for the ruling was that the Muslim faith qualified as a religion because of its belief in a supreme being (Allah) controlling the destiny of man (Cripe, 1990; Vogelman, 1971).

This ruling paved the way for the decision in *Cooper v. Pate* (1964), wherein inmates successfully sued for the right to use the Koran, and for a place and opportunities to worship. In *Cruz v. Beto* (1972), the meaning of religious freedom was further examined as a due process issue, as inmates contested a state policy of paying only for Catholic, Jewish, and Protestant clergy and Jewish and Christian bibles. The court ruled that inmates must be afforded "reasonable opportunities" to exercise their faith of choice in a way comparable to others, as required by the Fourteenth Amendment's equal protection clause. Yet, it was also decided that the state did not need to provide everyone the resources (i.e., staff and space) for this to occur.

Communication Rights, Legal Resources, and Access to the Courts

The First and Fourteenth Amendments were also employed in the struggle against the censorship of inmate mail. The broad question to be addressed was whether the First Amendment provided protection against censorship of inmate mail (Branham and Krantz, 1994). This question related to the Fourteenth Amendment issue of due process, namely, the implications of the censorship of mail for communication with lawyers. In short, did mail censorship violate due process rights by impeding access to the courts? In *Palmigiano v. Travisono* (1970), the federal court established restrictions on the censorship of mail (Wallace, 1992), but the matter was given further clarification by the Supreme Court in *Procunier v. Martinez* (1974) and *Wolff v. McDonnell* (1974). In the former case, inmates charged that existing state regulations governing the censorship of mail were overly restrictive. Existing regulations prohibited letters wherein inmates "unduly complained" or "magnified grievances," or engaged in writings that expressed inflammatory political, racial, religious, or other views (Branham and Krantz, 1994). Institutional regulations also prevented the mailing of "otherwise inappropriate letters."

In *Procunier v. Martinez*, the Court ruled that restrictions on mail had to serve an "important" or "substantial" government interest not related to the suppression of expression. However, in demonstrating these interests, the state did not have to provide "certain" evidence that these interests would be threatened. Ultimately, the Supreme Court ruled in favor of the inmates by declaring the (aforementioned) regulations unconstitutional. To safeguard against unreasonable censorship, states were to provide the following: (1) a notice to an inmate when a letter written to or by an inmate is going to be censored; (2) an opportunity for the author to protest the censor decision; (3) and a review of censorship by another official other than the one who made the initial decision to censor.

Further clarification by the U.S. Supreme Court was given in *Wolff,* in which a Nebraska inmate challenged a prison rule that allowed correctional officers to open and inspect mail in the presence of prisoners. Justice Byron White wrote that it was permissible to open the contents of an envelope and put it on the table, as long as the readable portions (i.e., a letter) were not read (Smith, 2000).

Clearly, inmates were never denied access to the courts in a literal sense. However, several conditions, apart from mail censorship often made access difficult. These conditions included access to legal books and papers, delays, lack of assistance in preparing documents, and being restrained in efforts to obtain counsel even when the inmate could personally afford one.

The problem of access to legal resources was partially remedied in *Bailleaux v. Holmes* (1961). The court ruled that prison authorities could not stifle the study of law when it could be shown that this impeded one's right of access to courts (Vogelman, 1971). A major decision on access to legal resources was issued by the U.S. Supreme Court in *Johnson v. Avery* (1969). This case centered on the matter of inmate lawyering and, incidentally, inmate protection against staff mistreatment. Historically, prison rules had prohibited jailhouse lawyering. The power it afforded certain inmates challenged the staff's authority and contributed to potential abuse of other inmates (e.g., via extortion or sexual favors). Because jailhouse lawyers (JHLs) possessed this advantage, they were often subjected to harassment and abuse by institutional staff. Maltreatment eventually pushed jailhouse lawyering underground (Jacobs, 1997).

In *Johnson v. Avery,* the Court ruled that the absence of JHLs put an undue burden on other inmates' right of access to the courts. The Court ruled that prisoners were entitled to obtain legal assistance from other prisoners, unless the prison provided alternative means by which to file the necessary legal documents (Smith, 2000). The Court did put restrictions on when and where JHLs could render assistance, and it forbade formal compensation of any kind.

Right of access to the courts was addressed again in *Gilmore v. Lynch* (1970), *Haines v. Kerner* (1972), and *Bounds v. Smith* (1977). In *Gilmore,* the federal court ruled that limiting law books in prison libraries unreasonably denied prisoner's access to court (Wallace, 1992). In *Haines,* the court affirmed that special attention be given to inmate petitions. In *Bounds,* the court affirmed that adequate law libraries and trained personnel must be provided.

Disciplinary Measures and Due Process

The Fourteenth Amendment essentially asks the question, "What process is actually due citizens" (Branham and Krantz, 1994) so that they might be pro-

tected against the arbitrary action of government? One of the specific implications of the right to due process is that procedural steps must be followed
when life or liberty is threatened. Critical to the prisoner rights movement
was demonstrating the relevance of due process, even though guilt had already been established. In other words, did due process apply when someone was being punished?

In *Wolff v. McDonnell* (1974), the Supreme Court addressed the question
of whether prisoners were afforded due process protections under the conditions of disciplinary cell confinement (Rhine, 1990). The court ruled that
due process rights did apply (i.e., fair procedures), because the state did give
some valued things to prisoners that could later be taken away. It was not
necessary that the same standards of due process be applied as in the trying
of the original charge of conviction. Still, the court conceded that a "mutual
accommodation between institutional needs and objectives and the provisions of the Constitution" must be met. Translated into practice, an advance
written notice of the institutional charges against the prisoner was to be giv-
en at least twenty-four hours prior to appearance before the disciplinary
board. The court ruling also required that a written statement by the fact find-
ers as to the evidence relied upon and reasons for disciplinary action be provided. An inmate was also permitted to call witnesses and present
documentation in his or her defense as long as it did not pose a threat to institutional safety. Finally, *Wolff v. McDonnell* established that the prison disciplinary board be impartial and, if the inmate was illiterate, that substitute
counsel be provided (ibid.).

In *Hewitt v. Helms* (1983), the Supreme Court outlined the process "due"
inmates upon transfer to administrative segregation (i.e., segregation for the
protection of the inmate). In these circumstances, the inmate was to be giv-
en "some notice" of the reason for the transfer, though it did not have to be
in writing. The inmate was also to be given the opportunity to express his or
her views about the transfer, though it did not have to be in person (i.e., written notice sufficed). The court further established that the inmate be given
the opportunity to have the transfer decision reviewed by a prison official after the transfer, though the review did not have to be a formal hearing. Finally the court ruled that periodic reviews by prison officials were required
for the duration of the inmates' segregative confinement (Branham and
Krantz, 1994).

Overall, the courts agreed that due process rights did apply in a number
of situations, particularly disciplinary hearings that might result in a sanction
or grievous loss such as gain time. Due process requirements, in the form of
orderly procedures, also applied to classification assessments, intraprison
transfers, and transfers to administrative/segregative confinement. In effect,
procedural safeguards were to be applied to all actions taken by officials, but
the quality and quantity of the safeguards varied with the extent to which life,
liberty, or property was potentially denied.

Conditions of Confinement and Use of Force

Conditions of confinement in southern states drew the greatest attention of the courts. Lack of resources and institutional disrepair contributed not only to poor sanitary conditions and medical care, but abuse of inmates by other inmates who had been selected by prison authorities to govern the institution (Smith, 2000). But the South was not alone in having prison conditions challenged or in having judges issue remedial orders. Throughout the country, the Eighth Amendment was applied to a number of confinement situations, including deficiencies in medical care, failure to provide inmates protection from other inmates, and use of unreasonable force by correctional officers in situations of self-defense, protection of other inmates, and enforcement of rules.

Pugh v. Locke (1976) provided one of the most infamous examples of judicial decisions affecting general conditions of confinement. In his opinion, the presiding judge gave a scathing critique of the Alabama penal system. Among the litany of charges leveled, the judge noted the following: broken and unscreened windows that created a serious problem with flies and mosquitoes, old and filthy cotton mattresses that led to the spread of contagious diseases and body lice, exposed wiring, facilities overrun with roaches in all stages of development, one functioning toilet for more than two hundred inmates, toilets that did not flush and were overflowing, no working classification system, food stored in infested units, and the practice of packing six inmates into four-foot by eight-foot cells with no beds, no lights, no running water, and a hole in the floor for a toilet which could only be flushed from the outside (Judge Johnson, 1976; opinion quoted in Smith, 2000:189–191).

Lawsuits concerning conditions in isolated confinement, specifically, illustrate the complexities as well as the inconsistencies surrounding Eighth Amendment rulings. The points of contention in these cases generally revolve around the maintenance of personal hygiene, the physical conditions of the cell, exercise allowed, diet, and duration of isolation. For example, in Wright v. McMann (1967), the Supreme Court ruled that when inmates were deprived of soap, water, towel, toilet paper, toothbrush, and clothing, the conditions had become constitutionally intolerable (Palmer, 1991). However, another court found it was constitutionally acceptable to allow water and a shower only on every fifth day (Ford v. Board of Managers of New Jersey State Prison, 1969). Another court found it constitutionally acceptable to deprive an inmate of all hygiene materials for seven to ten days, with no reading material, and in a cell inhabited by mice and roaches (Bauer v. Sielaff, 1974). Though consensus was ultimately lacking on what qualified as unconstitutional conditions, the factors judged as relevant on a consistent basis were the physical conditions of the inmate, the condition of the cell, and the personal hygiene of the inmate (ibid.).

Estelle v. Gamble (1976) set the standard for many Eighth Amendment claims, particularly those relating to inmate medical care. The critical factor that emerged from this case's ruling was the standard of "not inadvertence or error committed" in good faith, but the presence of "obduracy and wantonness" (ibid.). In other words, the court ruled that to constitute cruel and unusual punishment, officials must act with deliberate indifference to an inmate's (medical) needs. If the official's actions only reached the level of negligence (i.e., the failure to act reasonably), an inmate would be directed to seek remedy in civil state courts.

It was not until much later in *Farmer v. Brennan* (1994) that the requirements of deliberate indifference were substantially clarified. They included the following stipulations: (1) official(s) must be aware of the facts revealing that an inmate faced a substantial risk of serious harm, (2) official(s) must have actually deduced from these facts that the inmate was at significant risk of being seriously harmed, and (3) official(s) must have taken reasonable steps to prevent the harm from occurring. Inappropriate action was generally defined as preventing an inmate from receiving care or delaying the administration of care, and taking superficial or no steps in responding to inmate complaints. What qualified as a medical deficiency went above and beyond an isolated instance to include systemic or institutional policies. For example, insufficient staffing, equipment or record keeping, or the employment of non–English-speaking physicians qualified as unconstitutional (Branham and Krantz, 1994).

Given the number of prison riots, strikes, and peaceful demonstrations that occurred between the 1950s and 1970s, the constitutionality of the use of force was particularly relevant. The standard rule was that prison officials could use force, but the reasonableness of the force was to be decided on a case-by-case basis (*Jackson v. Allen,* 1974; Palmer, 1991). Reasonableness of force hinged on such criteria as the degree of force being used by the inmate, the staff's reasonable perception of injury, and the means used to resist the assault. Following the bloody Attica riots, inmates alleged that officials had engaged in unreasonable and unprovoked brutality. The court agreed:

> Injured prisoners, some on stretchers, were struck, prodded, or beaten with sticks, belts, bats, or other weapons. Others were forced to strip and run naked through gauntlets of guards armed with clubs, which they used to strike the bodies of the inmates as they passed. Some were dragged on the ground, some marked with an "X" on their backs, some spat upon or burned with matches, and others poked in the genitals or arms with sticks. According to the testimony of the inmates, bloody or wounded inmates were apparently not spared in this orgy of brutality. (ibid.)

Equal Protection, Equal Treatment
The Fourteenth Amendment not only requires that due process be extended to citizen and inmate alike, but that it be equally applied, regardless of race,

gender, or religion. Inmates were also guaranteed equal protection (i.e., treatment) under the law. For example, mounting racial tensions in prisons during the early 1960s prompted correctional administrators to resort to racially segregated units. In *Washington v. Lee* (1966), U.S. District Court struck down segregative schemes for violating the Fourteenth Amendment equal protection clause. The court acknowledged that in certain "isolated instances," segregation may be justified, but for only a "limited period" of time. The Supreme Court affirmed the ruling of the lower court, by concluding that institutional safety concerns could sometimes override racial discrimination concerns. Nevertheless, subsequent rulings on racially segregated units generally required that institutions find some alternative means of securing order and safety, such as increasing the supervision of inmates, disciplining and isolating problem inmates, and decreasing the prison population (Branham and Krantz, 1994).

The Fourteenth Amendment also applies to gender discrimination claims and provided the basis for much of the women's prisoner rights movement. The "parity movement," as it was termed (Rafter, 1990), was distinctive from the male prisoner rights movement. In the words of Aylward and Thomas (1984), there were no "sisters in litigation." Female inmates were far less litigious and far less politicized than their male counterparts. In fact, it has been suggested that their interest in litigation bordered on apathetic. When litigation did come to pass, it had a unique focus. Their lawsuits dealt primarily with the issue of disparate treatment in the area of housing and programming, rather than abuse or maltreatment by staff (Wheeler, Trammell, Thomas, and Findlay, 1989).

Because so few women were incarcerated, and even fewer incarcerated for long periods of time, female facilities were scarce. Women offenders were often housed in converted hospitals, youth facilities, hotels, or in portions of male facilities (Chesney-Lind, 1991). Consequently, if the sentence was lengthy in duration, women were often transferred across state lines to facilities equipped for long-term incarceration. Feminist activists viewed this as unfair and unequal treatment, because women, unlike men, were housed thousands of miles away from their families and children. In *Park v. Thompson* (1976), the high court of Hawaii agreed, ruling that the prohibition on visitation constituted a "grievous loss." This ruling had a profound but unanticipated national impact. Counter to the feminists' decarceration objectives, the ruling led to a national campaign to build more female facilities.

The parity movement also focused on women's access to law libraries, vocational/educational programming, specialized treatment programs, and medical services. Inadequate prison services and programs were justified by system officials on the same grounds as the earlier transfer policies. The "demand" was simply not there and the numbers of female inmates were too few to bother. Outdated and substandard vocational programming were further justified by system officials on the grounds that women were not the major breadwinners of the family (Smart, 1976). In reviewing such claims, the courts required that females receive a "parity of treatment" (Branham and Krantz, 1994). Programs for females did not have to be identical to males, but they did need to be "substantially equivalent . . . in substance if not form" (*Glover v. Johnson,* 1979). For example, an auto mechanics course did not have to be provided in a female facility, but a program that made them equally economically viable upon release did have to be provided.

Probation and Parole

It is important to note that the prisoner rights movement did not deal exclusively with inmate issues. Offenders serving time in the community were still in custody of sorts, as their liberty could be quickly denied at the discretion of the probation or parole officer. The U.S. Supreme Court first addressed the issue of parole revocation in *Morrisey v. Brewer* (1972). The ruling in this case established that parolees had the right of due process and that the revocation process must unfold in two separate stages. In the first stage, the offender must be notified of the nature of the violation and the impending preliminary hearing. During this preliminary hearing, probable cause for the violation would be determined, and the offender was to be present, able to speak on his own behalf, and submit documents and cross-examine witnesses (Branham and Krantz, 1994). At the second stage, the revocation hearing, the same rules and protections applied as in the preliminary hearing, but the due process standards did not need to reach the level of those afforded at a full criminal trial. *Mempa v. Rhay* (1967) established that probationers had a right to counsel during revocation hearings (Palmer, 1991) and, in *Gagnon v. Scarpelli* (1973), the Supreme Court asserted that the procedural protections articulated in *Morrisey* applied to probation revocation proceedings as well.

This period of high judicial activism in the area of offender rights extended to the administration of capital punishment as well. Just as discrimination, injustice, and unfair practices were at the heart of the civil rights movement and the prisoner rights movement, these same issues framed the controversy surrounding the death penalty.

ABOLISHING CAPITAL PUNISHMENT

Prior to 1965, the death penalty had not been challenged on constitutional grounds. To illustrate, in postrevolutionary America, the death penalty was abolished for the majority of offenses on humanitarian and utilitarian grounds. In the 160 years that followed, particular methods of administering death were challenged and abolished (Bedau, 1997a). It was not until the Warren Court that the question of the constitutional validity of capital punishment (Nakell and Hardy, 1987) was raised. The questions of constitution-al validity were procedural (Fourteenth Amendment) and substantive (Eighth Amendment) in nature.

The hearing of *Rudolph v. Alabama* (1963) provided the first hint that the Supreme Court might consider the constitutionality of the death penalty. This case addressed whether death was an appropriate sanction for the crime of rape, but was germane to the broader cause of civil rights; those who had been sentenced to death in rape cases consistently were black men whose victims were white women (Bedau, 1997a). In the *Rudolph* case, the Court failed to declare the statute in question unconstitutional, but the constitu-tionality of capital punishment was revisited in *Maxwell v. Bishop* (1965). The courts again ruled that death in the case of rape was constitutional on procedural grounds because the intent of the said statute was not discrimi-natory. However, before *Maxwell* was settled, efforts to end the death penal-ty in rape and other cases had spread to Florida, California, and all other death penalty jurisdictions. For example, in *Akens v. California* (1972), the state struck down the death penalty as unconstitutional in its application. Several states followed California's lead, believing the nation's death penal-ty was under constitutional review.

Finally, in *Furman v. Georgia,* the Supreme Court ruled that in all the cases before the court, the death penalty as administered violated the Eighth and Fourteenth Amendments. Of the five Supreme Court Justices, William Bren-nan and Thurgood Marshall were alone in declaring the death penalty unconstitutional as a form of punishment entirely. Justice Brennan was sweeping in his indictment, claiming the death penalty was unconstitution-al for any crime, any person, using any method. All five justices concurred on the grounds of arbitrariness. Specifically, Justice Stewart proclaimed that the decisions were randomly made as if "being struck by lightning" (Bedau, 1997a). At the same time the death penalty was declared random, it was also declared discriminatory in its application. The administration of the death penalty was without guidelines (i.e., random), thereby facilitating its arbitrary and discriminatory application. It disproportionately disfavored the poor and minorities, leading the court to conclude that one could readily observe the difference between those who received death and those who did not (Bran-ham and Krantz, 1994). The Supreme Court perceived a gross lack of proce-dure in all decisions relating to the administration of the death penalty. Given its irreversible nature, the Court declared that "super due process" was sub-sequently warranted (Bedau, 1997a).

The *Furman* decision invalidated the death penalty statutes in several states. Thirty-five states responded to this ruling, not by abolishing capital punishment, but by using *Furman* as a guideline for developing a constitu-tionally acceptable statute (Nakell and Hardy, 1987). During this moratori-um, hundreds of sentences were commuted to life imprisonment. *Gregg v.*

Georgia (1976) served as the test case for many of the newly crafted death penalty statutes. Several features of the Georgia statute made it acceptable to the Supreme Court. First, it provided limits on discretion by requiring that the sentencer find beyond a reasonable doubt that at least one of ten aggravating factors be present. A second feature was a provision of automatic review by the state supreme court in all death penalty cases. The statute also featured a two-phase trial system whereby guilt/innocence was decided in one phase and sentencing in the second phase (Bedau, 1997a).

The Georgia statute provided a point of comparison for the state statutes that did not pass constitutional muster. For example, in *Woodson v. North Carolina* (1978) the Supreme Court cited three reasons why a mandatory death penalty statute was unacceptable even though it addressed the problem of arbitrariness: (1) when the law conflicted with standards of decency such that juries would acquit defendants in order to avoid the imposition of sanctions, (2) when the law merely shifted the discretion to juries, and (3) when the law removed the right of a defendant to an individualized sentencing hearing where mitigating circumstances could be presented (Branham and Krantz, 1994).

The validity of mandatory death statutes was repeatedly addressed in *Roberts v. Louisiana* (1976), *Coker v. Georgia* (1977), and *Eberheart v. Georgia*. *Roberts* abolished mandatory death for the killing of a police officer, *Coker* abolished mandatory death for rape, and *Eberheart* abolished mandatory death for kidnapping. Incidentally, in all these cases the defendant was black and the victim was white. However, the Supreme Court did not strike down all mandatory death statutes. The decision to uphold the legality of such statutes rested on whether the statute in some way prohibited the presentation of mitigating circumstances (Branham and Krantz, 1994). The Supreme Court's position was that legislatures were prohibited from defining certain crimes for which death must be imposed, but they were not prohibited from identifying when death could not be imposed (ibid.).

SUMMARY AND DISCUSSION

In 1968, *Life* magazine journalist John Lindsay wrote that it was "a matter of concern when Americans find the ordinary channels of discussion and decision so unresponsive that they feel forced to take their grievances to the street" (quoted in Skolnick, 1969). The activism of the 1960s and early 1970s was not entirely unprecedented (American history is filled with instances of political and economic revolt), but the activism of this generation did possess some unprecedented qualities. It lasted longer, involved more people, and was more militant and hostile to established authority and institutions (ibid.). The same can be said of the rights movement for offenders and pris-

oners. What made this movement distinctive was the volume of filings and
the willingness of the courts to clarify and expand prisoner rights and provide tangible relief when necessary. However, as social activism in general
diminished, so too did activism on behalf of offenders and prisoners. The ro-
manticism of the offender/prisoner rights movement gave way to divisions
within the movement itself. Many attorneys were not paid for their efforts,
nor did they always get along with those they represented. Activists soon
learned that most prisoners were not political leaders in the making. They
were often simply criminals who were typically unskilled and uneducated
(Wald, 1980).

The impact of the prisoner rights movement has since drawn both praise
and criticism. Advocates of judicial intervention have contended that activism of any kind has rightfully expanded public access to the courts and
given voice to traditionally powerless groups (Feeley and Hanson, 1990). Judicial reform advocates applaud court rulings that redress past harms and
prevent future harms by restructuring the responsible bureaucracies (Bradley,
1990). Consequently, they claim the prisoner rights movement resulted in
much needed improvements, including the abolishment of the southern
prison plantation (slave) model of confinement, increased professionalism
of correctional staff, increases in correctional accountability, more uniform
policies via accreditation standards, and improved jail conditions (Feeley
and Hanson, 1990).

Critics have charged that such activism undercut the power given to the
executive and legislative branches. Advocates of judicial restraint believe the
courts overstepped their authority by changing social policy and the rules
that governed social institutions. They maintain that the rightful role of the
courts is the interpretation of the law, not the governance of malfunctioning
bureaucracies (ibid.). Consequently, restraint advocates assert that prisoner
rights resulted in greater loss of control by institutional authorities, which
contributed to greater inmate on inmate and inmate on staff violence. They
also claim that it led to increases in staff turnover, lower staff morale, a breakdown in effective management, not to mention the prohibitive costs associated with court compliance.

What both of these interpretations overlook is that many of the abuses the
prisoner rights movement attempted to correct are as prevalent today as they
were before, during, and immediately following the movement. The current
conservative position of the courts, in many cases, has inadvertently given
sanction to these abuses. Courts are now opting to curtail rights, rather than
enforce the ones in place, and have even reversed prior decisions. For example, courts have turned back arguments that criminals can prevent parole
boards from considering illegally obtained evidence during revocation hearings. Courts have also rejected the argument that a prisoner should be given
adequate notice and a hearing before disciplinary action is taken. In *Lewis*

v. Casey (1996), Supreme Court Justice Thomas even asserted that prisoners have no constitutional right to legal resources and assistance and that right of access to the courts should be limited solely to protection against interference in filing legal papers.

It is also the case that medical care in prisons may be better than what it was, but it is far from good. Surely, the gross negligence of the past makes a poor justification for present inadequacies. Across the United States, two-thirds of prison doctors are not board certified, and physician and nursing positions are considerably understaffed. Inmate deaths still result from negligent medical care. Moreover, inmate beatings and killings by guards are not as uncommon as presumed. In *Hudson v. McMillian* (1992), Justice Thomas and Scalia questioned whether the Eighth Amendment even provided protection for prisoners against abusive actions by correctional officers (Smith, 2000). Overall, access to the courts, health care, visitation, and communication are increasingly impeded through policies that require inmates to absorb more and more of the costs of their confinement. Further, the use of the death penalty during the 1980s and 1990s enjoyed a renewed and broad public and political support.

11

Decentralizing Corrections in the Age of Discontent (1960s–1970s)

INTRODUCTION

UNPRECEDENTED AND FAR-REACHING LEVELS of public discontent characterized the 1960s. Revelations of government corruption, participation in an unpopular war, strained race relations, civil disobedience, urban riots, and the inability of the criminal justice to lawfully respond to escalating civil disorder culminated in a crisis of legitimacy in American institutions. It was from this crisis in American institutions that the prisoner rights and decentralization of corrections movements developed.

What emerged in relation to these events and realizations was a growing interest and recognition of the relevance of labeling theory. Labeling theory shifted criminology's focus from the offender to the criminal justice system. Essentially, labeling theory argued that interaction with criminal justice was an integral element in the process of creating, intensifying, and perpetuating criminal and delinquent behavior (Cicourel, 1968; Emerson, 1969; Schur, 1971).

The previously unquestioned rehabilitative agenda for correctional reform, More Is Better, was viewed as suspect. The new call, Less Is Best, provided the fundamental rationale for decentralizing corrections. The reasoning was that the correctional system had not only failed to stem crime but, even worse, was doing more harm than good. It labeled and stigmatized offenders, and subjected them to damaging criminal associations that perpetuated criminal and delinquent careers.

The decentralization movement was to replace formal correctional system processing of offenders with various informal and preferably voluntary forms of community treatment. With legislative authority, funding assistance, theoretical justification, and broad professional and public support, various decentralized strategies transformed correctional practice throughout the 1960s and 1970s.

This chapter reviews the social context and associated theoretical reasoning, development, goals, practices, and selected consequences of the major program components comprising the decentralization of corrections movement. The review documents that while the theoretical justification and expressed goals of decentralized corrections were very different from the theory and goals of preceding penal reforms, the practices and consequences were not only familiar but more far-reaching.

LABELING THEORY: JUSTIFYING DECENTRALIZATION

Though labeling theory was popularized during the 1960s and 1970s, the general theory had appeared much earlier, with key elements reflecting the symbolic interactionist tradition (Mead, 1934; Blumer, 1969). Frank Tannenbaum (1938) is frequently credited for providing the first statement of labeling theory. Tannenbaum referred to the process of labeling that leads to subsequent deviant behavior as the "dramatization of evil." According to Tannenbaum, the "dramatization of evil" is initiated following acts of normal youthful misbehavior (e.g., playing baseball in the street and hitting a ball through a neighbor's window). Tannenbaum argued, "the process of making the criminal, therefore, is a process of tagging, defining, identifying, segregating, describing, emphasizing, making conscious and self-conscious; it becomes a way of stimulating, suggesting, emphasizing, and evoking the very traits that are complained of" (ibid.:20).

Tannenbaum identified several formal justice system consequences that provided a focus for later diversion, deinstitutionalization, and other community-based efforts. The author contended that youth entering the criminal justice system are subjected to a forced "companionship" with other children similarly defined, which results in "a new set of experiences that lead directly to a criminal career" (ibid.). Tannenbaum concluded that the best policy was "a refusal to dramatize the evils" (ibid.). Diversion, deinstitutionalization, and other community-based programs were officially intended as a means to eliminate the potential for the "dramatization of evil." They would reduce the numbers of offenders exposed to criminal justice system processing and the damaging labels and associations wrought by that exposure.

In *Social Pathology* (1951), Edwin Lemert introduced two fundamental concepts that refined labeling theory. These concepts were primary and secondary deviance. Primary deviance encompassed a range of deviant acts committed for a variety of situational or personal reasons. Those who committed primary deviant acts did not consider their deviance as fundamental to their identity. Rather, deviant acts were spontaneous or situational behavior. In contrast, secondary deviance occurs when the actor no longer dissociates his deviant behavior from his self-identity. Of particular importance to Lemert was the explanation for the shift from primary to secondary deviance.

Lemert argued that this shift involved a sequential process of primary deviant acts followed by gradually amplified negative social audience reactions. As a result, and over time, the deviant actor assumes a deviant self-identity that is followed by secondary deviance that reaffirms the individual's deviant identity.

Neither Tannenbaum's nor Lemert's labeling theory contributions received major attention when they were first published. However, as the decade of the 1960s unfolded, interest and writing reflecting labeling theory proliferated. These writings included contributions by Howard Becker (1963), John Kitsuse (1964), and Kai Erikson (1966). According to Cullen and Agnew (1999), this group of scholars argued in their respective extensions of the earlier work of Tannenbaum and Lemert, that societal reaction, not the offender, should be the focus in criminology's quest to determine the causes of crime (pp. 270–271).

During the course of the 1960s, labeling theory's popularity grew to the point of challenging the dominant functional perspective. John Hagan (1973) contends that labeling theory's rise to prominence in the 1960s can be attributed to its interesting argument. Hagan argues that criminologists are drawn to those particular ideas that challenge the conventional wisdom on causal sequence (ibid.:456). Cullen and Agnew (1999) elaborate

> Common sense would dictate that arresting, trying, imprisoning, and rehabilitating offenders would make crime less likely; after all, the manifest function of processing offenders through the criminal justice system is to reduce their recidivism and to make society safer. However, the unique twist to labeling theory was the claim that these very efforts to prevent crime actually cause crime. (ibid.:272)

But labeling theory's "interesting argument" had been articulated decades earlier without gaining even a moderate foothold in criminology. In the 1960s, however, the times were ripe and, and as result, labeling theory had a captive and receptive audience. Labeling theory was, indeed, "the" theory for the times. Given the developing crisis in American institutions, a theory that directly and forcefully critiqued one of these major institutions, namely, the criminal justice system, was broadly embraced. In effect, "a theory that blamed the government for causing more harm than good struck a chord of truth that resonated with the times. Labeling theory, of course, did precisely this in arguing that the criminal justice system stigmatized offenders and ultimately trapped them in a criminal career" (ibid.). The policy directive emerging from labeling theory was clear: reduce the criminal justice system's intervention into the lives of offenders. Young offenders were to be diverted from the system whenever possible, and all offenders (adult and juvenile) were to be dealt with in ways that kept them out of reformatories and prisons.

DEVELOPMENT OF THE DECENTRALIZATION MOVEMENT

Feeley and Sarat (1980) have argued that the issue of crime and what to do about it became a signature political issue with the presidential campaign of 1964. The national government was caught up in a "war mentality"—against domestic social ills and foreign enemies—and the preferred weapon to deploy was the massive mobilization of national resources. The federal government's response to the problem of crime was found in the application of the war metaphor and culminated in the passage of the Omnibus Crime Control and Safe Streets Act of 1968 (ibid.:3–4). This act established the Law Enforcement Assistance Administration (LEAA) to implement a national strategy for waging America's war on crime.

Before the Safe Streets Act, a small grant-in-aid program was created in 1965 to assist state and local law enforcement. The LEAA authorized the attorney general to provide grants to improve law enforcement. Following the 1965 passage of the act, the attorney general created the Office of Law Enforcement Assistance (OLEA), and over the three-year operation of OLEA, twenty million dollars in grants was awarded. While OLEA did not have a specific congressional mandate to guide its funding decisions, it did demonstrate the federal government's commitment to do something about the problem of crime without increasing federal control over state and local government (Feeley and Sarat, 1980:36).

During 1965, President Lyndon B. Johnson established the President's Commission on Law Enforcement and the Administration of Justice. In 1967, the commission completed its assignments, which resulted in nine individual reports on specific crime problems and aspects of the administration of criminal justice. These reports were the result of two years of work by more than five hundred professionals working as staff or in consultant capacities (Feeley and Sarat, 1980:37). The commission was organized into a series of task forces that dealt with such crime problems as organized crime, drugs and crime, and components of the criminal justice system including police, courts, penology, and juvenile justice.

Ultimately, the various task force results were integrated into a series of two hundred conclusions and recommendations, and published as *The Challenge of Crime in a Free Society* (U.S. President's Commission on Law Enforcement and Administration of Justice, 1967a). These conclusions and recommendations, unlike previous justice reform thinking, shared the view that crime in America would not be remedied by merely expanding the capacity of the criminal justice system. In fact, a number of the task force reports concluded that because of the negative effects associated with labeling by the criminal and juvenile justice systems, reform efforts should be directed toward the development and implementation of various alternative, "pre-judicial dispositions." Pre-judicial dispositions meant handling cases "unofficially" through the use of various nonsystem alternatives such as diversion, deinstitutionalization, and various other community-based programs.

For example, the U.S. President's Commission Task Force on Juvenile Delinquency and Youth Crime concluded that formal juvenile justice system action

> may actually help to fix and perpetuate delinquency in the child through a process in which the individual begins to think of himself as delinquent and organizes his behavior accordingly. That process itself is further reinforced by the effect of the labeling upon the child's family, neighbors, teachers, and peers, whose reactions communicate to the child in subtle ways a kind of expectation of delinquent conduct. The undesirable consequences of official treatment are heightened in programs that rely on institutionalizing the child. The most informed and benign institutional treatment of the child, even in well-designed and staffed reformatories and training schools, may contain within it the seeds of its own frustration, and itself may often feed the very disorder it is designed to cure. (U.S. President's Commission on Law Enforcement and Administration of Justice, 1967b:8)

To begin nationwide implementation of various decentralization reforms and other presidential task force recommendations, the 1968 Safe Streets Act was passed. The Johnson administration desired quick action to demonstrate resolve in effective crime policies. The Safe Streets Act, located within the Justice Department, provided a major grant-in-aid program to assist states and local government in their efforts to effectively confront crime. The first step was to develop a comprehensive procedure for dealing with state and local crime problems that incorporated the numerous recommendations of the President's Commission task forces. Ultimately, the procedures involved a state and local matching fund requirement under the administration of LEAA. The average annual funding for LEAA from its inception through 1980 was approximately $850 million a year.

Beginning in the late 1960s and continuing through the decade of the 1970s, the decentralization of corrections strategies of diversion, deinstitutionalization, and community corrections was the "name of the game" in the federal funding of penal reform initiatives. In direct contrast to the assumption guiding penal reform from 1900 to the 1960s, the President's Commission concluded in 1967 that infusion of more resources for expanding correctional services would not result in more effective individualized treatment and offender rehabilitation. Rather, the commission argued that such individual treatment and rehabilitation goals were unrealistic expectations. Such expectations were seen as reflective of a grossly overly optimistic view of what is known about the phenomenon of crime and what a fully equipped correctional system could do about it. The commission maintained that experts in the field of correctional treatment agreed that it was most difficult to develop effective offender treatment programs because of the continuing lack of understanding of the causes of crime and delinquency. The commission concluded that until the field of human behavior developed well beyond its existing stage, sufficient understanding was not likely to be provided (U.S. President's Commission on Law Enforcement and Administration of Justice, 1967b:8).

Criminological research was found by the commission to support the view that crime and delinquency are not merely acts of individual deviance as they are patterned behavior resulting from a variety of societal influences well beyond the reach of probation officers, correctional counselors, or psychiatrists. Moreover, because the justice system was believed to be doing more harm than good by labeling and perpetuating subsequent crime and delinquency, various types of decentralized reforms that were aimed at avoiding the system altogether became the mainstream of LEAA-funded correctional reforms. The implementation sequence of LEAA's decentralization of correctional reforms began with juvenile diversion program efforts that proliferated throughout the country in the late 1960s. During the mid- to late 1970s, deinstitutionalization of status offenders and various community treatment programs for both juvenile and adult offenders experienced major growth. Reformers within and outside LEAA proposed that federal funds be used to divert offenders from the criminal justice system. Between 1968 and 1978, LEAA funded over 1,200 community programs at an estimated cost of $112 million (Beckett, 1997).

GOALS AND PRACTICES OF DECENTRALIZATION REFORMS

Diversion

Juvenile diversion programs were the early mainstream of the decentralization movement. As envisioned by the President's Commission, diversion was to result in a narrowing of official juvenile justice jurisdiction to only those cases of "manifest danger," with the bulk of troubled youth being diverted into neighborhood youth serving agencies formally designated as Youth Service Bureaus. Referral to the bureaus could be from parents, schools, or other sources, with the majority of referrals originating from the police and juvenile court and with mandatory acceptance by the bureaus.

The commission specified that the bureaus' services could include individual, group, and whole-family (parents and siblings) counseling, placement in group or foster homes, and work, recreational, special remedial education, and vocation training services. "The key to the Bureaus' success would be voluntary participation by the juvenile and his family in working out and following a plan of service or rehabilitation" (U.S. President's Commission on Law Enforcement and Administration of Justice, 1967a:20).

The major model of operation followed by diversion programs was that of system modification (Obrien and Marcus, 1976:17–36). System modification meant that diversion programs were intended to provide police and juvenile court intake staff with alternatives to traditional juvenile justice system processing, thereby minimizing youth contact with the formal juvenile justice system. Actual referrals to diversion programs were by police, probation, juvenile court, parents, schools and, surprisingly, many self-referrals by youth. Cressey and McDermott (1973) found in their study of diversion intake practices that juvenile court intake officers occupied the central role in the diversion referral process. The authors concluded that the nature of the informal relationships between diversion programs and court intake units was ultimately significant in the rate of diversion.

While the treatment modalities of most diversion programs included a range of individual, group, and family services, the distinction between individual youth and their families was not sharply maintained in the implementation of treatment. Typically, counseling and social casework approaches were employed with individuals, groups, and families, and this was supplemented with the use of various community treatment sources for referral including mental health, marital counseling, and welfare.

Rutherford and McDermott (1976) conducted a national assessment of diversion programs to develop a program typology. The typology included legal, paralegal, and nonlegal diversion program types. Police, juvenile court, and probation-provided diversion programs fell under the legal or paralegal program types, while private-agency-provided diversion programs fell into the nonlegal or paralegal program types. The authors identified the following characteristics for each program type:

> **Type 1: Legal.** Legal diversion programs, whether formal or informal, were administered by official justice agency personnel (i.e., police, probation, court); formal legal sanctions could be imposed; explicit or implicit coercion was present; programs were staffed by official agency personnel; and the programs were located on or within official agency premises.
>
> **Type II: Paralegal.** The paralegal diversion programs operated outside official agencies but were funded and administered by the official justice system and were staffed by official justice personnel (in kind, sabbatical, etc.). These programs were physically housed within official justice agency premises, had access to official justice agency records, received their clients from the official justice system, and maintained a formal or informal method of reporting on client progress in cooperation with official justice system.
>
> **Type III: Nonlegal.** The nonlegal diversion programs were client focused; client participation was voluntary; any form of program coercion was discour-

aged; no sanctions were imposed for nonparticipation or termination of program services; a client advocacy role was emphasized, and clients perceived
the program as nonlegal; the program determined staff appointments and maintained its goals without pressure from funding sources. (ibid.:12–15)

Legal diversion programs were the predominant models operating
throughout the country. Early studies portrayed diversion as an important alternative to the formal justice system primarily because of the anticipated reduction in negative labeling and subsequent crime on the part of those
offenders subject to diversion (Lemert, 1971; Polk, 1971; Rosenheim, 1969).
Several later studies by Mahoney (1974) and Morris (1974) critically speculated about the potential of diversion to produce unintended consequences.
Mahoney, for example, argued that the prevailing liberal reformist belief that
juvenile and adult offenders get a bad deal from the official justice system
could result in blindness to some of the less desirable aspects and potential
of diversion programs. In consideration of the negative potential of diversion,
Morris speculated that these alternative programs would ultimately result in
more pervasive but less severe control over a larger proportion of the base
population. Morris elaborated that if police are provided broader latitude to
decide whether to arrest or divert, there will be fewer arrests, but overall,
more individuals will be subject to arrest and/or diversion.

Toward the late 1970s, a series of empirical studies of the actual justice
system impact of diversion programs appeared. These empirical studies
demonstrated the patterned outcome of net-widening by diversion programs
(Austin and Krisberg, 1981; Blomberg, 1977; Hylton, 1982; Klein, 1979;
Lemert, 1981). Specifically, these studies documented that diversion practices were largely applied to youth and families who, prior to diversion,
would not have been subject to contact with the official justice system.

The finding of net-widening refers to the previously documented outcome
of penal reform alternatives to become implemented as supplements, thereby increasing the overall proportion of base population subject to some form
of correctional control. However, in the case of diversion, net-widening was
more pervasive and accompanied by additional unintended consequences.
Specifically, diversion programs not only drew the bulk of their clients from
groups previously not subject to imminent official justice agency processing,
but also placed many of these clients into family intervention services that
served not only diverted youth but their siblings and parents as well. As a result, diversion's net-widening was more expansive from that of previous penal reforms.

Klein (1979), in a review of studies reporting on client behavior changes
resulting from diversion programs, reported that three studies cited positive
findings of less delinquency (Baron, Feeney, and Thornton, 1973; Klein,
1974; Ku and Blew, 1977), two studies cited findings of negative effects of

more delinquency (Elliott, 1978; Lincoln, 1976), and eight studies cited equivocal findings (Berger, Lipsey, Dennison, and Lange, 1977; Binder, 1976; Carter and Gilbert, 1973; Elliott, 1978; Forward, Kirby, and Wilson, 1974; Klein, 1974; Lincoln, Teilman, Klein, and Labin, 1977; Stratton, 1975). The only study employing random assignment to diversion and nondiversion alternatives was that of Lincoln et al. (1977), which reported substantially lower rates of recidivism for diverted youth as compared to youth who received official juvenile court processing. However, those youth released outright, without any form of program services, were found to have the lowest recidivism rates.

In assessing the specific client effects of diversion because of net-widening, several studies reported upon diversion's capacity to increase client jeopardy, official system penetration, and subsequent behavior difficulties. For example, in a comparative study of adult offender diversion programs, Mullen (1975) found that offenders referred to diversion programs who were unable to meet the program's requirements were subjected to a form of double jeopardy; they were returned for prosecution on their original charge, prosecuted vigorously, convicted, and placed on probation supervision. Mullen pointed out further that most of the offenders handled in this manner would not have been subject to formal court processing if not for the net-widening outcome of diversion.

Similar findings in juvenile diversion programs were reported, particularly in relation to youth whose families were unable or unwilling to comply with the various requirements of diversion programs' whole-family intervention efforts. Specifically, Blomberg (1977) found that when families were unable to comply with diversion's family intervention requirements, the children in those families were routinely referred to the juvenile court for suitable out-of-home placement. He cites the following case to illustrate this potential:

A fourteen year old boy with no prior record was referred to family intervention from probation intake on a runaway charge. His father and stepmother subsequently agreed to participate in the family intervention counseling program. During the counseling sessions the fourteen year old, his sixteen and ten year old brothers, the stepmother, and father were all required to be present. The case worker indicated that the father felt that by working and earning the living he was carrying out his family responsibility and that his wife should be able to handle the boys. The stepmother did not feel she could control the boys, especially the two older ones. The case worker felt there was a general sibling rivalry for the stepmother with sexual overtones in the case of the sixteen year old. Following the mandatory five counseling sessions, the case worker recommended continued family therapy which the father refused. The case worker made several follow-up visits to the home and subsequently recommended that all three boys be removed from the home because of continued difficulties between the boys and stepmother. Ultimately the two older boys were placed in the home of a relative. The ten year old was placed in a group home from which he ran away twice attempting to return home. Following the second runaway, he was referred back to the juvenile court and because of the runaway record and what was determined to be general behavior deterioration, he was found to be incorrigible and subsequently placed in a custodial institution. (ibid.:280)

Further, Polk (1981) reported that, in many instances, when families encountered difficulties in complying with diversion's program requirements, the parents were referred to criminal court on charges of contributing to the delinquency of minors or moral neglect.

The potential associated with diversion's net-widening to create or intensify subsequent behavior difficulties related to justice system contact and increased visibility was supported by Klein (1975) in his study of the relationship between rates of rearrest and alternative dispositions. Klein found that providing diversion services to net-widening youth who would otherwise have been released outright may well have increased their subsequent rearrest rates, because of their increased visibility to their diversion treaters and police, rather than because of increased rates of misconduct.

Deinstitutionalization

Diversion reforms opened the window to the sweeping decentralization of corrections trend that included deinstitutionalization and various forms of community programming. The Juvenile Justice and Delinquency Prevention Act of 1974 initiated a second wave in the decentralization of corrections movement that demonstrated federal resolve in delinquency control and juvenile justice reform. The 1974 act was based upon the recognized need for a comprehensive, continual, and well-funded approach. To accomplish this goal, Congress established the Office of Juvenile Justice and Delinquency Prevention (OJJDP) as a semiautonomous agency within LEAA.

Underlying the 1974 act was the belief that a major shortcoming of the juvenile justice system was excessive use of secure confinement in detention facilities and juvenile justice institutions. The excessive use of secure confinement was further complicated by the indiscriminate mixing of minor and serious offenders often with adult offenders (Sarri, 1983). The major reform initiative emerging from the 1974 act called for termination in the use of juvenile detention or correctional institutions for juveniles who have committed acts that would not be criminal if committed by adults, namely, status offenses.

OJJDP's twofold goal in the deinstitutionalization of status offenders was (1) to reduce the use of secure confinement and (2) to encourage the development of community treatment alternatives for status offenders. The first goal was derived directly from labeling theory's contention that when minor offenders are formally processed by police, courts, and corrections, these offenders take on a delinquent identity and organize their subsequent behavior accordingly. The second goal reflected legal concerns for equity and justice. The belief was that it was not appropriate to hold in secure confinement those who have not committed criminal acts. These two program goals as summarized by Kobrin and Klein (1983) involved a strategy that connected a primary concern "with deinstitutionalizing status offenders, that is, with diverting them from detention and correctional institutions and, having done so, with bringing about a reduction in their subsequent offense behavior by providing the backup of community-based remedial services" (p. 11).

Several deinstitutionalization program efforts preceded the 1974 act: the 1972 Massachusetts Program, the 1960s California Community Treatment Program, and a number of other program efforts (for further discussion, see Empey, 1982:487–489). The most cited and controversial effort was that of Massachusetts. In 1972, Jerome Miller, director of youth services in Massachusetts, responded to a series of crises in the state's training schools by simply shutting them down. All of the functions of the closed training schools were transferred to the community. However, it was the 1974 act that led to nationwide recognition and implementation of deinstitutionalization of status offenders.

Hellum (1983) summarizes that, in 1971, Wisconsin and Alaska prohibited postadjudication commitment of status offenders, and New Mexico followed in 1972. In 1973, three states—South Dakota, Texas, and Nevada—prohibited postadjudication commitment of status offenders, as did five additional states in 1974: New Jersey, Massachusetts, Iowa, Maryland, and Illinois. New Jersey and Maryland prohibited postadjudication detention as well. In 1975, three additional states prohibited detention, and three prohibited commitment. However, between 1975 and 1978, seventeen additional states prohibited or reduced the use of detention, and twenty-five prohibited or reduced the use of postadjudication commitment for status offenders (Hellum, 1983:35). In effect, by establishing eligibility for federal delinquency funds contingent upon deinstitutionalization progress, the 1974 act provided a major incentive that led to nationwide legislative and policy implementation of the deinstitutionalization of status offenders.

The 1974 act also mandated the development of various community treatment alternatives to incarceration. As envisioned, these community treatment alternatives would include youth advocacy programs as well as various other education, family intervention, counseling, and employment assistance programs.

Corry (1983) identified the deinstitutionalization programs in Pima County,

Arizona; Alameda County, California; and Spokane County, Washington as exemplary program sites. The Pima County effort, while opposed by local politically powerful groups, had the power of a crusade. A charismatic juvenile court judge who was determined to end the excessive use of detention and institutionalization in the jurisdiction led the so-called crusade. The program was focused upon the development of youth advocacy and delinquency prevention in the county's high-delinquency areas. In Alameda County there existed a long-held belief in avoiding detention and institutionalization whenever possible. As a result, the probation department was successful in developing a family crisis intervention program with a high level of professional competency. The program's community focus was centered in the county's youth service centers located in high-delinquency areas. In Spokane County, there was a substantial degree of community receptivity to the deinstitutionalization of status offenders program. A constituency of community leaders assisted in the development of Youth Alternatives, which provided round-the-clock program services for status offenders. These services were focused upon family crisis intervention and case diagnosis with the use of some private sector youth service agencies.

During the late 1970s, a series of evaluation studies appeared that reported on the results of the deinstitutionalization of the status offenders program reform movement. Like diversion and numerous other penal reforms before it, the deinstitutionalization program movement's deeds did not match its words or goals. Postprogram recidivism rates showed little difference between deinstitutionalized and institutionalized youth (Coates, Miller, and Ohlin, 1978). However, in a systematic review of the literature that reports on the shortcomings of this program movement, Klein (1979) persuasively argued that deinstitutionalization as well as diversion were not implemented as intended and, as a result, what is reported as program failures were actually failures to properly implement the programs.

In assessing national trends in the general use of detention during the 1970s, Sarri (1983:335) concluded that, while there has been substantial federal and state effort to reduce reliance on detention, detention and jailing are used much more extensively than is necessary. More specifically, regarding the 1974 act calling for the deinstitutionalization of status offenders, Sarri concluded that, while leading many states to legislate and develop deinstitutional programs, "it is still the case that the act too had far less impact than was desired. If we are to comprehend why so many policies and programs have failed to achieve their objectives, we must investigate more thoroughly societal views about social control of youth development" (ibid.:318). Consequently, whether we accept Klein's interpretation as a failure to implement or Sarri's societal views on youth control, the end result was the same for the deinstitutionalization reform movement. The goals were not readily visible in the practices.

Decentralizing Adult Corrections

The earliest and most visible decentralization reforms were juvenile diversion and deinstitutionalization. These programs set the stage and provided specific rationales and program models that adult programs came to embody during the 1970s. In fact, diversion and deinstitutionalization rationales and program components were fundamental to adult community-based reform efforts.

In 1973, LEAA initiated the Exemplary Projects Program, which identified programs of proven merit, verified their achievements, and widely disseminated information about these programs. The Des Moines Community-Based Corrections Program was both the first Exemplary Project and the first to be replicated in five jurisdictions across the county. The Des Moines program was not a crime-fighting program as such or a program that targeted habitual or violent offenders. Rather, the program addressed some of the problems presented by the bulk of the criminal caseload for which it was counterproductive to employ traditional criminal justice sanctions. Specifically, the Des Moines program provided several graduated community-based service alternatives to traditional criminal justice sanctions for minor and nonviolent offenders. Even though many prosecutors and judges were inclined to be lenient with such offenders, they were often impeded because of the limited alternatives available to them. Like diversion and deinstitutionalization programs, the Des Moines program provided alternatives to confinement before and after trial and included various helping services for defendants and convicted offenders who wished these services. The Des Moines program was to help make the management of criminal justice more efficient and increase rehabilitation potential by enabling more individualized and proportionate sanctions and services for offenders.

The Des Moines program's four graduated components were release on recognizance, supervised release (i.e., pretrial release), intensive probation, and residential facility services (e.g., work release centers). Offenders' eligibility for a particular graduated component was based upon a numerical score that reflected seriousness of offense, prior record, employment record, and several other community tie variables. LEAA selected five sites to replicate the Des Moines program: Salt Lake City, Utah; Duluth, Minnesota; Orange County, Florida; San Mateo County, California; and Baton Rouge, Louisiana. Evaluation of the five replication efforts documented that not all of the Des Moines program components were susceptible to replication. The local residential facility was replicated successfully in all five sites, but probation services proved unsuccessful in replication because of the different laws governing probation at the national, state, and local levels.

Overall, the evaluation of the five sites' replication found that each site implemented the Des Moines program as a means to supplement and fulfill some of their respective criminal justice needs rather than as a commitment to the Des Moines program concept. As concluded by LEAA (1979),

The communities that received a replication grant originally sought the grant in order to meet immediate needs of its own criminal justice agencies. And as each replication addressed those special needs, it tended to assume its own distinctive character. It is safe to say that the manner in which, and the extent to which, each replication varied from the Des Moines model pretty accurately reflected the special local problems the replication was expected to resolve. (U.S. Department of Justice, 1979:43)

What LEAA concluded from the Des Moines program replication results was that communities that did not share some of the characteristics of the Des Moines community and criminal justice system provided an unfavorable environment for replication. Specifically, some of the characteristics in Des Moines that shaped the character of the program included an overcrowded jail, substantial geographic distance from urban centers, slow rate of geographic and demographic change, strong sense of community and receptivity to reform, and allowing local officials to administer corrections in their own way. Stated specifically, the more the replication site varied from the prototype, the less likelihood of successful replication.

The decentralization of adult corrections into the community was not slowed by the mixed results of the Des Moines replications. However, rehabilitation efforts, or the development of any program deemed lenient or rehabilitative in focus, were slowed by the findings of a major study by Martinson (1974). In this study on what works in correctional treatment, many more questions were raised about the results of community-based and institution-based corrections programs. Martinson's study was aimed at determining the most effective means to rehabilitate offenders. His major conclusion was that, with few exceptions, various rehabilitation efforts have had little effect on recidivism, from which the phrase "nothing works" emerged. In fact, such claims as those by Martinson and the questionable record of such LEAA-sponsored correctional reforms as diversion, deinstitutionalization, and community corrections led Congress to abolish LEAA in 1980. The perception at the end of the 1970s was that, despite the pouring of millions of dollars into reforms that aimed to divert or rehabilitate, crime was still escalating. This perception of failure was a driving force in the law and order approach that was to follow.

SUMMARY AND DISCUSSION

This chapter has briefly described the social context and associated theoretical reasoning, development, practices, and selected consequences of a series of decentralized correctional reforms that emerged during the 1960s and 1970s. These reforms were officially intended not as additions to the correctional system, but as alternatives to a potentially damaging and counterproductive system. This shift in the thinking and character of punishment was reflective of a larger crisis in American society and its major institutions. With the decentralization of corrections movement, a new era of penal reform was initiated. Rather than continue with the more than half-century-old tradition of "more is better," the new approach was to avoid contact with the formal correctional system altogether through the use of decentralized community alternatives. Only the most serious offenders or those who posed a "manifest danger" to the community were to receive traditional correctional processing. The bulk of offenders, or the less serious offenders, were to be rerouted into alternative programs based on often voluntary participation. Ultimately, all of these reform efforts were to reduce negative labeling and criminal associations as well as to increase justice and equity in the handling of less serious offender groups.

This new era in penal reform, however, produced not only more of the same results, but they were also laden with more ominous overtones and implications. Rather than differentiating the handling of offenders, diversion, deinstitutionalization, and community programs substantially expanded corrections populations often to include entire families. The resulting net-widening and associated negative latent functions extended well beyond the words versus deeds disparities of earlier penal reforms. To elaborate, in the case of diversion's role in formalizing methods that led to the control of whole families, significant policy implications arose. Family intervention resulted not only in extended control of parents and siblings through net-widening, but also in accelerated penetration into the justice system for those youth, siblings, or parents unable to comply with diversion's family intervention program requirements. As a result, because of diversion's widening of the net to include youth and families previously not subject to contact with the penal system, troubled youth and their families were put at risk of accelerated penetration into the justice system merely by their inability or unwillingness to comply with various family intervention requirements. Sanctions for the failure to comply ranged from informal threat of enforcement to formal contempt charges and more severe out-of-home institutional placements for children of parents failing to comply (Blomberg, 1977:281–282).

The net-widening pattern associated with the decentralization of correction's movement is illustrated by a comparison of correctional caseloads between 1965 and 1976. Total caseload for both incarcerated and community-supervised adults and juveniles in 1965 was 1,281,801 or 661.3 per 100,000 population. However, and after more than a decade of experiences with diversion, deinstitutionalization, and community corrections, the 1976 total correctional caseload had increased to 1,981,229 or 921.4 per 100,000 population, representing an increase in numbers of 54.6 percent and a rate increase of 39.3 percent. During this eleven-year period, the increase in the numbers incarcerated was 83,782, while the number on probation and parole increased by 190,557. These figures are an underestimate of total populations subject to some form of correctional control because they do include many minor offenders, their families, and others subject to diversion, deinstitutionalization, or various community correction services. Moreover, this major growth in correctional clients was occurring during a period of stable crime rates (Austin and Krisberg, 1981:183).

Another important policy issue that arises in relation to the various net-widening consequences of the decentralization of corrections, concerns how this larger umbrella of control relates to reducing, creating, or accelerating criminal and delinquent behavior. This policy issue reflects, in part, the very concerns that labeling theory has raised and the decentralization of corrections programs were aimed at eliminating. Labeling theory contends that formal contact and interaction with formal justice agencies is an integral component in the intensification and perpetuation of crime and delinquency. What has resulted from diversion's net-widening and family intervention efforts has been expanded control over larger numbers of youth and families receiving some form of formal and informal control, as well as accelerated control by the out-of-home institutional placement of youth and potential contempt charges against the parents in those families unable or unwilling to comply with diversion's family intervention requirements. In these instances, parents and siblings with no prior criminal or delinquent histories are accelerated into the formal justice system and are subject, therefore, to criminal and delinquent labels. The potential of this practice to create, perpetuate, or intensify subsequent crime and delinquency raises important research and policy questions (Blomberg, 1977:279–280).

At the end of the 1970s and with the 1980 elections fast approaching, crime again emerged as a decisive political issue. Amid the claims of "nothing works" in correctional treatment, calls to "get tough" went virtually unopposed by those in policymaking circles. Paying no heed to the unintended consequences of past policies, local, state, and federal officials proceeded to implement get-tough schemes of a sweeping magnitude.

12

Conservatism and Law and Order Punishment (1980s–1990s)

INTRODUCTION

BY THE END of the 1970s, there existed a far-reaching sense of societal failure. A "crisis of legitimacy" faced the nation in the forms of the Vietnam War aftermath, the Iran hostage crisis, Three-Mile Island, high unemployment, crippling inflation, and the unrelenting problem of crime. The belief that the 1960s had left the nation morally bankrupt only deepened the sense of cynicism and despair.

The cultural, political, and economic trends of the 1980s and, to a lesser degree, the early 1990s must be viewed against this bleak social backdrop of failure. To restore a sense of national pride, nothing short of a social about-face seemed to be necessary. The mandate was simple: retreat from the liberalism of previous decades. The new plan of action called for a smaller and more conservative government, sexual restraint, drug abstinence, rugged individualism, traditional values, and affluence. In many ways, tolerance gave way to intolerance, and one of the most notable examples of this intolerance was the proverbial war on crime. The emergence of a "zero tolerance" posture led to a string of reforms that collectively became known as the get-tough movement. The purpose of this chapter is to describe and discuss the social context, ideas, practices, and consequences resulting from America's tough-on-crime movement.

A REVERSAL OF FORTUNE

The 1960s and 1970s were defined by social activism and civil rights. In stark contrast, the 1980s were defined by supply-side economics and a "culture of greed." True, economics did not unilaterally shape the culture, but the two were unquestionably intertwined and Reagan emerged as the architect of both. The 1981 presidential inauguration of Ronald Reagan and the debut of

169

the nighttime soap opera *Dynasty* (Feuer, 1995) were coincidental but telling indications of the "great U-turn" (Harrison and Bluestone, 1988) that lay ahead.

Political Economy

Reagan's vision for the nation was to reverse the policies of welfarism and liberalism. His first order of business was to reduce government size, taxes, business regulations, and inflation (Ashford, 1990). Toward these ends, he advocated the privatization of certain government operations, the reduction or elimination of welfare and job programs, and the rebuilding of warfare programs. Monetary assistance to the poor was no longer seen as helping the downtrodden or the alienated, but rather as subsidizing the undeserving. Reagan conservatives trumpeted the self-made man, who acquired his wealth through determination and merit, rather than inheritance and parentage. Overall, Reagan's policies could be summarized as prowealthy and probusiness.

The consequences of these various policies were positive for a few, but devastating for others. Economic polarization increased dramatically, as a sliver of society amassed unfathomable wealth. The richest fifth of families earned nearly 43 percent of the nation's total money income, nine times more than what the poorest fifth took in (Steinberg, 1997). By 1990, the term "millionaire" was rendered meaningless. There were over 100,000 decamillionaires, and the number of billionaires increased from a handful in 1981, to 26 in 1986, to 49 in 1987, and to 52 by 1988 (Phillips, 1991). Altogether, the number of millionaires and billionaires increased by more than 250 percent, and average annual CEO compensation increased from $373,000 to $773,000 (ibid.).

Much of this wealth was generated from what was known as "paper entrepreneurialism." As corporations profited from mergers, hostile takeovers, downsizing, multinationalizing, and deindustrializing, product output and reinvestment suffered. Between 1973 and 1985, junk bonds and stock trading increased ninefold, while the nation's total output only increased threefold (Harrison and Bluestone, 1988). The end result was that the rich got richer, the poor got poorer, the middle-class got squeezed, and foreign competitors, namely Japan, dulled the competitive edge of American industry.

Between 1978 and 1992, plant closings eliminated four million high-paying blue-collar manufacturing jobs (Steinberg, 1997). In 1982, one in ten Americans were unemployed (Harrison and Bluestone, 1988). "Corporate downsizing" also forced the white-collar sector into unemployment or part-time work. By 1984/1985, every one of the forty-two different categories of U.S. industry had introduced either wage freezes, wage cuts, or other concessions, such as part-time work. Quality jobs and the nation's manufacturing base were vanishing and being replaced with low-paying service sector jobs, or what the *Washington Post* termed "McJobs" (ibid.). Between 1979 and 1984, three in five jobs (58 percent) paid $7,400 a year or less, compared to only one in five jobs between 1963 and 1979 (ibid.).

From 1980 to 1993, the number of persons living in poverty increased from 29 million to 39 million, an increase of 34 percent. Of those living in poverty, one in five were children (Irwin and Austin, 1997). From 1977 to 1988, the average after-tax family income for the bottom 10 percent fell by 10 percent, yet it increased 74 percent for the top 10 percent (ibid.). Wages for middle America stagnated, with the average family income falling to levels found in the 1970s (Phillips, 1991). Worsening economic conditions had even more ravaging effects on the poorest sectors of society. The loss of unskilled manufacturing jobs, the flight of the black middle class from urban America, and the federal government's check on the growth of safety-net programs contributed to a class permanently stuck in ghetto living, or what Wilson (1987) dubbed the "underclass." The underclass, as defined in a *New York Times* article, was "the miserable human residue, mired in hard-core unemployment, violent crime, drug use, teen-age pregnancy, and one of the world's worst human environments, [which] seems to be a partial perverse result of the very success of other blacks" (quoted in Lilly, Cullen, and Ball, 1995).

The age of conservatism was not without its successes, but the downside was noticeably steep. The accumulation of individual wealth came at the expense of the majority of the population, and the more universal gains were largely deceptive. Though Reagan halted the recessionary cycle by fortifying national defense, the recovery was orchestrated under the precarious condition of deficit spending. During Reagan's tenure, the government spent $1.3 trillion more than it collected in taxes or other government receipts (Harrison and Bluestone, 1988). The total cumulative national debt later soared to $7 trillion (Malabre, 1987). In four years, the United States went from being the leading world creditor to being the leading world debtor (ibid.). Interestingly, this pattern of deficit spending was not limited to the government. Deficit spending was a broader cultural phenomenon in a society that valued material excess.

Valuing Decadence

In 1985, Ivan Boesky assured the graduates of Berkeley that "you can be greedy and still feel good about yourself" (quoted in Sewall, 1997:xi). In 1988, a California stock broker declared that "only a sucker would work for less than $200,000 a year" (cited in ibid.). In the movie, *Wallstreet,* Michael Douglas's character proclaimed, "Greed is good," and a pending graduate of Harvard confided to his minister, "I'm not greedy, I just want all I can get, legally, of course" (quoted in Gomes, 1996). These statements summed up the philosophy of life for many Americans in the 1980s, a decade variously termed the "decade of narcissism" and "the society of the spectacle."

As the young idealists of the 1960s aged into mainstream America, the credo of "less is more" was pushed aside by the goal of "getting mine" (Sewall, 1997). The hippies and yippies (Youth International Party) of the 1960s had become the yuppies (*young urban professionals*) of the 1980s. Pursuing a very different version of the good life, yuppies donned Rolex and Cartier watches, Izod casual wear, and Ralph Lauren suits. They revered physical fitness, upward mobility, a busy lifestyle, and BMW automobiles. These values were repeatedly played out on the television screen, via *L.A. Law, Dallas, Dynasty, Miami Vice,* and the *Family Ties* character, Alex Keaton. In real life, these values were played out in Donald Trump's real estate pyramids, Michael Milken's junk bond profiteering, and the cityscape's "glass temples to the gods of commerce banks, insurance companies, and brokerage houses" (Gomes, 1996:177).

Material excess was fashionable, and moderation was for those who could not afford otherwise. In the "he who dies with the most toys wins" culture, those who could not afford it simply charged it. Not unlike the bloated deficits of the federal government, by 1986 the average American family had accumulated personal debts of more than $11,500, not including its mortgage (Harrison and Bluestone, 1988). The total amount borrowed by consumers between 1981 and 1986 increased from $394 billion to $739 billion. Credit card debt alone increased from $55 billion in 1980 to $128 billion in 1986 (ibid.).

By the time George Bush assumed the presidency, the "casino society" (dubbed by Strange and quoted in ibid.) that produced the stock market crash of 1987, the savings and loan scandal, and the incarceration of high-profile entrepreneurs was on the decline. Expressing his own disdain for the flagrancy of the nouveau riche, Bush promised a "kinder, gentler" America. Americans, too, were beginning to raise their eyebrows at the displays of conspicuous consumption. Bruce Babbitt declared that when Rhodes scholars are arrested for insider trading, that contributes to the populist sentiment that a privileged class is getting rich at the expense of the rest of the economy (Phillips, 1991). Nevertheless, Bush largely retained the policies of Reagan, by advocating no new money for education, the elderly, transportation, or children in poverty (ibid.). The Bush presidency tempered cowboy capitalism and the vanity of the privileged, but a "kinder, gentler" posture toward crime and criminals was not forthcoming. In this regard, a rugged individualism ideology still prevailed.

NEO-CONSERVATIVE CRIMINOLOGY

The Reagan/Bush years witnessed a revitalization of criminological theories of centuries past. This is not surprising, considering the Reagan and Bush administrations went to great lengths to dispel the notion that street crime—and other social problems—had socioeconomic causes (Beckett, 1997). Reagan declared that "here in the richest nation in the world, where more crime is committed than in any other nation, we are told that the answer to the problem is to reduce our poverty. This isn't the answer." He went on to say that the American people had "lost patience with liberal leniency and pseudo-intellectual apologies for crime" (quoted in ibid.:48). George Bush similarly declared that "we must raise our voices to correct an insidious tendency—the tendency to blame crime on society, rather than the criminal" (quoted in ibid.).

On these words, classicism, moralism, and biological positivism all gained a new hearing, as each located the roots of crime within the individual. For example, rational choice theory, as articulated by Cornish and Clarke (1986), was largely a restatement of the doctrine of free will. It assumed that criminals were opportunistic actors, capable of calculating the consequences of their behavior. Based on the "expected utility" principle of economic theory, rational choice held that human decisions were determined by the maximization of profit and the minimalization of loss. This theory further posited that the decision to engage in criminal activity also included the selection of specific crimes at specific times and places. However, in contrast to the free will of the enlightenment age, rational choice theory allowed for certain intrusions on the thought process, such as fear, inaccurate information, and a morality that could disrupt the hedonistic calculus (Lilly et al., 1995).

A second theory giving credence to free will ideology was routine activities. However, routine activities theory, as developed by Cohen and Felson (1979), offered a more complex view of crime than rational choice perspectives. Cohen and Felson maintained that crime was an event precipitated by several factors, including freely motivated offenders, suitable targets, and the absence of capable guardians of persons or property. As increases in these three factors converged, victimization rates would accordingly increase. Hence, decreases in victimization rates would occur when there was a consistent drop in the rates of one of these criminogenic factors.

In the conservative climate, morality became a pertinent factor in the crime debate as well. Predictably, crime was viewed as a function of declining morality in society, due largely to a breakdown of the family. While the "social breakdown" thesis (Sassoon, 1995) explained crime in environmental terms, the presence of a "willing self" was again assumed. Criminal behavior was attributed to a deficient personal character that was outwardly reflected in the sum total of one's deeds (Lamb, 1996). Crime was nothing more than immoral behavior brought about by poor child-rearing.

Also making a comeback were theories that focused attention on the biological attributes of the offender. Advances in biotechnology revealed the intricacies of genetics, brain functioning, and the nervous system, enabling a more scientific explanation of human behavior. Examinations of DNA, neurotransmitter activity, hormonal imbalances, cranial damage, and learning patterns in the brain produced biological explanations that were far more sophisticated than their Lombrosian predecessors (see Cloninger and Gottesman, 1987; Cloninger, Sigvardsson, Bohman, and von Knorring, 1982; Mednick, Gabrielli, and Hutchings, 1984; Mednick, Volavka, Gabrielli, and Iti, 1981; Rowe, 1985; Venables, 1987). Though viewed with great skepticism in mainstream criminological circles, biological perspectives were co-opted by those courting a conservative agenda because it too focused attention on the individual.

For example, in *Crime and Human Nature,* Wilson and Herrnstein (1985) defended both moral and biological perspectives. They argued that certain individuals were more disposed toward criminality than others, as evidenced by their repeated involvement in crime. They proposed that criminal dispositions began prior to infancy and were only later nurtured by (negative) family, school, labor market, and/or criminal justice experiences. In their estimation, what ultimately separated the predisposed offender population from the law-abiding, or generally law-abiding, population were the factors of genetics, class, and morality.

With the aid of the academic arguments presented by Wilson and Herrnstein and other neo-conservative scholars, the liberal social determinism's influence on crime control policy ceased to exist. The offender was now envisaged as a rational actor, a morally deprived actor, and/or a biologically predisposed actor. This theoretical base handed conservatives an academically "certified" rationale for law and order punishment.

LAW AND ORDER PUNISHMENT

As the previous chapter demonstrated, the war on crime inspired by the Reagan/Bush administrations was not the first. Lyndon Johnson waged a war on crime in 1965, and a lesser known war was waged by Richard Nixon in 1969. However, the Reagan/Bush administrations' war on crime was arguably the most notorious. What set the Reagan/Bush wars apart from their predecessors was their thoroughly punitive content. The strategy of the "war" was to deter potential offenders with severe penalties and incarcerate to control current offenders. With enough punishment and enough incarceration, crime could be controlled (Clear, 1994). If not, punishment for its own sake would do. This "win-win" strategy drew its logic from a combination of conflicting philosophies that were all made compatible under the flood of antirehabilitation sentiments. The philosophies, or rationales, that were given to punishment included retribution, deterrence, and incapacitation.

Penal Rationales

In a report issued by the Committee for the Study of Incarcerations, the final blow to rehabilitation was delivered. In the report entitled *Doing Justice* (von Hirsch, 1995), retribution was crowned the new philosophical successor. As a rationale for punishing, retribution appealed to liberals and conservatives by resolving the problems wrought by rehabilitation, namely, disparity, discretion, and ineffectiveness. Assuming a meaning beyond mere vengeance, contemporary retributive philosophy called for "just deserts" or proportionality, and like sentencing for like offenders. In the words of von Hirsch, "Proportionalism gave notions of fairness a central role in penal theory" (1995:124).

Proportionalism rested on the idea that penal sanctions should be calibrated according to the reprehensibleness of the crime. It held that offenders should never receive a sanction that exceeded the harmfulness of the act. Retribution, so defined, did not call for an equal exchange of harm, as suggested in the doctrine of *lex talionis*. Rather, it implied an imposition of suffering that was limited but graduated on a scale of crime seriousness. Retribution asserted that a person's claim to just and fair treatment should always supersede the achievement of societal aims. Therefore, punishment was only justified as censure for deeds already committed.

At the same time that retribution was being touted by both liberals and conservatives, the merits of deterrence were being upheld by those with more conservative leanings. A product of enlightenment utilitarianism, the philosophy of deterrence remained relatively unchanged in its contemporary application. Still premised on the notions that man possessed free will and that criminal behavior could be prevented through certain and swift punishment, deterrence supplied much of the rhetoric for the decade's get-tough reforms. In contrast to retribution, however, deterrence called for the escalation of penalties until the desired individual or general prevention effects were achieved.

Resigned to the idea that *effective* punishment was not a certainty, incapacitation also found favor as an overriding justification for punishment. Incapacitation, like retribution, did not require understanding of the causes of crime or the delicate balances involved in the cost/benefit calculations of mankind. Its sole aim was to interrupt the criminal career of the offender. Therefore, its effectiveness was guaranteed. Whereas rehabilitation aimed to prevent crime by way of tailored assistance, and deterrence by manipulating hedonistic impulses, incapacitation assured crime reduction by way of lost opportunity and physical constraint.

The interruption strategy of incapacitation was conceived on two different levels. General incapacitation approached crime control through policies that increased incarceration for all categories of offenders. Selective incapacitation proposed that only certain offender groups—either habitual or the most dangerous—be targeted, given the costly and other counterproductive effects of incarceration. Integral to selective incapacitation, then, were risk assessment instruments that could consistently and accurately determine which offenders would persist in their criminal careers.

Though at odds conceptually, these philosophies of retribution, deterrence, and incapacitation coexisted if for no other reason than they were not "rehabilitation." This is not to say that the resulting penal reforms and practices were always true to their philosophical namesake. However, their varying degrees of influence were clearly visible in the major penal reforms and practices of the day. The most notable reforms and practices were the war on drugs, abolition of parole, mandatory minimums, determinate sentencing, habitual offender statutes, intermediate punishment, and the expanded use of capital punishment.

The War on Drugs

The war on drugs was not a penal strategy, per se, but it affected the correctional system profoundly. In an attempt to reduce the crime and lawlessness thought to be associated with drug use, the war on drugs was waged in nearly every corner of society. Search and seizure protections were eroded so as not to "handcuff" police, and drug testing became more ordinary than exceptional. The workplace, amateur and professional athletics, the educational system, and the criminal justice system were all transformed by the grip of a "drug-induced" panic, despite the fact that overall drug use was on the decline.

Drug use, as measured by the percentage of Americans reporting using illicit drugs in the past thirty days, had dropped from 14 percent in 1979 to 6.2 percent in 1991. Marijuana usage, in particular, had dropped from 13 percent in 1979 to 5 percent in 1991. During this time, cocaine usage also dropped from 2.4 to 0.9 percent (Bennett, 1994). The percentage of high school students using cocaine was up from 1975, but stayed relatively constant between 1981 and 1984, dropping substantially after 1987 (ibid.). Crack cocaine use, however, had increased among the urban underclass. Consequently, claims of a crack epidemic were not entirely unfounded (Walker, 1985). Between 1985 and 1989, cocaine-related emergency room incidents increased from 10,248 to 42,145 and cocaine-related deaths increased from 717 to 2,496 (ibid.). What was regarded as a crack cocaine epidemic then provided much of the rationale for the war on drugs.

Efforts to control the supply and demand of drugs proceeded without hesitation. Federal antidrug expenditures increased from $873 million in 1979 to $12.7 billion in 1995 (U.S. Office of National Drug Control Policy, 1995). Under the Bush administration, the commitment to the war on drugs was formalized through the passing of the Anti-Drug Abuse Act of 1988 and the appointment of a "drug czar" in 1989. The drug czar presided over the newly formed U.S. Office of National Drug Control Policy, which was charged with the execution of the following objectives: Street-level drug enforcement was to be intensified, and federal, state, and local enforcement efforts were to be integrated. Cooperative arrangements with foreign countries were also to be forged to halt the flow of drugs into the country. An attack on soft drugs was to be renewed, coupled with expansion of antidrug education programs. Finally, tougher drug penalties were to be implemented (Walker, 1985).

Guidelines, Get-Tough Legislation, and Prison Overcrowding

Legislative Intents
The sentencing reforms of this period were motivated not only by the call to moral rearmament, as typified in the war on drugs, but by perceptions of leniency, ineffectiveness, and sentence disparity. Gradually, states began to dismantle key pieces of rehabilitation by eliminating or restricting parole use and indeterminate sentencing. Sentencing guidelines and determinate sentences were subsequently introduced, with the intent of bringing fairness and uniformity to sentencing. Under this sentencing structure, like offenders were to receive like sanctions, and prison release dates were to be determined at the outset of the sentence. To put it in extreme terms, release and sentence reductions were to be established by mathematical calculation, rather than by human interpretations of rehabilitative progress.

Between 1976 and 1979, seven states abolished all or most of their paroling authority's discretion (Ringel, Cowles, and Castellano, 1993). By 1979, eighteen states had restricted their use of parole, and six additional states had abolished it altogether. Between 1979 and 1982, sixteen more states restricted parole use and three more states abolished parole (Clear, 1994). By 1990, six more states, including Illinois, California, and Minnesota, had joined this national trend.

Other states, such as New Jersey and Pennsylvania, abolished indeterminate sentencing but retained parole. Most states retained some form of post-prison supervision, though it was often carried out under a different name (e.g., control release) or as a split sentence (i.e., incarceration followed by a term of probation). For example, in 1977, 72 percent of all state and federal prisoners were released under the parole system. That figured had dropped to 48 percent by 1983, to 40 percent by 1988, and to 39 percent by 1993. Still, during this period of declining parole use, the proportion of releases to some form of postsupervision was 82 percent (Holt, 1998).

While the primary objectives of sentencing guidelines and determinate sentencing were proportionality and fairness via standardized sentencing, their objectives were often blurred with the get-tough movement in general. While these two sentencing reforms did not necessarily lead to more punitive sanctioning, habitual offender statutes and mandatory minimums had punitiveness as their express intent.

Habitual offender statutes were to punish repeat offenders of any kind more harshly. These statutes were not a form of structured sentencing, but they permitted sentence enhancements for offenders classified as habitual. In contrast, mandatory minimum statutes required tougher sanctions for selected offenses. Mandatory minimums overwhelmingly targeted drug and firearm offenses, but often extended to burglary, rape, murder, or some combination of these offenses. By 1983, forty-three states had mandatory prison terms for one or more violent crimes, and twenty-nine states and the District of Columbia had such terms for narcotics offenses (Gordon, 1990). The Rockefeller drug laws adopted by New York in 1973 were the first in the nation. They called for a fifteen-year mandatory prison term for anyone convicted of selling more than two ounces of a controlled substance or possessing more than four ounces of a controlled substance (Hansen, 1999). Delaware also enacted its mandatory minimums in 1973, but added new provisions in 1981. Ultimately, more than 222 mandatory sentencing provisions were enacted in Delaware, though only eighteen were responsible for 94 percent of the prison admissions (O'Connell, 1995). By 1990, Florida had ten separate mandatory laws. Three of these related to drugs, two related to habitual offenders, and three related to the use of firearms. Six of the Florida laws were passed in 1988/1989 alone (Walker, 1985). For example, selling drugs within one thousand feet of a school drew a mandatory minimum sentence of three years. The operation of a drug enterprise drew a mandatory sentence of life or no less than twenty-five years. Use or possession of an automatic firearm or machine gun resulted in an eight-year sentence (Bales and Dees, 1992).

In 1984, Congress enacted mandatory minimums for federal drug offenses and offenses involving the use of a firearm (Schulhofer, 1993). The formal objectives of the federal code paralleled those of their state counterparts. They were to assure "just" (i.e., appropriately severe) punishment, effective deterrence and incapacitation, elimination of sentence disparity, incentive for offenders to turn in others, and courtroom efficiency resulting from pressure to plead guilty (ibid.). This first round of federal legislation took effect in 1987, but through 1990, new mandatories were added and existing ones were enhanced (ibid.). The result of this congressional activity was one hundred separate mandatory minimum sentence provisions, located in sixty different statutes. The majority of the provisions were never used, as 94 percent of the cases processed were attributed to controlled substances and firearm possession (ibid.).

Penal Impact

The impact of these policies was not as decisive as the rhetoric and legislation that enabled them would suggest. As for achieving broad deterrent effects, the evidence was equivocal at best. For example, in Delaware, despite a 45 percent increase in the number of felony drug offenders incarcerated, reductions in drug activity were not realized (O'Connell, 1995). As for curbing unwarranted disparity in sentencing, the reforms merely shifted the discretion of judges and paroling authorities to prosecutors. In several states, prosecutors decided whether to invoke the mandatory law, and, in all states, prosecutors decided whether to invoke the sentence enhancements permitted by habitual offender statutes.

The incarceration of unprecedented numbers of offenders, drug offenders in particular, was one of the most consistent and compelling consequences of this reform activity. In 1979, only 6 percent of the entire U.S. prison population was comprised of drug offenders (Blumstein, 1995). Throughout the 1980s, drug arrests increased by 88 percent, with the result that a quarter of all inmates were serving time or awaiting trial for a drug offense (von Hirsch, 1995). By 1994, 25 percent of the state inmate population was serving time for either drug possession or the sale or manufacturing of drugs. In the federal system, 60 percent of the inmate population was serving time on drug charges (Blumstein, 1995; von Hirsch, 1995). According to the Federal Bureau of Prisons, between 1980 and 1994, the number of drug offenders incarcerated in federal prisons rose from 4,749 to 46,499.

The likelihood of incarceration and actual time served increased for other offenses as well. Between 1981 and 1987, the probability that a conviction would lead to a prison sentence increased by 41 percent for burglary and by 166 percent for rape. Actual time served also increased by 54 percent for burglary and by 129 percent for rape (Clear, 1994). In 1985, the average sentence for a first-time admission to prison nearly doubled to sixty-seven months (Clear and Cole, 1993:197). Prior to federal penal code reform, 52 percent of federal convictions resulted in prison, compared to 74 percent following reform (Walker, 1985). Average time served in federal prisons also increased from twenty-four months in 1984 to forty-six months in 1990 (von Hirsch, 1995). In the four years immediately following the implementation of the new federal laws, the proportion of sentences to prison increased from 52 to 60 percent, sentences to probation decreased from 63 to 44 percent, time served for violent crimes increased by an estimated 37 percent, and time served for drug crimes increased by 123 percent (McDonald and Carlson, 1992). Nationally, according to the Criminal Justice Institute, as of 1992,

13,937 inmates were serving "natural life" sentences. Another 52,054 were serving sentences of life without the possibility of parole. An added 125,995 were serving sentences of twenty years or more, and 200,000 were serving "extremely long sentences" (Irwin and Austin, 1997).

As more offenders were admitted to prison and for longer periods of time, the aims of incapacitation were realized. In fact, the numbers of individuals under correctional supervision of any kind increased by 188 percent between 1975 and 1990. During this period, the number of probationers, specifically, increased by 203 percent. In 1980, 1.1 million offenders were on probation and 220,000 were on parole. By 1990, according to the Edna McConnell Clark Foundation, 2.5 million offenders were on probation and 457,000 were on parole or postsupervision by some other name (quoted in Rothman, 1995a). Between 1980 and 1992, the number of individuals incarcerated in jails and state and federal prisons increased from 330,000 to 883,000, constituting an increase of 168 percent. Jail populations alone increased by 46 percent between 1978 and 1984. In 1987, 8.6 million people were admitted to jail (Clear, 1994). In the federal system exclusively, the prison population jumped from 24,000 in 1980 to 95,000 in 1994 (U.S. Bureau of Justice Statistics, 1995b). Stated differently, between 1980 and 1987, the U.S. incarceration rate increased from 139 to 228 incarcerated individuals per 100,000 citizens. In 1985, 1 in 63 American citizens was subjected to some form of correctional supervision (e.g., prison, probation, parole) (Clear, 1994).

Table 12-1 illustrates that skyrocketing incarceration rates were a uniquely American phenomenon. By 1993, the U.S. incarceration rate equaled 519 men and women per 100,000 citizens. Russia's incarceration rate was 558 per 100,000, while apartheid-divided South Africa maintained an incarcer-

Table 12-1. International Incarceration Rates, 1993

Country	Incarceration Rate per 100,000
Russia	558
United States	519
South Africa	368
Poland	196
Canada	116
Mexico	97
England/Wales	93
France	84
Germany	80
Japan	36

Source: Mauer (1996).

ation rate of 368 per 100,000. The entire industrialized world had significantly lower incarceration rates than the United States.

The rate of increase in the U.S. prison population was not the only remarkable feature of the "imprisonment binge" (Irwin and Austin, 1997). The change in the composition of the prison population was equally dramatic. In 1982, 1 in 49 black males between the ages of 20 and 29 was incarcerated in a state prison, a ratio that was 8 times higher than that for whites. In 1989, nearly one-quarter of black males age 20 to 29 years old was under some form of correctional supervision (Mauer, 1990). In 1993, blacks made up 44 percent of the state and federal prison population, but only 12 percent of the U.S. population. Moreover, 18 percent of the prison population was Hispanic, though Hispanics made up only 10 percent of the U.S. population. Whites, on the other hand, constituted 74 percent of the U.S. population, but only 36 percent of the state and federal prison population (U.S. Bureau of Justice Statistics, 1995b).

The racial disparity in the prison population was inevitably a function of the focus of the war on drugs. Though survey data show that 13 percent of all monthly drug users were black, 35 percent of those arrested for drug possession, 55 percent of those convicted of drug possession, and 74 percent of those sentenced to prison for drug possession were black. When the Hispanic population is added, the percent of minorities sentenced to prison for drug possession increases to over 90 (Beckett, 1997). This pattern of disparity is explained in large part by the fact that one gram of crack is the equivalent of one hundred grams of powdered cocaine in the eyes of sentencing guidelines. Because the drug war focused on crack cocaine, which was mainly sold and used in inner-city communities, the overwhelming majority of offenders sentenced to prison for drug possession were poor blacks and Hispanics (Irwin and Austin, 1997).

With little forethought given to the consequences of getting tough and in the absence of a dedicated funding source, the U.S. penal system literally collapsed. Burgeoning prison populations reached unconstitutional levels, subjecting numerous states to lawsuits. By 1993, forty states and the District of Columbia were under court order to alleviate overcrowded conditions and/or improve other substandard living conditions. On average, state correctional systems were operating at 31 percent over capacity, while the Federal Bureau of Prisons was operating at 46 percent over capacity. By 1994, eleven states exceeded capacity by 150 percent, with only nine states operating below capacity. One-third (135) of the nation's jails were also under court order (Irwin and Austin, 1997; Rothman, 1995a).

To accommodate the demands of escalating prison populations and constitutional requirements, federal, state and local governments embarked on costly prison-building campaigns. For example, California taxpayers would have to pay $4.1 billion to fund prison construction over an eight-year period (Morain, 1994). In the state of New York, 33,458 prison beds were constructed, with construction costs over the next thirty years estimated at nearly $6 billion (Correctional Association of New York, 1995). Between 1990 and 1994, the nation's prison capacity increased by nearly 200,000 beds. In 1994, federal legislation earmarked $7.9 billion to aid state prison construction (Edna McConnell Clark Foundation, 1995).

Adding operational expenses to the bill, the costs associated with managing offender populations grew beyond the reach of many state budgets. According to the 1992 *Corrections Compendium,* Connecticut, Florida, Maine, Illinois, and Michigan were unable to operate newly constructed facilities because of insufficient funds (CEGA Services, Inc., 1992). Fiscal shortfalls forced five other states to delay institution openings, while other states could only use half the space available in the new facilities. This was not altogether surprising when one considers the expense associated with staffing correctional facilities. According to the U.S. Bureau of Justice Statistics (1995a), the number of corrections personnel (including probation and parole) increased by 70 percent between 1984 and 1990, amounting to a total monthly payroll of almost $1.3 billion (ibid.). Altogether, correctional costs nationwide, including prison construction and maintenance, and probation and parole, increased from $6 billion in 1979 to $24.9 billion in 1990. Prior to 1979, correctional costs had increased at a much more gradual pace, growing from $2.3 billion in 1971, to $3.8 billion in 1975, and then to $6 billion in 1979 (Edna McConnell Clark Foundation, 1995).

While correctional systems across the country responded to their respective crises with considerable expenditures, there were obvious limits to the spending. Because Americans had developed an almost equally despised enemy in government taxation, the enormous costs incurred by the get-tough strategies were partially defrayed by reduced spending on education, welfare, and various other social programs. However, the relief provided by such budgetary maneuvering was both minimal and temporary. Ultimately, the simultaneous public demand for protection from crime and from higher taxes prompted the development of an alternative reform strategy known as intermediate punishment.

Intermediate Punishment
Intermediate punishments provided a major line of defense in the overcrowding dilemma. In fact, it was argued that in the absence of fiscal crisis and prison overcrowding, there would have been little incentive to develop intermediate punishments (Lurigio and Petersilia, 1992). Home confinement, electronic monitoring, boot camps, intensive supervision probation, and day-reporting centers were among the many intermediate punishment programs implemented to reduce reliance on incarceration, save money, be punitive, and control crime in the community. Though not a catalyst for intermediate punishment's development, proportionality in sentencing was an

added but lesser reform objective. Intermediate punishments filled the void in sentencing options that was created by the dual system of nominal probation and prison, by providing graduated sanctions that fell between prison and nominal probation.

Given the potential of intermediate punishments to fulfill a wide range of objectives, their adoption proceeded with little opposition. With intensified manual and technological monitoring, home detention with multiple conditions (e.g., community service, treatment, restitution), and drug tests, intermediate punishments were to provide a veritable continuum of custody. The "punishment package" approach sought to incapacitate offenders within the community by controlling their movement in time and space. It was also hoped that intermediate punishments would deter offenders by being more punitive than nominal probation and thus more effective at reducing recidivism. It was assumed that *rational* offenders would refrain from criminal behavior, knowing that increased surveillance would lead to rapid detection of wrongdoing and rapid response by the criminal justice system.

By 1989, forty states and Washington, D.C., operated intensive supervision programs, and twenty-six states and Washington, D.C., operated separate house arrest programs. Of these twenty-six states, twenty-three and the District of Columbia coupled house arrest with electronic monitoring. Shock incarceration (i.e., boot camp) and/or split sentencing were being practiced in sixteen states, while other intermediate punishment–based programs were used in ten additional states (Byrne and Pattavina, 1992). Currently, intermediate punishments have become a regular feature of punishment systems in nearly every state, by whatever name chosen by the particular jurisdiction (e.g., community control, house arrest, home confinement, intensive supervision probation).

Consistent with the other get-tough reforms of the day, intermediate punishments fell short of their anticipated potential. Rather than reducing prison overcrowding and corresponding costs, intermediate punishment programs often contributed to the very problems they sought to alleviate. Few states or jurisdictions could claim true diversionary effects following the implementation of intermediate punishment programs (Blomberg, Bales, and Reed, 1993; Lucken, 1997). In Florida, the probability of a prison sanction actually increased following the implementation of the state's community control program (Blomberg et al., 1993), though Baird and Wagner (1990) contend prison overcrowding in Florida would have been worse in its absence. Georgia's intensive supervision program claimed a 10 percent diversion rate in the program's infancy (Petersilia, 1987), but was unable to sustain even this small diversionary record in the long term.

Not only were intermediate punishment programs generally implemented as supplements to incarceration, but any initial diversionary effects were likely negated later by the prevalence of technical violations (Petersilia and Turner, 1993). Thus, whether implemented as alternatives or supplements, intermediate punishments compounded the problem of institutional over-crowding. Jail and prison populations alike were aggravated by the recycling of technical program violators who could not withstand the rigors of "piled up sanctions" (Lucken, 1997). The combined requirements of substance abuse treatment, cost of supervision, restitution, community service, anger management, drug tests, daily logs, and/or curfews often proved to be too onerous and costly for "socially disorganized" offenders (Blomberg and Lucken, 1994b). In jurisdictions across the country, intensive supervision probation programs were producing nearly twice the number of technical violations as routine supervision, though rates of reoffending for both programs were essentially equal (Petersilia and Turner, 1993). Georgia, in fact, was forced to prohibit returns to prison that were due to technical violations. Almost from the outset, then, intermediate punishment's success was jeopardized by its contradictory objectives. It was not possible to strictly enforce the conditions that made intermediate punishment more punitive than probation without also undermining the goals of reducing prison overcrowding and correctional costs.

Death Penalty

The 1980s also witnessed a surge in the use of capital punishment as a sanction. Within four years of the *Gregg v. Georgia* (1976) decision, thirty-five states opted to modify, rather than abolish, capital punishment. Several states, including Colorado, Illinois, Maryland, and Montana, made further revisions that increased the number of aggravating circumstances that could be considered in capital cases. At the federal level, new capital offenses were designated. For example, the Omnibus Anti-Drug Abuse Act of 1988 extended the sanction of death to homicides occurring in the course of drug activity.

Even with the persisting problem of racial bias in the sanction's application, federal and state governments were unwavering in their support of the death penalty. In recognition of this bias, the Anti-Drug Abuse Act required that the role of race in capital punishment be examined. Responding to this legislative mandate, the Federal General Accounting Office (GAO) reported that 82 percent of capital punishment studies showed that race was a relevant biasing factor, especially when the victim was white and the defendant was black (Vito, 1995). The GAO analysis further concluded that race was a biasing factor at all stages of the criminal justice system, and that offense variables could not fully account for the racial disparity in the use of the sentence of death (ibid.).

Despite a showing of racial bias, the now conservative Supreme Court ruled that a remedy would best be provided by a legislative body. In 1991, the House of Representatives drafted the Fairness in Death Sentencing Act. This draft act required that defendants provide evidence of racial bias, and,

Figure 12-1. U.S. Execution Rates, 1977–1993.

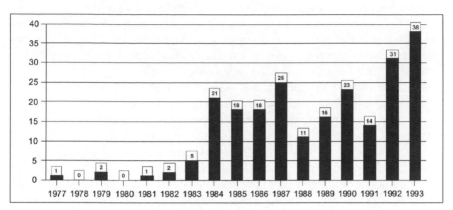

Source: Vito, 1995.

if bias was demonstrated, the sentence would be reduced to life in prison (ibid.). With little to no public fanfare, the act was summarily defeated (ibid.).

Enabling legislation and a willing public combined to send more and more offenders to death row. In 1987, 299 prisoners were admitted to death row, bringing the total number under sentence of death to more than 2,000 by 1988. By 1993, that figure increased to 2,802 (Gordon, 1990; Vito, 1995). Though the execution rate did not initially keep pace with death row admissions, the pace of executions did noticeably hasten, as shown in Figure 12-1. An equally noteworthy pattern was the variability in the use of capital punishment by region. Of the ninety-three executions carried out between 1977 and 1987, eighty-seven occurred in the South. Seventy-five percent of them took place in Texas (26), Florida (17), Louisiana (15), and Georgia (12) (Gordon, 1990). The remaining six executions were in Utah, Nevada, and Indiana. As with the many other get-tough measures, the realization of deterrent effects was inconsistent, if not negligible. Evidence of deterrent effects were found in select older studies (e.g., Sellin). However, more recent research indicated that there were no effects or, worse, there were "brutalizing" effects. In the latter case, it has been argued that capital punishment actually increases violent crime, namely, murder.

SUMMARY AND DISCUSSION

Few dispute the fact that the 1980s were a triumph for upper America. Kevin Phillips, a Republican official in the Reagan administration, even concluded that the policies that shaped the distribution of wealth created a "nation of billionaires and homeless" (Phillips, 1991). Philosopher and criminologist, Jeffrey Reiman (1990), took this assessment a step further by declaring that the "rich got richer and the poor got prison." Ironically, by 1992, there were more than 500,000 correctional employees nationwide, which amounted to more than any Fortune 500 company other than General Motors (Beckett, 1997). The American Correctional Association membership doubled between 1982 and 1988, and even more startling was the increase in the number of criminal justice system employees. In 1965, there were 600,000 employees. By 1993, there were more than 2 million (ibid.).

Without question, the war on crime involved a mass mobilization of resources that were narrowly focused on low-level drug offenders and street criminals. Getting tough on "them" was the bread and butter of local, state, and federal political campaigns. Entertainment and news programing fed the frenzy into the 1990s, by drenching the public with criminal profiles and crime reports. For example, media coverage of crime tripled from 632 crime stories reported in 1991 to 1,949 in 1994. Surprisingly, 63 percent of respondents in a public opinion poll indicated that the media accurately depicted the crime problem in this country.

Though crime levels in the 1980s and early 1990s were much higher than crime levels in 1964, crime rates were not increasing categorically. Between 1973 and 1991, robbery and household burglary rates declined by 17 and 42 percent, respectively. Household larceny dropped as well. The murder sprees and drive-by shootings that fueled the national hysteria indeed increased murder rates, but these incidents were highly isolated and confined to a few areas in a just a few cities. The urban wastelands of Washington, D.C., New York City, and Los Angeles (Walker, 1985) bore the brunt of these violent escapades, not the nation as a whole. Between 1980 and 1993, murder, robbery, and burglary rates across the nation were stable and, in some instances, were declining (Blumstein, 1995). Nevertheless, the nation blindly accepted the claim that unprecedented levels of serious crime justified the unprecedented levels of punishment

The offenders who entered the penal system during this get-tough period were frequently new offenders caught in the drug enforcement crackdown. For example, in Florida, 45 percent of the state's prison admissions had no prior prison commitments. Another 23 percent had only one prior commitment (Florida Department of Corrections, 1994). Nationally, a number of repeat offenders were remanded to prison under the tough new laws, but a sizable proportion of these admissions to state and federal prison came from parole violations. In 1983, 20 percent of prison admissions were returning parolees. In 1987, the percentage of parole violators admitted to prison increased to 26 percent and in 1993 to 30 percent, yet these parole returns

Table 12-2.   Adult Correctional Population, Adult Population, Crime Rates,
               1980–1994

	1980	1994	Change (%)
Adult Correctional Population	**1,832,350**	**5,196,505**	**184**
Probation	1,118,097	2,962,166	165
Jails	163,994	490,442	199
Prison	329,821	1,053,738	219
Parole	220,438	690,159	213
Adult U.S. Population	**162,800,000**	**192,600,000**	**18**
Crime Rates			
Adult arrests	6,100,000	8,900,000	46
Reported index crimes	13,400,000	14,000,000	4

Source: Irwin and Austin (1997).

were generated primarily by technical violations rather than new offenses
(Holt, 1998).

If crime rates did not drive punishment rates, then what did (see Table 12-
2)? Scholars have rightfully wrestled with this question, as this penchant for
punishment had no historical or geographic equivalent. To explain this punitive trend, Scheingold (1984) and Beckett (1997) look to the dynamic between the media and the political juggernaut. Politicians exploit easy
noncontentious issues like crime to gain broad public support, while the media report the "problem" in earnest. The public is manipulated into believing
that crime is an urgent problem and thus rank it as a top national priority.
This essentially manufactured preoccupation with crime is subsequently
used as cause for advancing a punitive agenda. However, it is argued that if
left to its own devices, the public's preoccupation with crime, and the fear
that drives it, would subside.

Others have offered a quite different explanation for escalating punishment levels. When progressivism's promise of a science and government
cure to crime failed to materialize, society was stripped of all hope and expectations. As a result, frustration, rather than reason, determined crime control policy. Tucked away in current formulations of deterrence, retribution,
and incapacitation is evidence of the resignation and confusion that presumably typifies modern society. For example, reliance upon increasingly severe punishment suggests an abiding public faith in the logic of deterrence,
in spite of the public's awareness of its uncertain effectiveness. Retributive
strategies, on the other hand, avoid the "what works" predicament because
their goal is to merely express condemnation through sentences that are proportionate to the harm committed. Incapacitation strategies also avoid the effectiveness question by redefining success altogether. Success is no longer

judged by observable changes in offender sensibilities or thought patterns, but by substantial interruptions in the offender's criminal career.

While scholars continue to grapple with the Why? and What's next? in punishment, the impact of law-and-order policies continues unabated. The consequences of getting tough are more than what this chapter has described. In particular, there has been a growth in *special* inmate populations, whose unique needs and risks put additional and disproportionate burdens on the penal system. The treatment and management of these special populations are discussed in detail in the subsequent chapter.

13

The Prison as Nursery, Hospital, and Asylum

INTRODUCTION

DEMOGRAPHIC AND SOCIETAL SHIFTS have converged with law and order policies to change the composition of the prison population in significant ways. The needs and risks of young active male offenders have always dictated the demands on the penal system and still do. However, the needs and risks of females, the elderly, the diseased, and the mentally ill are adding to those demands, making imprisonment a more complicated and difficult practice. The increasing prevalence of these special populations is altering the norms of correctional management and transforming the look and function of the prison. Like the detailed discussion in Chapter 9 of the prison subculture and inmate perspectives on the nature and consequences of imprisonment, this chapter provides detailed discussion of special inmate populations. In part, the rationale for this detailed discussion is that these special inmate populations have unique characteristics and burdens that make the psychological and physical experience of prison all the more difficult and harsh. Moreover, given the ever-increasing practice of incarcerating more and more of the population, it is likely that newer and other special prison populations will emerge in the near future with little appreciation of their numerous policy implications.

Admittedly, these special populations are not truly new, as women, the infirm, and the insane have always been a part of the prison's history. But the increasing incarceration and release of these special populations pose different controversial challenges for correctional officials and society at large. This chapter considers how the increasing incarceration of these various special populations has not only changed the character of the prison but may signal other changes in penology and the larger society.

MOTHERS BEHIND BARS

"In the drama of criminal justice, most leading players have been men" (Friedman, 1993:211). Women offenders have always been in short supply, and it is their relative absence that has dictated, historically and currently, their treatment in the penal system. Strangely, the relative absence of women has worked to their gross disadvantage (Belknap, 1996). Up until the twentieth century, women were incarcerated in facilities for males or in adjoining units, where they were raped and prostituted at the hands of their keepers and other male inmates. Not surprisingly, prison pregnancies were a recurrent scandal (Friedman, 1993; Zedner, 1995). By sharing the facilities for and the resources provided to male inmates, female inmates' access to physicians and chaplains was typically restricted. The ill effects of confinement were also more exaggerated for female inmates, as indoor domestic chores left little reason or opportunity to participate in outside activities. To instill proper social behavior, the language, conversation, purity, and femininity of female inmates were also monitored with greater scrutiny. Consequently, female inmates were punished for rule infractions involving behaviors that were overlooked in male inmates.

In light of this history, and the stagnation of current conditions, Carlen and Tchaikovsky (1985) have concluded that the regime of women's prisons, then, and now, is one that seeks to "discipline, infantilize, feminize, medicalize, and domesticize." The adjoining efforts of the prisoner and civil rights movements sparked modest reform, but women remain an afterthought in corrections. Only the recent rising incarceration rates of women have kept the interest in female inmates alive. Between 1981 and 1991, the increase in the incarceration rates for women surpassed that of men, with female incarceration increasing 254 percent, compared to 147 percent for men (ibid.). In 1980, there were 12,331 women incarcerated in federal, state, and local facilities; in 1989, there were 40,566; and, by 1991, there were 87,000 (Bloom and Steinhart, 1993). Between 1985 and 1998, the dramatic increases in adult women under correctional supervision continued. To illustrate, in 1985, 1 in 227 women were under correctional supervision (including jail, prison, probation, or parole), 1 in 267 were on probation, 1 in 4,762 were on parole, 1 in 4,762 were in jail, and 1 in 4,167 were in prison. By 1998, those figures were as follows: 1 in 109 women were under any correctional supervision, 1 in 144 were on probation, 1 in 1,262 were on parole, 1 in 1,628 were in jail, and 1 in 1,230 were in prison (Greenfeld and Snell, 1999).

The growth in the incarceration and community supervision rates of women offenders is not the result of an emerging violent breed of female criminal. Nearly all of the women imprisoned during this surge have been nondangerous, petty property offenders, or drug offenders. Moreover, incarcerations for murder have generally involved the killing of an abusive spouse or significant other. Far from being criminal predators, female inmates tend to be impoverished, drug addicts, victims of sexual or domestic violence, and mothers (Belknap, 1996; Bloom and Steinhart, 1993; Immarigeon and Chesney-Lind, 1992). It is this latter quality of motherhood that firmly sets the confinement experience of women apart from men.

Approximately 80 percent of the women entering prison are mothers. On average, each incarcerated woman has two or three dependent children (American Correctional Association, 1993), and many of these women were with their children prior to incarceration. Only 60 percent of incarcerated men are fathers, and less than half of them had custody of their children at the time of their incarceration (Belknap, 1996). In 1986, it was estimated that more than 37,000 children had mothers who were incarcerated. In 1989, more than 52,000 children had mothers who were incarcerated (Bloom and Steinhart, 1993). The National Council on Crime and Delinquency estimated that, on any given day in 1991, approximately 167,000 children had mothers who were incarcerated in prisons or jails. Approximately 90 percent, or more than 125,000, of these children were under eighteen years old. By 1997, that figure increased to 194,000 (Greenfeld and Snell, 1999).

A profile of mothers in prison is provided in Table 13-1. This table shows these women indeed pose a low-security risk and bear a number of psychological, economic, and physical burdens. Nevertheless, as Zedner (1995) ar-

Table 13-1. Profile of Inmate Mothers (%)

Ethnicity		Employment/Welfare Assistance	
African American	39	Not Employed	65
White	34	Employed	35
Hispanic	16	Not on AFDC	58
Native American	8	On AFDC	42
Other	3		
		Annual Income	
Marital Status		Under $10,000	64
Never Married	33	$10,000–$25,000	28
Married	19	Over $25,000	9
Divorced	18		
Separated	13	**History of Abuse**	
Common-Law	11	Physical	53
Widowed	6	Sexual	42
Education		**Offense of Conviction**	
8th or Less	11	Drugs	39
Grades 9–11	44	Felony Property	23
H.S. Graduate	34	Serious/Violent	15
College Education	11	Serious/Violent	15
		Other	21

Source: Bloom and Steinhart (1993).

gues, penal accommodations are continually guided by the principles of least effort and least expense. The neglect of care that has prevailed in women's prisons, in general, is highlighted by the neglect of care that prevails in the distinct areas of motherhood and pregnancy.

The problems introduced by the fact of motherhood are many. They begin with questions regarding the care and custody of existing children. Who will assume custody upon incarceration? What kinds of visitation arrangements are available? The questions become more complicated when dealing with the care of pregnant inmates and the care and custody of their newborn infants. Will the woman be coerced into having an abortion, or will restricted access prevent her from having an abortion? What services or care are available during the pregnancy? What services or care are available for pregnant women who are addicted to drugs or infected with HIV? Should newborns be permitted to stay with their incarcerated mother?

The issue of maintaining family ties looms large, since children do experience psychosocial problems as a result of separation (Gabel, 1992). However, studies have shown that the frequency of mother-child visits is exceedingly low. Snell and Morton (1994) and others (Bloom and Steinhart, 1993) found that approximately 52 percent of incarcerated women had never been visited by their children. Snell and Morton (1994) also found that only one in five received mail and one in four had never spoken with their children. Other studies have indicated that only 10 percent of mothers see their children on a weekly basis, 17 percent see them only once a month, and 12 percent see them only once every four to six months (Bloom and Steinhart, 1993).

A number of factors account for the lack of communication between mother and child. In some instances—approximately 25 percent of cases—the parent had not been regularly taking care of the child prior to incarceration (McCarthy, 1980). However, the conditions surrounding visitation are more likely to blame for the infrequency of family visits. Most families must travel hours to reach the facility, only to wait several more hours before the actual visit can begin. Callous treatment by prison officials and invasive searches for contraband, at a minimum, make the visit unpleasant. Nor is the visitation atmosphere conducive to meaningful interaction. In the majority of facilities (approximately 66 percent), visitation typically occurs in a common open area. In other facilities (approximately 9 percent), visitation occurs through partitions. Despite the long distances traveled by families, only 12 percent of facilities permit overnight stays (Bloom and Steinhart, 1993).

More controversial are the problems that surround the soon-to-be-mother. It has been estimated that one of every four women in prison was either pregnant at intake or gave birth at some time in the previous year (Wooldredge and Masters, 1993). Approximately 6 percent of the women at prison intake and 4 percent of women at jail intake are pregnant (Bloom and Steinhart, 1993). In 1987, there were an estimated 1,265 pregnant women across thirty-eight facilities (Ayers, 1999). A 1992 survey of jailed and imprisoned women revealed that approximately 9 percent of them give birth while incarcerated. By 1997, it was estimated that 6 percent of females admitted to jail were pregnant, compared to 5 percent of female admissions to state prison (Greenfeld and Snell, 1999).

Of all the problems encountered by female inmates, the treatment of pregnant inmates has drawn the most criticism. The absence of twenty-four-hour medical care or gynecological care, special diets, nutrition, and prenatal classes are some of the concerns cited. Table 13-2 reports the overall lack of prenatal programming and care based on a nationwide survey of correctional facilities. The unsterile searches of pregnant (and nonpregnant) inmates, which can lead to damaging infections to mother and fetus, have also come under attack (Holt, 1982). Equally troubling to critics is the indifference shown to the particular needs of the pregnant inmate who is a drug addict. In the absence of proper obstetric care and health care, in general, officials have overlooked the fact that the fetus experiences the same symptoms of withdrawal that the mother does (Ryan and Grassano, 1992). However, it is the use of shackles and restraints during transport to hospitals and child delivery that has most outraged Amnesty International and other offender advocacy groups.

The problems attendant to pregnant inmates are further compounded by the prevalence of HIV and AIDS among female offenders. In a study conducted by the Centers for Disease Control (CDC) and the Johns Hopkins

Table 13-2. Services for Pregnant Inmates

Service	Institutions Providing Service (N = 61)[a]	
	Number	Percentage
Prenatal Care	29	48
Lamaze	10	16
Special Diet	9	15
Abortions/Counseling	5	9
Prenatal/Counseling	13	21
Full-Time Nurse or Midwife	5	9
Counseling for Placement	9	15
Separate Living Quarters	8	13
Postnatal Counseling	7	11

[a]Institutions responding incarcerate 76% of all the females in U.S. prisons.

Source: Wooldredge and Masters (1993).

School of Public Health, it was found that rates of HIV infection in jails and prisons ranged from 2.5 to 14.7 percent for female inmates, compared to 2.1 to 7.6 percent for male inmates (Lawson and Fawkes, 1993). In 90 percent of the facilities surveyed, the infection rate for women—particularly women under the age of twenty-five—was two times higher than the rate for males. The same pattern emerged in a 1994 study, which found that 3.9 percent of women in state prisons were infected with the virus, compared to 2.4 percent of men in state prisons (Chesney-Lind, 1997). Between 1991 and 1994, the number of female inmates with AIDS increased by 69 percent, versus a 22 percent increase for males (ibid.). While it cannot be stated with certainty that AIDS is passed on to all babies, approximately 51 percent of newborns do acquire the disease from their mother (Lawson and Fawkes, 1993).

Added to this, the correctional system must deal with the predicament of unwanted pregnancies. While current law does not prevent abortion, except under certain circumstances, the problem for incarcerated women is in gaining access to the necessary resources so the right can be exercised. Because incarcerated individuals must rely on the state for all their needs, ranging from the trivial to the vital, a critical and legal question that arises is whether the state—which is not required to fund abortions for free, indigent women—is required to fund abortions for incarcerated women. In trying to make this determination, it must be considered that the incarcerated woman has become a ward of the state, and is therefore unable to raise the resources needed to pay for an abortion. Moreover, because the female inmate must rely entirely on the state to make the arrangements, Vitale (1980) has argued that failure to do so may violate the right to have an abortion.

Vitale has also argued that forcing an inmate to have an unwanted child is tantamount to cruel and unusual punishment. He contends that a forced pregnancy violates the Eighth Amendment on two different grounds. First, it imposes an unnecessary and wanton infliction of pain, and second, it constitutes a failure to treat medical needs. Vitale submits that if the prison must treat dental conditions, sinus conditions, ulcers, fevers, and varicose veins, then an unwanted pregnancy surely qualifies as a health condition deserving attention. Moreover, the state's termination of the pregnancy in no way undermines the state's custody or punishment interests.

There is, however, a crucial irony in the debate surrounding inmate abortions. Holt (1982) notes that female inmates who do not want to terminate their pregnancies are often forced to do so through coercive or deceptive means. To induce abortions, prison officials have threatened solitary confinement or given women medication without their knowledge. In either case, the inmates are stripped of important constitutional and individual rights.

Should the pregnancy proceed, another controversial government decision lies ahead. Should the mother be permitted to keep the child for a limited period of time? Prior to the twentieth century, inmates were often allowed to keep their child until the child reached the age of two years. In such circumstances, prison regulations warned that mothers were not to be "rewarded" through preferential treatment in work detail or rules of silence. While there was concern over the impact of the environment on the child, such as a lack of stimulus by the real world (Zedner, 1995), the promise of resocializing deviant women overrode this concern. The conditions in many institutions may have been wholly unsuitable for children; at Sing Sing, most babies died (ibid.), but the presence of children was viewed as an important rehabilitative tool for wayward women.

In nearly all states today, the child is taken away within twenty-four to forty-eight hours. Prison nurseries have become an anomaly rather than a fixture, as facilities have emphasized a punitive rather than a rehabilitative philosophy. Prior to 1981, Florida law allowed a female inmate to retain her child within the institution until the child was eighteen months old. This provision was repealed in *Delancy v. Booth* (1981) on the grounds that the mother had no constitutional or statutory right to raise the child in prison (Schupak, 1986). Since 1929, California law allowed the child to remain with the mother until the child was two years old, but in 1978 California repealed this law as well. As an alternative, California created the Community Prisoner Mother-Infant Care Program (halfway-house), but the program was grossly underfunded (ibid.). In 1992, there were approximately five thousand mothers in prison and only one hundred community-based mother-infant care beds (Bloom and Steinhart, 1993).

At present, only New York and Nebraska allow children to remain with the mother. The children are permitted to stay on the premises until the age of eighteen months to two years. The state retains the right to revoke this privilege if the mother has a history of separation from the child or is facing multiple and lengthy sentences (Holt, 1982). Whether the child is immediately taken from the mother or permitted to temporarily stay, most children are ultimately placed with their maternal grandparents. Others are placed with friends or in foster care. Only 17 percent stay with their fathers (Bloom and Steinhart, 1993).

The problems associated with incarcerating mothers are many, ranging from child custody issues, pregnancy, the transmission of HIV to unborn children, and drug withdrawal effects on the unborn, to specialized (obstetric) health care. State facilities have been slow in responding to these problems, making it apparent that the historical problems of poor programming, poor health care, and rape have maintained a foothold in the modern women's prison. As costs associated with expanding facilities for males have dominated budgets, programs that are vital to women have been cut, even though they were substandard to begin with. A more comprehensive system of medical and social services is available at the federal level. Birth control and abortions are available, but the newborn is not permitted to return to the institution except as a visitor. Also, the inmate is responsible for the child's placement (Holt, 1982).

ELDER INMATES

The elder inmate, like the female inmate, still represents a comparatively small proportion of the overall inmate population, but the presence of elder inmates has grown dramatically in the past two decades. They now represent the fastest growing segment of the inmate population (Wheeler, 1999), giving rise to the popular colloquialism "the graying inmate population."

Between 1981 and 1991, the number of inmates over the age of fifty-five increased by 50 percent (Flynn, 1993). In 1992, state prisons held 5,606 inmates over the age of fifty-four and 532 inmates over the age of seventy-five (Edna McConnell Clark Foundation, 1995). This constitutes a 21 percent increase from 1988. In the year 2000, 125,000 of the nation's inmates are over the age of fifty and another 40,000 to 50,000 are over the age of sixty-five (Aday, 1994). It is further estimated that, by 2005, 16 percent of the nation's prison population will be over the age of fifty (Soderstrom, 1999). The increase in the elder population has been particularly pronounced in Florida, which has the third largest inmate population over the age of fifty in the country. For example, in 1982, there were only 895 inmates over the age of fifty. By 1990, that number had reached 2,064, an increase of 131 percent. During that same period, the overall inmate population increased by only 68 percent (Rossell, 1991).

Like the rise in the number of female inmates, the growth in the number of elder inmates does not stem from an outbreak in elder crime overall. Flynn (1993) has argued that while absolute numbers of the elderly in prison are indeed increasing, the percentage of crime committed by the elderly is not. While some scholars conversely argue that age-specific crime has increased somewhat, they acknowledge that this increase is disproportionate to the increases in the incarceration rate (Burnett and Chaneles, 1989).

Nor does the answer to the question of growth lie solely with the nature of the offenses committed. Fifty-three percent of all elder arrests are for drunkenness, DUIs (driving under the influence), larceny/theft, and other offenses directly related to alcoholism (Feinberg, 1984; Wilbanks, 1984). The greatest increases in crime among this population have been in drug and property offenses (Feinberg, 1984; Wilbanks, 1984). For example, in Florida, there were only seventy-three elderly incarcerated for drug offenses in 1983/84. Beginning in 1986/87, drug offenses became the primary offense of incarceration for those over fifty years of age. Consequently, by 1989/90, there were 312 elderly imprisoned for drug offenses (Rossell, 1991).

This does not mean that offenses committed by the elderly are rarely violent or serious, but evidence regarding the nature of their criminal behavior is mixed. For example, in Florida, the second most common offense of the incarcerated elderly was for illicit sexual conduct, followed by theft and forgery (ibid.). McShane and Williams (1990) have found that 60 percent of an elder inmate cohort were violent, yet other studies reveal the opposite to be true. Kratcoski and Pownall (1989) have found that only 13 percent of elder inmates are violent. Soderstrom (1999) has found that offenders over the age of fifty were responsible for only 3.6 percent of violent crime.

While the source of the increase in elder inmates cannot be determined precisely, what is certain is that prison is a microcosm of society. Just as there are many more elderly present in the population as a whole, their presence in prison can be expected to increase as well. Equally evident is the impact of get-tough legislation that sentences more offenders to prison for longer periods of time without the possibility of parole or some other form of early release. In 1991 alone, 11,759 inmates, across thirty-two prison systems, were serving natural life sentences (Flynn, 1993). In forty-four U.S. jurisdictions, 44,541 inmates were serving life sentences, and, across forty-seven systems, 105,881 were serving sentences of twenty years or more.

Growing concern with the elder inmate population is rooted in the prohibitive costs associated with their incarceration. It is estimated that the annual physical and mental health costs for elder inmates is approximately $70,000 compared to $23,000 for the nonelder inmate (Durham, 1994; Rossell, 1991). The Federal Bureau of Prisons estimates that, by 2005, the annual cost of treating common cardiac and hypertensive conditions will reach $94 million, constituting a fourteenfold increase over 1988 costs (Rossell, 1991).

The health care needs that contribute to these costs are wide-ranging. Many of these offenders have a long history of substance abuse, alcoholism, depression, poor health habits, and untreated medical conditions. Consequently, they enter the system in a state of health that is far worse than their nonoffending counterparts. In fact, it has been suggested that a fifty-year-old inmate is the physical and emotional equivalent of a nonoffending sixty-year-old (Kratcoski and Pownall, 1989). Health care issues that arise throughout an elder inmate's stay only compound these costs. For example, approximately 80 percent of those over the age of sixty-five will acquire at least one chronic illness that requires some form of long-term care.

While it is often serious chronic health care needs that draw the most attention, accommodations for the elderly do not always involve the critical care associated with hospitalization or round-the-clock nursing. It is the day-to-day "normal" accommodations for the elderly that require the most adjustments on the part of prison officials. Prosthetic devices, glasses, dentures, hearing aids, ambulatory equipment, special shoes, or wheelchairs are what shape the daily existence of the elder inmate. Structural modifications may also be required, such as changes in lighting, the installation of hearing de-vices in telephones, and the installation of grab bars and guard rails. For those inmates who are disabled or in wheelchairs, cells must be enlarged or beds fixed at different heights.

It is this collection of needs and accommodations that has prompted the question of whether elder inmates should be housed in facilities apart from the general inmate population. At present, the establishment of separate fa-cilities has not been the standard policy. Only twenty-one state systems have special units or dedicated housing for elder inmates. A nationwide survey reveals that most states make their housing determinations at the point of classification (Aday, 1994). In other words, custody classification, medical classification, housing, or release decisions are not based on age alone. Most assignments to specialized housing are for health-related reasons, not pure-ly age considerations. For example, the Federal Bureau of Prisons has de-signed geriatric units only for elderly who are no longer able to function without constant specialized medical care. Within these units, specialized diets are provided along with ongoing monitoring of health problems such as diabetes and cardiovascular dysfunction. Work and leisure programs are also modified in accordance with declining vision and hearing and bone de-terioration. These facilities are designed to accommodate walkers and wheel-chairs as well.

Though the standard practice is to integrate elder inmates with the gener-al population, several arguments for creating separate housing and pro-gramming exist. Elder inmates prefer separate housing because they fear victimization and have difficulty coping with the fast-paced, noisy, and abra-sive prison environment. Distance and confusing institutional design also pose problems for elder inmates trying to find their way to common areas (i.e., infirmary, dining hall, canteen, recreation areas). The difficulty they en-counter navigating the prison environment often forces the elder inmate into isolation (ibid.). They are often not part of the inmate subculture and, thus, rely on staff for their institutional adjustment (Kratcoski and Pownall, 1989). Their isolation is further aggravated by the fact that most elder inmates have been abandoned by family and, thus, have few or no visitors or ties to the community. They generally enter and leave the prison system single, wid-owed, separated, or divorced.

Physical activities, and the daily regimen as a whole, are also typically ill-suited. The elderly generally refrain from recreational activities designed for younger inmates out of frustration or embarrassment. Notably missing as well are programs geared toward rehabilitation, reentry, and vocational training. Given that elder inmates are not likely to return to the workforce, prison of-ficials may discourage them from participating in educational and vocation-al programs so they can be used by the younger offenders (Rossell, 1991). Prison programs simply are not geared to the survival issues that shape the

elder inmate's day, including death, illness, and remaining alert. Special programs for the elderly are few in number, with the exception of compassionate leave programs. Compassionate leave is available in some states and
generally applies to inmates who have six months or less to live. However,
compassionate leave or medical leave releases are rarely used. For example,
in Florida, in 1994/1995, only sixteen inmates were released early for medical reasons. Yet even this overture can be problematic, as nursing homes are
frequently unwilling to accept individuals with a prior record.

Again, the problem in dealing with elder inmates lies in the scarcity of resources. While prison health care facilities are equipped to deal with acute
illness and injuries of all kinds for all ages, they are just now beginning to
deal with the management of the regular, chronic long-term health problems
associated with aging and dying. Correctional systems are now convening to
deal with the hospice needs of dying inmates. Anticipating that more offenders will be dying in prison, whether due to age or disease, officials from
twelve departments of corrections convened last year to address the development of formal prison hospice programs.

THE MENTALLY ILL

In 1939, European scholar L. Penrose declared that "as a general rule, if the
prison services are extensive, the asylum population is relatively small and
the reverse also tends to be true" (quoted in Steadman, Monahan, Duffee,
Hartstone, and Robbins, 1984:474). What Penrose was describing was a
process that would later become termed "transinstitutionalization." While
transinstitutionalization did not occur in the United States as Penrose envisaged it, the impact of the decarceration movement of the 1960s and 1970s
came close. To illustrate, the number of beds in public and private mental
hospitals decreased from 451,000 in 1965 to 177,000 in 1985 (McCorkle,
1995). In roughly the same period, state and federal prison populations increased from 210,000 to 420,000. At the end of 1968, there were approximately 399,000 patients in state mental hospitals alone and 168,000 in
prison. Within a decade, the asylum population dropped by 64 percent to
147,000, while prison populations increased by 65 percent to 277,000
(Steadman et al., 1984). The shift in California provides a more startling example of this purported transinstitutionalization effect. In 1966, there were
27,000 individuals in California's state mental hospitals and 27,000 incarcerated in the state's jails and prisons. Today, there are only 4,500 state hospital beds and 160,000 incarcerated in the state's prisons ("California mental
hospitals," 1999).

Again, these figures seem to corroborate Penrose's observation that mental hospitals and prisons directly share and/or exchange populations based

upon the relative allocation of resources. However, research has shown that these two institutions are not as interdependent as was previously thought (quoted in Hartman et al., 1984). Nevertheless, these figures do reveal a historical truth about the relationship between prisons and asylums, namely, their similarity of function.

In the 1960s and 1970s, decentralization efforts led to the closing of most state hospitals for the mentally ill. While fiscal crises served as the prime motivation for the closings (Scull, 1977), the decarceration of mental hospitals was publicly justified on humanitarian grounds. It was held that the mentally ill could be better served at the local level, under the auspices of nonstigmatizing community centers. These centers were to dispense symptom-relieving psychotropic drugs and monitor the mentally ill on an outpatient basis. However, in large measure, local jurisdictions failed to develop these centers, leaving the criminal justice/penal system to absorb the fallout. The mental hospitals that remained were reserved for the most dangerous of the criminally insane. The penal system, local jails in particular, acquired the less dangerous mentally ill who no longer qualified for civil commitment (Steadman et al., 1984).

The long arm of get-tough policies had extended to yet another disadvantaged group. Campaigns against public disorder crimes, such as panhandling, jumping subway turnstiles, disturbing the peace, trespassing, and vagrancy (i.e., homelessness), were, in effect, campaigns against the mentally ill. This "publicly bothersome" population often spends three to four months in jail without trial, though its crimes are generally related to survival needs (e.g., "dine and dash"). In Idaho, it was estimated that approximately three hundred mentally ill were jailed in 1990 for an average of five days without criminal charge. A 1992 survey revealed that this pattern of incarcerating the mentally ill occurs in roughly 29 percent of the nation's jails. Because the mentally ill rarely post bail or qualify for other forms of release, they often remain in jail at least twice as long as the average inmate (Torrey, 1995). The jail essentially becomes a dumping ground for the mentally ill until other caretaking arrangements can be made.

According to the National Coalition for the Mentally Ill in the Criminal Justice System, there are approximately 33 percent more mentally ill individuals in jails than in mental hospitals. In a study that has provided some of the best evidence to date on the prevalence of the mentally ill in jail, Teplin (1990) has found that among 728 randomly sampled inmates in Chicago's Cook County Jail, almost 6.4 percent manifest some form of psychosis (e.g., schizophrenia, mania, or severe depression). However, less than 1.8 percent of society suffers from such disorders. More significant is the fact that these findings are not unique to Chicago. In the San Diego County Jail, 14 percent of the 4,572 male inmates and 25 percent of the 687 female inmates are on psychotic medication (Torrey, 1995). In Seattle's King County Jail, it is estimated that on any given day, 160 of the 2,000 inmates are severely mentally ill. In the Travis County Jail in Austin, Texas, approximately 14 percent of the inmates are afflicted with a serious mental illness. Dade County Jail in Miami separately houses approximately 350 inmates with mental illness, which is more than any state mental hospital in the country. In the Los Angeles County Jail, 3,300 of its 21,000 inmates require mental health services on a daily basis (ibid.). It was estimated that in 1988, 100,000 people in jail required treatment for serious mental illness.

Though the problem of mentally ill inmates is concentrated primarily in the jail system, it is not exclusive to local facilities or institutional corrections. The community corrections system is equally distressed by the supervision of mentally ill offenders. As of 1998, approximately 547,800 mentally ill offenders were under probation supervision (Ditton, 1999). Further, the war on drugs also contributed to bringing more of the mentally ill into the prison system. For example, on any given day, Florida's prison system houses more than two times as many mentally ill as state mental hospitals (Wickham, 1999). It is estimated that between 10 and 35 percent of inmates held in U.S. prisons have significant mental disorders (McCorkle, 1995). An additional 17 percent have less severe but still serious mental illness (Edna McConnell Clark Foundation, 1995). In California, 8 percent of the state prison population had at least one of four major mental disorders.

The presence of the mentally ill in state and federal facilities illustrates that the crimes of the mentally ill go beyond nuisance crimes. In fact, the mentally ill were more likely to be incarcerated for violent offenses, including robbery, assault, and murder (Ditton, 1999). However, in instances where the crime committed is more serious and requires some degree of planning, it becomes hard to tell the difference between a criminal who happens to have a mental disorder and a person who has a mental disorder that causes them to commit crime (Kagan, 1990). It is also unclear whether the increase in the number of the mentally ill in prison is due more to the war on drugs or to an increase in the mentally ill population in society. For many mentally ill offenders, extended drug use has created neurological damage, or the drug use has served as a way of escaping the realities of mental illness. Absolute numbers of mentally ill in penal facilities are increasing, regardless of the fact that the proportion of inmates who are mentally ill is not. Nevertheless, the penal system must still find ways of adapting to a population that is more schizophrenic, depressed, obsessive-compulsive, paranoid, and personality-disordered.

As with female and elder inmates, the penal system has been slow to respond to the exceptional problems posed by the mentally ill. Increased health care costs are partly responsible for this slow response. For example, in the Orange County Jail in Orlando Florida, treatment costs amount to $1.3 million a year (Wickham, 1999). But there are other problems that make this population special. Suicidal tendencies are greater, as is the potential for security threats because of unruly behavior. The mentally ill are often reluctant to come out of their cells because they view their cells as safer and less stressful. They are also more prone to expressing their outrage through destruction of property (Adams, 1986), or injuring themselves by slamming their bodies to the floor, gouging their skin or genitals with nails, gashing their heads on stainless steel toilets and/or smearing feces on themselves or their cells.

The mentally ill, more than their non–mentally ill counterparts, are likely to have an escape history, assault infractions, and prison punishments. Though the incidence rate for these problems is very low, disciplinary measures may be precipitated by overreaction on the part of guards. They know the inmate has a mental health history and so view him as inherently more dangerous (Adams, 1983). There is, however, some truth to this perception. The mentally ill tend to be more violent toward fellow inmates, staff, and themselves (Baskin, Sommers, and Steadman, 1991), thereby inciting physical and verbal abuse by guards and other inmates (Hartstone, Steadman, Robbins, and Monahan, 1984; Steelman, 1987; Toch, 1977). As one California official noted, the "mad" and the "bad" do not mix well (Torrey, 1995).

The penal system is insufficiently equipped to deal with the problems posed by the mentally ill. In fact, for much of the twentieth century, mental health services were provided by the inmates themselves (Ferrara and Ferrara, 1991). Services provided by institutional staff were limited to crisis intervention, leaving other inmates to act as providers of counsel, restraint, and even medication. It was not until the prisoner rights movement that courts abolished this practice and began dictating the nature and scope of required mental health services. It is this court-driven treatment model that governs most mental health policies in institutions today.

Under the threat of violations of the Eighth Amendment and the Fourteenth Amendment, most institutions provide services that focus on the prevention and relief of pain and suffering. In other words, tranquilizers, barbiturates, and sedative-hypnotic drugs help avert crises by serving as "chemical straightjackets" for controlling, rather than treating, aberrant behavior (Sommers and Baskin, 1990). Fifty percent of mentally ill inmates in state and federal facilities reported having taken prescription medicine, while only 44 percent reported having received counseling (Ditton, 1999). However, only trained and licensed professionals are permitted to provide treatment of any kind (Ferrara and Ferrara, 1991). Federal guidelines have also established policies overseeing patient-to-staff ratios and the use of psychotropic medication. The guidelines are additionally intended to prevent the denial of equal access to work, recreation, and other programs, and the use of segregative confinement as a housing practice for the mentally ill.

Despite the existence of legal prescriptions, many states concentrate their mental health services at high-security facilities. Consequently, the mentally ill are overclassified, when in fact their true risk or dangerousness level does not warrant the upgrade (Adams, 1993). Even more common is confusion, mishap, and negligence in the treatment of the mentally ill. The deaths of mentally ill inmates at a California medical prison in 1991 illustrate this point (Specter, 1994). In one weekend, three inmates died from heatstroke caused by a combination of extreme temperatures in the cell blocks (over 108 degrees) and psychotropic medication that inhibited the body from dissipating heat. The risk of heatstroke from these particular medications was well documented in the literature and well known to prison officials; a few years earlier, another prisoner on the same medication suffered extensive brain damage for the same reason. Other inmates had been left without their medication entirely, prompting a three-million-dollar study of the California prison system's treatment of the mentally ill. Though the conclusions were resounding in their denunciation of the care provided, the California prison system ignored the recommendations of three commissioned studies (ibid.).

In 1999, the Florida Department of Corrections was still grappling with the housing and treatment needs of the mentally ill. The one facility that was designed to house the state's most chronically mentally ill inmates was closed. Upon its closing, the inmates were transferred to a facility that had been cited with eighteen deficiencies in its treatment of the mentally ill. Some of the most severe citations were for nurses dispensing prescription drugs without a licensed pharmacist on duty, failure to ensure that inmates would receive the treatment needed, and large numbers of mental health evaluations that were never conducted on the most severely mentally ill inmates. Nationwide, few states have gone beyond the basic minimum requirements. Consequently, there is little programming that involves case management. Moreover, only a handful of states have incorporated rehabilitative strategies aimed at bringing the individual to optimal functioning in anticipation of release.

PRISONS, AIDS, AND TUBERCULOSIS

The factors that put one at risk of contracting HIV and TB are often the same factors that put one at risk of being incarcerated. Poverty, and its associated problems of overcrowded living arrangements, poor health care, and drug use, are among these factors. As these various public health problems come together in the prison, the problems of AIDS and TB are greatly magnified. This fact has rendered the safety of the institutional environment even more precarious.

Though TB was nearly eradicated worldwide, its resurgence has been responsible for more deaths globally than any other disease. The rise in TB infections in the United States can be attributed in large part to increases in poverty, homelessness, drug use, and immigration from countries with high TB infection rates. The spread of TB has also been facilitated by the spread of HIV/AIDS, as HIV infection is likely to move TB from less active and dangerous stages to more active and deadly stages. Once TB has progressed from the infection stage to the disease stage, symptoms are displayed, and the disease becomes highly contagious. Consequently, the 5 to 10 percent lifetime risk of disease increases to an 8 percent risk per year (Blumberg and Langston, 1995). HIV also contributes to the spread of TB because it makes the diagnosis of TB more difficult. Thus, the infection accelerates without treatment.

Because TB tends to flourish in overcrowded and impoverished settings, where health care is deficient, it is only natural that penal systems would inherit this problem. Prisons are overcrowded, suffer from poor ventilation, and house individuals whose health and drug habits make them particularly vulnerable. Not surprisingly, the rate of TB among inmates is much higher than that of the general population. In one California prison, 30 percent of inmates are infected with TB, a rate that is ten times higher than the statewide average (ibid.). In New York, 27 percent of the inmate population is infected with TB, and a drug-resistant strain developed between 1990 and 1992, killing thirty-six inmates and a correctional officer. Penal systems throughout the country have reported 45 current and 140 cumulative cases of drug-resistant strains that strike inmates as well as staff.

As of 1996/1997, the total number of TB-infected inmates at intake in all U.S. facilities was 20,226. The total number infected with TB that was detected at times other than intake was 7,668. With 4,233 cases detected at intake, Illinois had the highest number of TB infections of any state (Criminal Justice Institute, 1997). At 1,514, Florida had the highest number of inmates with TB infections detected at times other than intake. New York had the highest number of inmates with active TB at intake (14), and Texas had the highest number of inmates with active TB detected at times other than intake (51) (ibid.).

Because TB is highly contagious, the methods of containing the spread of the disease are costly. The Center for Disease Control (CDC) has recommended mass screening and mandatory segregation for those inmates with active cases of TB (Blumberg and Langston, 1995). Ninety-six percent of all correctional systems have followed these recommendations. For example, to accommodate their active TB cases, New Jersey and New York were forced to build 150 isolation units. In 1995, there were 805 active cases of TB being treated in U.S. prisons. The ability of the system to detect and treat the disease before it progresses to dangerous levels is important when one considers the following projection. According to the CDC, in one year, as many as 133,000 persons with TB may be released to the community from state and federal facilities (Hammett, Harrold, and Espstein, 1998).

While HIV/AIDS poses a lesser problem than TB in terms of prevalence

and ease of transmission, HIV/AIDS introduces controversies over prevention and regulation that TB clearly does not. In 1991, 16,921 inmates in state
facilities were known to be HIV positive (Brien and Beck, 1998). In 1994,
there were 21,749 HIV positive inmates in state facilities. Between 1991 and
1994, the number of HIV positive inmates in the Federal Bureau of Prisons
increased by 53 percent, from 630 to 964. By 1997, that figure increased to
1,030 (Maruschak, 1999). In terms of absolute numbers incarcerated, New
York and Florida house the largest number of HIV-positive inmates in the
country. Together, these two states house nearly half of all HIV-positive inmates in the nation (Brien and Beck, 1998). Texas and North Carolina, however, have witnessed particularly large growth rates. Between 1991 and
1994, the number of HIV-positive inmates in Texas increased from 615 to
1,584, and 351 new HIV-positive cases entered the North Carolina system.

As with the other special needs populations discussed thus far, inmates
who are HIV positive or have full-blown AIDS constitute a relatively small
proportion of the prison population. Nationally, HIV-positive inmates constituted only 2.3 percent of the state prison population in 1991 and 2.5 percent in 1994. In 1997, these figures remained relatively unchanged at 2.2
percent (see Table 13-3). In twenty-six states, HIV-positive inmates constituted only 1 percent of the overall inmate population (Brien and Beck, 1998).
The highest percentages were found in New York (12.4), Connecticut (6.6),
Rhode Island (3.8), Maryland (3.7), and New Jersey (3.6). The prevalence rate
in the federal system was approximately 1 percent for every year between
1991 and 1997 (Maruschak, 1999).

The statistics for HIV-positive inmates, however, do not reveal the number of confirmed, full-blown AIDS cases in the penal system. The number of
inmates with full-blown AIDS in state and federal facilities totaled approximately 1,682 in 1991. At the end of 1994, there were 4,848 confirmed cases
in state and federal prisons. By 1997, there were 6,184 confirmed AIDS cases

Table 13-3. Percentage of Inmates Known
to be HIV Positive in State and
Federal Facilities (1991–1997)

Year	State	Federal
1991	2.3	1.0
1992	2.6	1.2
1993	2.6	1.2
1994	2.5	1.1
1995	2.4	0.9
1996	2.3	1.0
1997	2.2	1.0

Source: Marschak (1998).

Table 13-4.   Number of Confirmed AIDS
Cases in State and Federal
Facilities (1991–1997)

Year	Cases
1991	1,682
1992	2,644
1993	3,765
1994	4,849
1995	5,099
1996	5,874
1997	6,184

Source: Maruschak (1998).

in the overall prison population (ibid.) (see Table 13-4). This AIDS prevalence rate is 5.5 times higher than that found in the U.S. population.

Though research indicates that institutional transmission rates are low (Blumberg, 1990; Hammett et al., 1998; Vlahov, 1990), preventing the spread of the disease remains a paramount concern. Tattooing, needle sharing, and unprotected sex are commonplace. Further, it is estimated that 131,000 men are raped each year in prison (Donaldson, 1994; Dumond, 1992). As a result, the manner in which penal systems seek to prevent and contain the spread of the disease has implications for the institutional environment as well as society at large.

The initial response to the HIV/AIDS "crisis" in prisons was to engage in mass screening and mandatory segregation. However, these policies quickly became subject to judicial review. Constitutional attacks on testing and segregation policies were primarily grounded in the First, Fourth, Eighth, and Fourteenth Amendments and the notion of the right of privacy. Lawsuits also reflected two different concerns. Inmates who were HIV positive claimed testing and segregation policies were discriminatory and invaded privacy, while noninfected inmates claimed the absence of such policies violated their constitutional rights (Haas, 1993).

In *Occoquan v. Barry* (1986), a federal court held that the failure to test for HIV could constitute a violation of the Eighth Amendment for noninfected inmates, if it could be shown that the failure to test demonstrated a "deliberate indifference" to the health of the inmate population (ibid.). Support for testing and segregation was affirmed and strengthened with the decision in *Turner v. Safley* (1987). The decision gave prison officials the right to enact *any* policy, if it could be shown to be reasonable and have a rational relationship to penological purposes. The standard established by the Turner decision was affirmed in *Harris v. Thigpen* (1993) when the courts upheld Alabama's practice of forced mass screening and segregation of HIV inmates.

Walker v. Sumner stands alone as one of the few cases that ruled against testing, but not because of a blanket objection to the policy in and of itself. Rather, the courts declared that prison officials could not test inmates because the penal system in question had failed to demonstrate why the screening was necessary. In effect, prison officials must be able to clearly articulate what they plan to do with the test results.

The courts have overwhelmingly sided with prison officials and non-infected inmates on the matters of mandatory testing and segregation policies. Inmates seeking to challenge these policies have found little relief, particularly if the expectation of relief was linked to the Fourteenth Amendment right to equal protection. Most Fourteenth Amendment claims have failed because they require inmates to first establish that they are "similarly situated." In *Cordero v. Coughlin* (1984), the court established that HIV-positive inmates were not "similarly situated," and, even if they were, the policy of segregation was reasonable for the protection of all involved.

The most successful attacks against testing and segregation have been launched under the notion of the right to privacy. Courts have generally agreed that one has a right against unauthorized disclosure of one's medical condition or records. Because segregation by nature discloses one's condition, segregative policies have been successfully reversed on privacy grounds. In *Dough v. Coughlin* (1988), it was established that segregation was not permitted if treatment was not received. The court ruled that segregation was only permissible for the purpose of diagnosis and that release back to the general population must follow (ibid.).

Though the courts have cleared the path for mandatory testing and segregation, the majority of states have opted not to implement mandatory testing and segregation. It is recognized that testing may be a dubious policy given the indeterminable incubation period associated with HIV antibodies. Consequently, testing may do little more than produce false negatives and a corresponding false sense of security. Unless the penal system engages in ongoing periodic testing of all its inmates—Federal Bureau of Prisons, Alabama, Missouri, and Nevada conduct tests upon release as well—the benefits to such a policy are limited. Because early detection is important, inmates with high-risk behavior are often encouraged to voluntarily submit to testing. The testing policy of most states is to encourage testing for those who have engaged in high-risk behaviors. Most states will require testing if the inmate is pregnant, clinical tests have raised suspicion, or an exchange of body fluids has occurred. Currently, only seventeen state prison systems and the Federal Bureau of Prisons conduct across-the-board testing.

Given that few states conduct mass screening, it follows that few states segregate. Unless the inmate has full-blown AIDS and his or her medical condition requires separate housing, most states integrate HIV-positive inmates with the general population. Not only is it costly to erect separate facilities, it is likely that fewer inmates will volunteer for testing if they know they will be set apart from the rest. The integration strategy of present has not always been the preferred one. In 1985, forty-two state systems, the federal system, and 60 percent of jails maintained segregation policies. By 1992, only 8 percent of state systems had segregation policies. Alabama and Mississippi are now the only states to isolate all known cases regardless of whether the inmate is asymptomatic. As of 1997/1998, only 278 inmates with confirmed AIDS were housed in separate medical facilities, while 354 were housed in nonmedical facilities (Criminal Justice Institute, 1997).

Education, as opposed to testing and segregation, is regarded as the more effective way of preventing the spread of the disease. There is little controversy over the soundness of education programs for both staff and inmates, and thus all states provide some form of education to both groups. A promising educational format that has proven successful is peer education. Peer education programs use HIV-positive inmates to teach other inmates about the disease. However, between 1990 and 1994, the number of such peer education programs in the United States declined significantly. Most systems, particularly local jails, rely on video instruction and written materials to educate inmates.

A far more controversial method of prevention is state-sanctioned condom distribution. To date, six local/state correctional systems distribute condoms, including Mississippi, New York City, Philadelphia, San Francisco, Vermont, and the District of Columbia. New York City and Vermont allow inmates one condom per medical visit. In Mississippi, an unlimited number of condoms may be purchased at the canteen. San Francisco makes condoms available only as part of its education program. The District of Columbia has a similar policy but also makes condoms available at the infirmary. Philadelphia provides condoms as part of its counseling program (Blumberg and Langston, 1995).

SUMMARY AND DISCUSSION

The circumstances of these special populations again raise questions regarding the appropriateness of prison as the default sanction of our penal system. Most incarcerated women are nonviolent property or low-level drug offenders with a history of physical and sexual abuse, chemical dependency, and poverty. Moreover, some are pregnant and nearly all are mothers who must relinquish custody of the children that many provided care for prior to incarceration. Many of the elderly who are incarcerated have aged in prison for a violent offense committed at a young age. Research consistently shows that criminal behavior declines dramatically with age, yet the release of many of these elders is not forthcoming. For the few offenders who have entered prison late in life, how should their stay be accommodated? Soderstrom (1999) argues against a policy of separate facilities, claiming the elderly have a stabilizing effect and are actually less likely than younger inmates to be victimized. He also claims that community-based programs are less able to deal with elderly offenders who are likely to be without housing, family, or employment.

The ability of community-based alternatives to adapt and respond to the particular circumstances of the mentally ill is equally problematic, though some supervision components have made the effort by developing specialized caseloads. Nevertheless, the mentally ill find the community corrections system just as complicated and frustrating as the prison, with its highly structured regimen and multiple conditions. This problem is exacerbated by the absence of mental health supervision that monitors medication compliance. In recognition of the limitations of existing options, Orange County, Florida, has attempted, thus far unsuccessfully, to construct a separate local facility for offenders caught in the trap of homelessness, substance abuse, and mental illness. The proposed facility would fill the service gaps that exist, by providing a place for the homeless who do not qualify for shelters because of their mental illness, and drug offenders, who are ill-suited for jail because of their mental illness.

For inmates who are HIV positive or afflicted with full-blown AIDS, the prison system is no longer in what is termed "crisis mode." Rather, the focus has shifted to the longer-term concerns of housing, programming, and medical care (Lawson and Fawkes, 1993). In the past few years, several correctional systems (e.g., Florida, South Carolina) have addressed the problem of medical costs by permitting researchers and pharmaceutical companies to conduct experiments and investigational drug studies on inmates. This new "brand" of privatizing prison health care may well be extending to the treatment of other illnesses as well, such as asthma and hepatitis. The potential for private industry (i.e., pharmaceutical companies and researchers) to assist in the management of the needs of each of the special inmate populations is both real and potentially disturbing because it is proceeding with little or no objective oversight.

Discussion of special inmate populations again begs the question of the appropriate role of the prison in society. The limitations of law and order punishment and the overreliance on prison become more glaring when one contemplates the incarceration of nonviolent mothers, the mentally ill, geriatrics, and the sick and terminally ill. Recognizing that resources are limited, even without the added burdens of special populations, one must ask the question, Who should be incarcerated and what can reasonably be expected of the prison in dealing with these populations? Will their increasing numbers lead to the development of specialized community alternatives to prison? Or, will these populations prompt the development of new and more specialized systems of confinement, as is the case in Florida where the elderly, the mentally ill, and those with infectious diseases are being transferred to separate facilities? While we may question who should be incarcerated and how, as the next chapter documents, we continue to incarcerate more and more of the overall populations that inevitably will result in still other special prison populations.

14

Penal Reform and the
Culture of Control (1990s and Beyond)

INTRODUCTION

THE FINAL CHAPTER of any book bears a unique burden, as the measure of a good story is often found in its ending. Readers may judge the ending as unexpected, predictable, provocative, or even unsatisfying for having raised more questions than it has answered. Nonetheless, because the ending may be what the reader most remembers, the impression left is important.

In this final chapter, we hope to remind the reader of several themes, encapsulated within the broader question of "what do the preceding chapters tell us about American penology and the future?" One such theme concerns the relationship between different historical contexts and punishments ideas and practices. Another theme concerns the patterned and repetitive disparity between the ideas and practices of various punishment reforms. A third theme concerns the cumulative consequence of net-widening that results from the disparity between the ideas and practices of various punishment reforms.

From these themes, a connection will be made between American penology's past, present, and future. To make this connection, we briefly review the current social context, and the penal ideas and practices associated with this context. One discovers from this brief review that current penal practices indeed serve as a window to the recent and distant past, and the practices of the past ultimately serve as a window to the not so distant future. In this future, one can expect that these past and present penal practices and their patterned social control outcomes will no longer be confined to only the formal penal system. Rather, these practices are and will continue to be systematically extended into our larger culture and society, thereby affecting the lives of all American citizens.

A POSTMODERN SOCIETY

Throughout the book, it has been our custom to frame the discussion of particular penal reform movements and practices with discussion of the historical/social context and ideas relevant to the development of these reform movements and practices. In identifying the most recent penal practices, this custom is continued, albeit in abbreviated fashion. Our comments regarding the current social context are purposely kept to a minimum, because we do not yet have the benefit of hindsight. While it is not clear where we stand in the grand scheme of historical designations, a broad overview of the current social context helps frame current ideas on crime and penal practice, as well as the larger culture of control that we are now experiencing in American society.

To communicate what appears to reflect the spirit of the 1990s, we rely on several observations made by Gross in his book entitled *The End of Sanity: Social and Cultural Madness in America*. However, we preface his observations with a short explanation of the concept of postmodern, as his arguments are situated within a "postmodern" framework. Postmodern is a concept used to describe the state of post–World War II society. The concept implies that society has broken from its [modern] past, with modernity being understood as the period beginning with the enlightenment and ending roughly around the 1960s. Modernity or modern society is characterized by the application of reason and science to discover singular truths in all areas concerning man, society, and the universe. Thus, whether the subject is art, architecture, religion, education, politics, or penology, if it has come to reflect the conditions of postmodernity, it is said to be characterized by eclecticism, pluralism, fragmentation, relativism, and ambivalence rather than the singular truths characteristic of modern society.

One can hardly do justice to the meaning of this complex and controversial concept in a single paragraph, but Gross's observations illustrate, in part, what is meant by the condition of postmodernity. Gross concludes that disorder and irrationality are pervading all institutions of society, including art, the military, higher education, churches, the workplace, and criminal justice. As dramatic instances of this irrationality, he cites the following cases:

> In California, parents of a disruptive child who threatened to kill fellow students sued when the child was suspended. They won an award from the U.S. Circuit Court of Appeals for $20,000 for private school tuition and $360,000 in legal fees. A psychological therapist dredged up an "old memory" from a mentally disturbed adult woman that she had been sexually abused by her father in childhood. The therapist, who helped his patient sue the father, appeared on PBS television to explain that in memory that is repressed, then recovered, it made no difference if the act really happened. It was only important, he told the television audience, that his patient thought it had happened. At Harvard University, curriculum has been so weakened and "grade inflation" has so taken hold that 84 percent of a recent class graduated with honors. (Gross, 1997:9)

Sarup (1993) provides further understanding of postmodern society when he states that cybernetics, computer technology, and "soundbite" communications have generated a refusal to think historically. Jameson (1981) similarly claims that [postmodern] society has lost its capacity to retain its own past and has begun to live in a perpetual present. Whether one agrees or disagrees with the validity of postmodern arguments, the framework does provide a way of conceptualizing the array of changes occurring in society, not the least of which is ironically, reform without change. The ahistorical, perpetual present, or reform-without-change perspective is particularly helpful in interpreting the state of current criminology theory and penal practice.

INTEGRATED THEORIES OF CRIME

An assumption underlying efforts to develop integrated theories of crime is that previous theoretical accounts of crime, including biological, culture conflict, strain or anomie, learning, and labeling, have only some degree of explanatory support. Elements or components of particular theories are known to explain only certain aspects or variations of crime. As a result, it is believed that combining or integrating these particular theories provides more comprehensive and compelling explanations of crime.

The integration of theoretical perspectives is not completely unprecedented. But where current integrative efforts depart from their predecessors is in the degree of specificity and sophistication of the causal models. The relationships between the multiple relevant variables are more clearly delineated and measured. While recent attempts to integrate theories of crime have varied, several common approaches have emerged.

Cullen and Agnew argue that the most common approach to theory integration is the "end-to-end" strategy that seeks to identify the temporal order between variables leading to criminal behavior. For example, such temporal ordering would argue that high levels of culture conflict and associated strain or anomie lead individuals to develop and/or join delinquent subcultures, which, in turn, lead to criminal behavior (1999:207). Thus, the essential task in end-to-end theory integration is to forge relationships between theories that capture the temporal order or sequence that culminates in criminal behavior.

More broadly based efforts to develop integrated theories of crime involve "interdisciplinary integration." These include combining elements of biology, psychology, and sociology. Various biopsychological or biosocial theories contend that certain individual characteristics predispose individuals either toward criminal behavior or toward learning criminal behavior. These theories acknowledge that biological factors, whether genetic or nongenetic, shape individual traits that, in turn, influence the learning process. These types of integrated theories do acknowledge the fundamental role of the social environment, particularly early family circumstances, in shaping the learning process (see Wilson and Herrnstein, 1985).

Other theory integration examples have involved more microlevel efforts to integrate two or more theories to explain specific instances of individual criminal behavior (Tittle, 1995; Catalano and Hawkins, 1996). Conversely, macrolevel theory integration has attempted to explain group crime rates. For example, Rosenfeld and Messner's (1999) institutional anomie theory combines Merton's (1938) cultural emphasis upon the pursuit of money with social disorganization's focus on the inability of institutions to effectively provide social control. There has been interest in combining macro- and microlevel theories. Cullen and Agnew (1999) conclude that these particular integration efforts involve descriptions of the ways in which macrolevel variables affect the behavior of individuals, which, in turn, affects crime rates.

While the development of integrated theories of crime has enjoyed major interest and popularity at the end of the 1990s, our understanding of criminal behavior has only modestly improved. Even as efforts to establish empirical validation are ongoing, there is a sense that such efforts are proceeding in vain. Surely, any postmodern cynic would contend that if everything explains crime then nothing explains crime.

Because the multiple causes of crime can now be reasonably assumed, even if they can not be causally ordered, theory has only an indirect rather than a direct influence on current penal policy. As Gordon (1990:5) contends, eclectic is probably the best description of the theoretical underpinnings of the current penal system. While previous phases of crime control also exhibited ideological inconsistencies (classicism allowed some determinism, positivism allowed some punishment) there was at least a dominant set of ideas from which departures could be noticed. Now, "in the cheerless anti-theoretical realism of contemporary crime-control ideology, anything goes" (Cohen, 1985:158–59).

"ANYTHING GOES" PENAL STRATEGIES

While it has been argued that the search for the causes of crime has given way to the search for finding out "what works" (ibid.), it may also be that the search for what works is nearing its own dead end. Just as crime can be attributed to a little bit of everything, a little bit of everything has been used to subsequently combat crime. Policymakers have subscribed to a multiple-strategies approach that includes retribution, incapacitation, deterrence, restoration, and rehabilitation.

Truth-in-Sentencing and Three-Strikes
The truth-in-sentencing and three-strikes legislation of the past decade are little more than extensions of the habitual-offender statutes and mandatory minimum sentences that appeared in the previous decade. Still, this latest round of get-tough initiatives has been viewed as necessary to curb what

the public perceives as unchecked and widespread early releases of serious offenders. In 1987, the federal government was the first to enact truth-in-sentencing laws, with the aims of restoring public confidence in the sentencing process, and increasing time spent in custody in relation to the actual sentence meted out in court. The federal government further encouraged states to adopt their own truth-in-sentencing laws in return for federal aid for state prison construction. As of 1995, approximately half of all states had implemented such laws, while several other states had legislation pending.

Three-strikes laws impose even more severe prison sentences, including life with no possibility of parole for a third felony conviction. These laws were promoted as a means to keep habitual offenders off the streets. In 1993, the state of Washington was one of the first states to put a three-strikes provision on the ballot. This provision required life in prison without the possibility of parole for persons convicted of three or more serious or violent felonies.

A major national impetus for three-strikes laws followed the Polly Klaas murder in California in 1993. Twelve-year-old Polly Klaas was murdered by Richard Allen Davis, a California prison parolee who had been released after serving eight years of a sixteen-year sentence. Davis had numerous prior convictions for kidnapping, assault, and other crimes (Benekos and Merlo, 1994). Public outrage over Davis being released early from a sixteen-year sentence led to a three-strikes law in California with a number of states quickly following.

By 1997, twenty-four states and the federal government had some form of three-strikes legislation (Walker, 1998). The majority of these states include violent felonies, such as murder, rape, robbery, arson, and assaults on their list of "strikeable" offenses. Some states, however, include nonviolent offenses, such as the sale of drugs. There is also variation in the number of strikes needed to be "out." In eight states, only two strikes are required to bring about a sentence enhancement (Austin, Clark, Hardyman, and Henry, 1999). State laws also differ in their length of imprisonment when the offender "strikes out." For example, mandatory life sentences are imposed when "out" in Georgia, Montana, Tennessee, Louisiana, South Carolina, Indiana, New Jersey, North Carolina, Virginia, Washington, and Wisconsin (ibid.). In three other states, parole is possible after an offender is "out." In New Mexico, offenders that "strike out" are not eligible for parole until after thirty years. In Colorado, they are eligible for release after forty years.

Since the implementation of these laws, California has been the only state to extensively pursue their application. In California, the first two strikes are defined as "serious" felonies and the third strike is *any* felony. Six months following California's enactment of the three-strikes law, more than half of the three-strikes cases filed involved such nonviolent felonies as shoplifting, auto burglary, theft of cigarettes, and, in one Los Angeles case, theft of a pizza. Further, juvenile offenders convicted of, for example, two residential burglaries can be convicted years later, for example, of passing a bad check and be sent to prison for life. Six months after enactment of the California three-strikes law, the Los Angeles County jail, which was already under court order for overcrowding, had added an additional 1,700 inmates (Skolnick, 1995). However, this was not the only outcome. More cases were brought to trial instead of being plea-bargained, contributing to court backlog and higher financial costs related to increased processing of criminal cases.

Should other states follow California's vigorous enforcement of three-strikes, the impact could be devastating on the nation's penal system. As discussed in Chapter 13, more older offenders will be incarcerated, resulting in accelerated health care costs. Further, given that the age peak in criminal activity is fifteen to twenty-four years of age, it is unlikely that laws that result in longer prison sentences will have any major or sustained effect on crime rates. "The California Department of Corrections has estimated that 'three strikes' will require an additional 20 prisons to be added to the present 28 and the 12 already on the drawing board. By 2001, California anticipates 109,000 more prisoners behind bars serving life sentences" (ibid.:23).

However, to date, with the exception of California the application of these laws in other states has been more symbolic than substantive (Austin et al., 1999). Austin et al. point out that in all twenty-four three-strikes states, provisions for penalty enhancements were already in place. Therefore, they contend three-strikes legislation was not truly designed to have an significant impact on the system. For example, in Washington, only 115 offenders have been admitted to prison under the three-strikes law since 1993. In Georgia, a two-strike state, less than 10 percent of annual prosecutions in Atlanta are based on this law. The Federal Bureau of Prisons has not admitted any inmates under three-strikes since 1998.

Supermaximum Secure Prisons

Minimum mandatory, three strikes, and truth-in-sentencing laws reduce penal policy to the singular question of how much time in prison is needed before the requisites of retribution, deterrence, and incapacitation can be satisfied. How one does time is an equally important policy question that dates back to the debates of Auburn and Pennsylvania prison systems. Recall that both systems advocated isolation through silence and single-cell occupation, while Auburn ultimately permitted work in groups. Still, the emphasis in both systems was solitude. Supermaximum prisons have resurrected this feature of the penitentiary, but the aims of reform or repentance are nowhere to be found. Instead, total solitude serves the purposes of control and punishment.

While there is no common definition of the supermaximum secure prison, the National Institute of Corrections has identified three essential elements:

(1) accommodation that is physically separate, or at least separable, from other units or facilities, (2) a controlled environment emphasizing safety and security, via separation from staff and other prisoners and restricted movement, and (3) prisoners who have been identified through an administrative rather than a disciplinary process as needing special control on grounds of their violent or seriously disruptive behavior in other high-security facilities (King, 1999). Prison administrators claim the facilities largely house the highest-risk inmates, who have repeatedly exhibited violent behavior inside prison (Gavora, 1996). In effect, they claim to house the so-called worst of the worst who cannot be effectively managed in the general prison populations.

An example of how these facilities operate is found in Sheppard's (1996) description of the Illinois supermax secure facility. In the Illinois facility, inmates are locked alone in their cells for as long as twenty-three hours a day to keep them isolated from the staff and other prisoners. The design of the facility separates inmate and staff routes throughout the prison. Inmates are always shackled when being escorted outside their cells. All meals are delivered to the inmates in their cells. Inmates are allowed only three showers a week and one hour a day to leave their cell and use the library or a small exterior exercise area. Video surveillance cameras are positioned throughout the facility and cells, and security doors are computer-operated.

Growth in the number and use of these supermax facilities has met with some opposition by correctional leaders, the courts, and the media (Franklin, 1998). The National Institute of Corrections has even warned that states should proceed with caution, as the constitutionality of these facilities remains in question. Further, Amnesty International and Human Rights Watch have condemned these facilities without equivocation. The conditions surrounding supermax prisons currently violate the International Covenant on Civil and Political Rights, which the United States ratified, the United Nations Standard Minimum Rules for the Treatment of Prisoners, the Body of Principles for the Protection of All Persons Under Any Form of Detention or Imprisonment, and the Basic Principles for the Treatment of Prisoners, both of which were passed by the UN General Assembly (King, 1999).

One need only look to the pages of de Beaumont and de Toqueville's diaries on the U.S. penitentiary system in 1833 to grasp the devastating effects of this type of confinement:

> This trial, from which so happy a result had been anticipated, was fatal to the greater part of the convicts: in order to reform them, they had been submitted to complete isolation; but this absolute solitude, if nothing interrupts it, is beyond the strength of man; it destroys the criminal without intermission and without pity; it does not reform, it kills. (quoted in Marquart and Sorenson, 1997)

Not surprisingly, Haney's 1993 study of the Pelican Bay supermax facility in California yielded similar findings. Haney noted that not all inmates would experience the same degree of psychological damage, but that few would emerge unscathed. For example, Haney observed that prisoners placed in supermax units moved from being starved for social contact to being frightened of any social contact. Others acted out in ways to ensure they still actually existed, even if they knew their actions would elicit a negative response by correctional officers. Other supermax inmates became psychotic, filled with a perpetual fear of the correctional officers who "extracted" them from their cells for the slightest rule infraction. Still others engaged in suicidal or self-mutilating behavior. In Haney's study, one inmate reported that he had been slicing his arms several times a day for years just to see the blood flow.

Supermaximum secure prisons are increasingly affecting the way many prisoners serve their time. Approximately twenty thousand prisoners were housed in these facilities as of 1998, which constituted 1.8 percent of the total state and federal prison population (King, 1999). Even in the face of such psychological destruction, and knowing that the overwhelming majority of inmates housed in these facilities will be released to society, the facilities remain an increasingly popular tool with many elected officials. The supermax prison may even be embraced as the preferred construction alternative when there is a need for more prison cells (Franklin, 1998). Some states, once committed to providing some supermax accommodations, build more than is necessary because it is cheaper to build a five hundred-bed facility than a one-hundred-bed facility. Once the beds were available, they were filled, regardless of whether the inmate's behavior warranted placement in the facility. In 1997, thirty-four prison systems, including the federal government, were operating supermaximum secure facilities. At least four other states are prepared to construct these facilities and several other states are planning to expand their existing supermax units (ibid.).

Structured Rehabilitation

Throughout most of the twentieth century, the idea of treatment and rehabilitation dominated penal philosophy and practices. During the 1980s, treatment and rehabilitation efforts gave way to various get-tough penal strategies. Throughout the decade of the 1980s, and well into the 1990s, various get-tough strategies were largely unchallenged. As the 1990s progressed, however, a modified and more structured treatment and rehabilitation approach was added to the penal system's arsenal of diversified strategies.

Present treatment and rehabilitation programs involve offender reform as an implicit goal, but, as Seiter (1998) claims, they also center upon offender responsibility and accountability. These programs tend to be highly structured, with mandatory requirements, accountability measures, and numerous sanctions for noncompliance. For example, drug intensive supervision probation programs in Washington, New Mexico, Georgia, Virginia, and Iowa stress participation in substance abuse treatment, education, and employment programs. In the state of Washington, sex offenders must consent to treatment before being considered eligible for probation (Lucken, 1998) A drug treatment program in Volusia County, Florida, requires offenders to relinquish their driver's licenses for their first program violation and to serve a jail sentence for their second violation.

This same pattern of structured treatment can be found in the institutional setting. In Florida, funds appropriated for institution-based substance abuse programs have increased throughout the 1990s (Lucken, 1998). Morality building therapy programs have been implemented in correctional institutions in several states, including Tennessee, Florida, and Oklahoma. These programs seek to reeducate clients socially, morally, and behaviorally. Other institutions have incorporated a more subtle form of behavior modification. As was the practice in the nineteenth-century Elmira Reformatory, housing assignments are made according to the inmate's willingness to engage in self-improvement programs. Those who participate in these programs will be housed in units that have more pleasant surroundings and will be afforded more privileges, such as air conditioning, television, and exercise equipment.

While current treatment regimens are distinct from earlier progressive penology practices, such as sentence length being dictated by demonstrations of reform, they do bring many of the original progressive penology aims to life. The attempt to balance punishment with treatment has forced many state correctional systems to contract with private treatment agencies for a number of mental health and substance abuse services. These contracts include services for various drug and alcohol treatment, impulse control programs, anger management programs, life skills training programs, and job training and counseling programs. Consequently, the private treatment industry has expanded considerably to meet the high demand of offender referrals to various forms of treatment programming (Lucken, 1997). Community corrections officers are often required to possess degrees in psychology, social work, or criminal justice. Others are certified in various forms of specialized counseling. Specialized caseloads reflect the attempt to match offender needs and risks with officers that are more qualified to deal with those needs and risks. While the effectiveness of these various treatment programs remains in question, the renewal and refinement of rehabilitative efforts makes this trend noteworthy.

Restorative Justice

America's current system of justice is an adversarial one that pits the offender against the state. It is a justice model based upon conflict, and it seeks to hold the offender accountable through largely retributive means. Throughout this adversarial process, the victim and community are generally not key participants. Consequently, their role in administering justice is a minimal one.

Restorative justice is an alternative model for administering justice that takes into account the victim and the community. While restorative justice is an outgrowth of the victim rights movement, it incorporates the nonpunitive justice traditions of small tribelike communities. These traditions emphasize mediation, dialogue, reintegration, and reparation in the resolution of conflict. This does not mean that restorative justice ignores appropriate offender punishment, but it recognizes the need to supplement the punishment process with strategies that rebuild the damaged relationships between the offender, the victim, and the community.

By moving the focus of injury from the state to the victim and the immediate community, restorative justice is an example of decentralization to the extreme. In this regard, restorative justice and its associated programs reflect some of the premodern ideas of Colonial America. The parallels are best illustrated in reintegrative shaming (see Braithwaite, 1989) and citizen panels. Reintegrative shaming programs are focused upon community condemnation of the criminal acts of the offender (shaming), followed by acceptance of the offender back into the community (reintegration). Citizen panels use select citizens of the community to mete out community-based sanctions to offenders.

Other restorative justice–based programs, such as arbitration and mediation or victim offender meeting programs have taken a particularly strong foothold in the juvenile justice system. For example, by the end of 1995, twenty-four states had adopted or were considering adopting juvenile statutes and procedures that reflect restorative justice principles (Levrant, Cullen, Fulton, and Wozniak, 1999). Moreover, various restorative justice programs have been expanding as an option for adult victims of serious or violent crime.

Though restorative justice promises to offer something for everyone (i.e., victim, offender, and community), Levrant et al. (1999) have cautioned that restorative justice programs are limited in several respects. The authors argue that a fundamental weakness of restorative justice is its failure to provide a plausible blueprint for how to control crime. This failure of omission is critical because the success of the get-tough movement has rested on its promise to lock up as many people as possible. In contrast, restorative justice provides few answers on how to deal with serious and persistent offenders. Moreover, certain restorative justice programs (namely, victim offender meeting programs) will continue to have limited application, no matter how successful they may be, because they are best administered under voluntary conditions. It is because of this feature that restorative justice programs are generally implemented as supplements to traditional sanctions or as a victim service for less serious offenses.

Privatization

As discussed in Chapter 12, the get-tough approach of the 1980s and 1990s has led to unprecedented incarceration rates. Based on recent estimates, these high prison populations have cost the nation nearly thirty billion dollars a year (Smalley, 1999). This expensive price tag has made states and the federal government more willing to engage the private sector to help manage their penal systems (Bates, 1998).

The involvement of the private sector has come in the form of contracts for the provision of goods and services (e.g., food, health care, education, treatment); the operation of prison, jail, or community-based residential facilities (e.g., halfway houses, work release centers); and the production and sale of various technologies and materials to support the penal industry. There are now approximately twenty large companies in the country that operate prisons and jails, and private-controlled facilities are growing at four times the rate of government facilities (Lippke, 1997). In fact, in 1997, a private company made a proposal (which was ultimately rejected) to Tennessee to assume full responsibility for the state's entire prison system (Kyle, 1998). Whether it is the area of construction, operation, or providing various technologies to facilitate the more efficient control and surveillance of offenders, the private sector has become fully entrenched in the penal system.

As previous chapters indicated, private sector involvement in punishment is not new (Gowdy, 1997). The private sector was involved in the transport of convicts to various European colonies, America in particular, and was heavily involved in the penal system of the Civil War–torn South. Still, there remains an important difference between the private sector's previous and current involvement. Their current involvement is more fixed than intermittent, thereby forming an "iron triangle," or what Lilly and Knepper (1993) have termed a "corrections commercial complex." In this figurative complex, all parties to penal decision-making (e.g., legislators, lobbyists, private industry, corrections professionals) work together and to their own benefit, with little or no public scrutiny.

However, the increasing privatization of corrections has not occurred without opposition. Opponents of privatization claim that only state and federal government should be allowed to punish citizens (Gowdy, 1997), as the private sector is more interested in "doing well" than "doing good" (Robbins, 1987). For example, it is commonly argued that private facilities cut costs by not properly training their personnel, maintain only bare minimum staffs, reduce inmate programs, and save costs through reduced health care and food services (Smalley, 1999). In 1999, the largest private sector company, Corrections Corporation of America, settled a class action lawsuit brought by inmates because of inadequate medical care and abusive guard behavior (ibid.). The day following the settlement, a bill was introduced in Congress to prohibit any future use of private facilities for federal prisoners and to deny federal grants to states and cities that use private-run facilities. While the final outcome of this legislation is not yet known, it appears that private sector involvement will continue. Currently, in Florida, private companies are responsible for the care of over 80 percent of the state's more than ten thousand youth held in juvenile justice facilities.

Indeed, given the billions of dollars involved in privatized corrections, private companies have developed sophisticated lobbying efforts that wield substantial influence in penal policymaking. Opponents claim private companies will promote the escalated use of prisons and jails while denouncing other forms of viable and less costly punishment. These opponents contend that a private company's concern for profit and the associated need for more prisoners to fill their prison and jail beds will lead the companies to lobby for harsher punishments to keep prisoners as long as possible (ibid.). As Lippke (1997) suggests, the growth in private prisons indicates that, to some extent, governments are willing to modify their traditional roles in relation to legal offenders, though the U.S. Government Accounting Office has reported that, over time, there are relatively few differences in operating costs for public and private facilities (Robbins, 1987).

PENAL REFORM: PAST, PRESENT, AND FUTURE

Current penal practices illustrate not only the latest in American penology trends, but they also illustrate a connection between penology's past and future. The practices of three-strikes, supermax prisons, structured rehabilitation, restorative justice, and privatization demonstrate that our current approaches to crime control are, in many respects, a reconstruction of old ideas and practices. For example, Colonial America treated crime within the confines of the community, believing that punishment should elicit the shame of the offender and express the moral condemnation of the offended. In the period of transition, crime was viewed as a function of rational thought or free will. It was therefore assumed that the threat of long-term incarceration would deter rational men, particularly when applied in a uniform, swift, certain, and proportional manner. In the nineteenth century, crime was viewed as a moral disease caused by the breakdown of the family and a vice-ridden community. Confinement in a well-ordered asylum, known as the penitentiary, was promoted as a way to contain the spread of disease and to cure its victims. In Progressive America, and for more than half of the twentieth century, crime was viewed primarily as a consequence of the offender's social or psychological circumstances. These circumstances were to be overcome with targeted individualized treatment, administered through reformatories, parole, probation, and for the young the juvenile court. In the 1960s and 1970s, the thinking was that it was not the offender but rather the way society and the criminal justice system labeled (i.e., responded to) the offender that ultimately caused, perpetuated, or intensified subsequent criminal behavior. The resulting penal practices were aimed at decentralization in order to avoid or minimize formal system contact altogether. In the 1980s, a modified version of free will dominated the thinking on crime. Because offenders ultimately exercised "rational choice" in committing their offenses, all that was needed were get-tough strategies (more prison, intermediate punishment) that would make crime too costly.

What we currently have in place is a broad array of penal strategies that are reminiscent of the past and include, but are not limited to, fines, pretrial intervention, arbitration, restitution, community service, teen court, juvenile courts, victim/offender meeting programs, citizen panels, pretrial release, work release, probation and restitution centers, halfway houses, probation, parole, day-reporting centers, intensive supervision probation, boot camps, home confinement, electronic monitoring, jail, prison, supermax prisons, and various other community-based residential facilities. Perhaps the major difference in penology today and in the future will be the increasing role of technology in offender surveillance and control.

Speaking more theoretically, in considering penology's past, present, and future, the concepts of social amnesia, illusion of knowledge, and net-widening are applicable. Social amnesia reflects the tendency of American penology to ignore history and precedent when responding to the present or informing the future. Instead, discarded ideas and practices are reinvented and repackaged; meanwhile, the expectations for these practices remain the same, namely, effective crime control. Not surprisingly, social amnesia also refers to the tendency to interpret past events not as they were, but as we choose to remember them. Our interpretations of the past tend to be informed by current events and perspectives rather than how historical events actually unfolded. For example, the assumption that "nothing works" in rehabilitation is generally based on a flawed view of how rehabilitation was implemented in the first place. Specifically, we do not know if specific rehabilitation programs worked or not because the programs were never implemented as intended. Additionally, patterned declines in serious crimes during the late 1990s and into 2000 are being credited to various get-tough measures rather than the robust economy, low unemployment, and changing populations at risk of committing crime. As a result, many citizens and policymakers truly believe that getting tough on crime is the ultimate solution. Such broadly held beliefs continue to fuel new and more imaginative get-tough strategies, which in turn are producing far-reaching consequences that extend well beyond criminal offenders.

This pattern of "social amnesia" also reveals that we operate under a recurring "illusion of knowledge." What this notion suggests is that each generation of reformers thinks it knows what causes crime and therefore believes it knows how to effectively control it. In the book, *The Discoverers: A Histo-*

ry of Man's Search to Know His World and Himself, Boorstin (1983) chronicles man's historical quest for progress and finds that throughout history,
the biggest impediment to progress has been what he terms the "illusion of
knowledge." Boorstin concludes that mankind's progress rests not so much
in knowing, but quite the opposite, in recognizing how little indeed we do
know. Recognition of ignorance, then, is the fundamental first step in
progress. However, where in the history of American penology can we cite
a period in which recognition of ignorance tempered penal ideas, reforms,
and practices?

In the history of penal reform, not only have we suffered from social amnesia and failed to recognize our ignorance in putting forth ideas, reforms,
and practices, we neither do nor accomplish what we say we are going to do
and accomplish. As Cohen (1985:359) summarizes, "consequences so different from intentions; policies carried out for reasons opposite to their stated
ideologies; the same ideologies supporting quite different policies; the same
policy supported for quite different ideological reasons. And any possible
correspondence between ideas and policies will become even harder to locate." Theoretical models such as implementation impediments, organizational convenience, professional and ideological contradictions, or political
economy have attempted to account for this patterned outcome record
(Austin and Krisberg, 1981; Blomberg, 1987; Cohen, 1985; Feeley and Simon, 1992; Klein, 1979), but no matter what the interpretation, the conclusion about American penal reform history is that it has been gloomily punitive
and repetitive. The persistent disparity between ideas and practice, while
problematic in its own right, has contributed to an ongoing history of net-
widening. As a result, more and more of the population has become subject
to penal control.

To illustrate this historical pattern of net-widening, Figure 14-1 provides
the combined federal and state prison incarceration rates from 1850 to 1998.
The rate of incarceration increased from 29 per 100,000 population in 1850
to 461 per 100,000 population in 1998. The rapid and unprecendented increase of the 1990s in particularly noteworthy in light of the steady decline
in crime during the 1990s. Moreover, if local jail populations are added to
the state and federal prison populations, Tonry (1999) reports that at mid-year
1998, 668 residents per 100,000 population were incarcerated. This trans-
lates to 1,802,496 individuals incarcerated in local, state, and federal facilities throughout the United States. In other Western countries, between 50
and 135 residents per 100,000 population are in prison. As a result, the U.S.
rate of incarceration is between 6 and 12 times higher than other Western
countries.

Further illustrations of net-widening are provided by our use of probation
and parole. Between 1980 and 1996, when prison populations more than
quadrupled, probation populations increased from just over 1 million to over

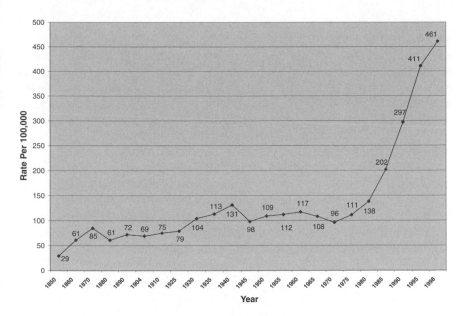

Figure 14-1. Federal and State Prison Incarceration Rates 1850–1998.

3 million, and parole increased from just over 220,000 to just over 700,000. In 1996, more than 5.5 million people were subject to either prison, jail, probation, or parole (U.S. Bureau of Justice Statistics, 1996). However, it is important to recognize that these alarming statistics are only a part of the actual extent of penal control. Most of the locally operated community-based programs are not included in these figures. Nor do these figures take into account the changes in the character of the control, such as the "piling up of sanctions" in the community and the increased punitiveness and duration of institutional confinement. For example, the number of people sentenced to more than a year in state and federal prisons almost tripled from 315,974 in 1980, or 139 per 100,000 population, to 823,414 in 1991, or 310 per 100,000 population.

A dramatic illustration of the changing character of penal control is the latest implementation of satellites to track probationers throughout Florida: Crime Trax (Rosica, 2000). The Crime Trax system will employ twenty-four satellites circling twenty thousand miles overhead to follow the state's 143,000 people on any form of court-ordered probation. Each offender will wear a wristlet that records his or her location once every minute by bouncing a signal off one of the twenty-four satellites circling overhead. At night, the wristlet acts as a remote control and transmits its information to a black box receiver located in the probationer's home. This box transmits the information through secure telephone lines to a state law enforcement computer. Simultaneously, law enforcement agencies throughout the state transmit the day's crime and incident information, including times and addresses, to this same state law enforcement computer. The computer, in turn, maps all the reported crime data and probationers' movement data to identify time, place, and individual probationer and crime incident matches. Florida has been using this technology for several years to monitor high-risk offenders in the community and the state is now substantially expanding its uses to all probationers in the state. No doubt other states will soon follow.

Together, these incarceration and community surveillance and control trends demonstrate that an ever-increasing proportion of America's population is becoming subject to some form of increasingly intrusive penal control. Between 1984 and 1988, the number of adults subject to some form of penal control (prison, parole, or probation) rose by 39 percent. Rosenfeld and Kempf (1991) report that the annual rate of change in the mid-1980s in the proportion of adult population under some form of formal penal control was 9.6 percent. This suggests that by 2006, one out of every ten Americans will be subject to formal penal control. There is considerable evidence to suggest that the annual 9.6 percent increase in formal penal control substantially underreports the actual annual increases during the 1990s. When these figures and projections are added to the increasing punitive penal measures employed with juvenile offenders and to the various other quasi-formal or informal public or private penal programs, it appears that we are becoming a medium-secure society in which all of us are increasingly becoming subject to elements of prisonlike surveillance, regulation, and control.

PENAL REFORM AND THE CULTURE OF CONTROL

While any discussion of the future must be viewed with a good degree of reservation, there is compelling evidence that American life in the new millennium will be subject to new and more far-reaching levels of control. Over a period of two hundred years, we have built a community of corrections that normalizes the presence of formal control, and even informal control, into the larger society. As Foucault suggests, perhaps the most important consequence of this community of corrections "is that it succeeds in making the power to punish natural and legitimate, in lowering at least the threshold of tolerance to penality" (1977:301). As this dispersal of control continues and becomes more widespread, the question that arises is: Are we experiencing a transformation in the character of crime control, such that a larger culture of control has developed, of which the formal penal system is only a part? Staples (1997) identifies several examples to illustrate the increasing blurring between penal control and the fast-developing culture of control in America:

Today, nearly ninety percent of U.S. manufacturers are testing workers for drug use. . . . In California and Texas, every citizen wishing to be issued a driver's license must have their thumbprint computer scanned. . . . In Kansas, school children are identified with "bar codes" so that a teacher can use a computer to track their daily behavioral and academic performance. . . . In Maine, a police officer whose name is simply raised in a local sex-abuse case is told he has to submit to a test designed to measure his sexual desire. . . . In Arizona, a "welfare mother" has a court-ordered contraceptive device surgically implanted in her arm. . . . And, in nearly every state in the country, convicted felons are placed under "house arrest," their movements monitored electronically by a transmitter attached to their ankles. (p. 1)

Today, technologically integrated profiles of individual citizens can provide detailed portraits of each of our lives, circumstances, and patterns. Information technologies can access various data on individual finances, employment history, medical history, marital status, consumer preferences, telephone records, welfare eligibility, nationality, ethnic background, educational record, and criminal history. Moreover, these databases and information enable the compilation of individual "histories" that, in turn, provide time-series analyses from which various predictions can be made about our future health, life span, earning capacities, consumer preferences, and other future behaviors. For example, in late 1999, media headlines throughout the country reported that data from a couple's premarital arguments can be used to accurately predict whether their marriage will succeed or end in divorce.

Corbett and Marx (1991) argue that these new technologies and their applications mean that we are living in a society that is becoming increasingly characterized by an implosion of previously accepted boundaries, resulting in the disintegration of the barriers that once offered individual sanctuary. Such "historic" or "modern" barriers as distance, darkness, time, walls, and even skin, which have all been basic to conceptions of privacy and liberty, are becoming outmoded in the current culture of control and its associated technologies and capacities. The contention here is that our communities, homes, workplaces, and bodies are becoming increasingly glasslike or transparent and therefore more easily regulated and controlled.

It appears we are indeed subject to a "lowered" threshold of tolerance to control and its many accompanying technologies. But why has our tolerance threshold to control become lowered? Clearly, it has not occurred because of a totalitarian takeover or collapse of worldwide democracy. But could it be the result of a quiet revolution in technology in which with "an invention here and a new computer application there, American culture is nearing the point forewarned by those who feared technology could breed a new kind of oppression" (Staples, 1997:128)? It is these new social control technologies and methods applied to the individual, the home, the workplace, the community, and other public places that, while appearing minor, necessary, and even helpful, are providing the infrastructure of a system of control with substantial intrusive and punitive potential.

The interesting paradox according to Staples is "that the gaze is increasingly secured through the very products and services that we are seduced into consuming. Portable phones are easily listened in on, and inexpensive video technology ensures that cameras and their tapes abound; meanwhile, emerging computer networks make our activities and correspondence easier to monitor" (ibid.:57). As summed up by Lyon (1994), this is all merely "pleasurable social control." Or perhaps even expedient social control. In Florida, for example, the state police asked citizens with cell phones to help police Florida's highways. The response was so great that the police had to instruct citizens not to report all minor infractions because of their lack of resources to respond to all calls ("Thousands of Eyes," 1994).

So, who then is behind this culture of control? Staples (1997) convincingly argues that there is no "Big Brother," and, instead, we, the citizenry, are behind the culture of control:

> Rather than having appeared simply "from the top down" or having originated from a small group of identifiable individuals or even a particular organization, disciplinary power has and is advanced, directly or indirectly, by all of us. It is not orchestrated by only a few or part of some master plan that is simply imposed on us; rather, disciplinary power is "bi-directional," flowing from top to bottom and vice versa. So, while Ronald Reagan can issue an executive order that demands that all federal workers be tested for drugs, an ex-auto mechanic can start marketing and selling video cameras to school districts for their buses. While the FBI can help push a wiretap bill through Congress, an employee in your hometown may initiate "integrity" testing of all job applicants. A government agency or giant corporation may set out to create a new surveillance gadget, but it seems just as likely that a university professor will develop one— or, importantly, the basis for a potential one—for no other reason than curiosity or to get a promotion. A young computer software designer may develop a new program because its capabilities are "cool," rather than seeing it as an employee monitoring tool. (pp. 129–30)

The growth of surveillance technologies and their broad dispersal, however, have not been without some setbacks and instances of protest and resistance. For example, today, Michigan welfare recipients are challenging a law that requires them to submit to drug tests to prove they are drug-free before they qualify for welfare funds. Further, media stories routinely report on the uncharted and potentially dangerous future of more broadly administered DNA tests for all arrestees, the developing medical technologies and the availability of individual test results, and the information technologies and databases that hold numerous data on individual citizens. Nonetheless, and despite these protests and media calls for restraint, in the late 1990s, development of DNA profiles from blood samples for all sex offenders was implemented. Entering 2000, the registering of DNA profiles for all jail and prison inmates was begun with future plans to enter DNA profiles on all American citizens to enable downloading to a database for solving any crimes with blood or other DNA evidence.

As the larger culture of control continues to grow, the ultimate question is, Will the culture of control that we all appear to be contributing to and are victims of have a ceiling or will it continue until democracy, privacy, and other individual rights become so weakened or disappear altogether? Heilbroner (1980) in his often-cited book, *An Inquiry into the Human Prospect,* argues that worldwide runaway population, which reached six billion in 1999, coupled with accelerating declines in natural resources do indeed signal both the demise of conspicuous consumption by some countries like the United States, and also such democratic values associated with individual rights and freedom of choice. Heilbroner contends that the public interest will and must take precedence over individual rights, resulting in increasing governmental regulation over our private lives. Given the current culture of control, we appear to be undergoing this very transition from democracy and individual rights toward some vaguely defined goal of order or public interest.

The historical quest by governments for preserving order while maintaining enough individual freedom to avoid tyranny appears particularly applicable to the current culture of control. While there are several views about what may temper the culture of control in the future, most futurists acknowledge that increasing control over the lives of all citizens will be forthcoming. Further, it appears safe to suggest that Americans are unlikely to stop wishing for the greater convenience, predictability, comfort, safety, or order that is associated with these various technological advances. However, as we become more experienced with these new technologies, their advances, and levels of control, perhaps we will become less careless, less open, and less trusting. This could result in each of us becoming more careful and skillful in what we disclose and agree to provide, not provide, or participate in. Additionally, it can be reasoned that, as we become more aware about the questionable prospects associated with the culture of control, we may become involved in more direct action, since much of this control originates in our local communities rather than in state capitals or the nation's capital.

CONCLUSION

The major events in the history of American penology have been reported before, with some contributions being more focused and some being more general. What this book has attempted to do is provide a middle ground between these two different extremes, in order to identify and communicate penal relationships and patterns emerging from two hundred years of American penal experience. By examining historical contexts and associated ideas about crime that gave rise to particular punishment practices, we have been able to identify several thematic patterns. It is these thematic patterns that provide us with insights into the likely future of not only penology but the large culture of control we face entering the new millennium. Throughout America's history of penal reform, various efforts to promote alternative practices have resulted in the implementation of supplements to previous practices that have sequentially been applied to an ever-growing proportion of America's base population. Today, we face a related but even more pervasive dispersal of control that is increasingly blurring the penal system with society at large. This culture of control and penology system poses clear threats to democracy, freedom, and privacy.

We are now living under increasing conditions of visibility, regulation, and control that continue to erode our privacy. For example, the capacity has now been developed to include a unique serial code in all personal computers that will enable tracking of all information within e-mail and other information flowing across the Internet. Concerns that have been expressed over privacy violations have been characterized by the designers of computer serial code numbers as "overrated." Another technology control system called Echelon, which involves a sophisticated electronic monitoring system employed by the U.S. National Security Agency in conjunction with governments in Britain, Canada, Australia, and New Zealand, is receiving considerable media attention. Echelon intercepts and sifts through daily electronic transmission (e-mail, faxes, and phone calls) for particular "keywords" that could signal a security threat. What concerns many is that unchecked monitoring and surveillance by the government, using Echelon or some other technology, poses a threat to individual rights to privacy (*New York Post,* October 21, 1999). Florida's current implementation of a satellite tracking system of all state probationers could be expanded to include troubled or wayward youth, the elderly, or others judged "in need" of supervision. The potential is that the various applications of new technologies can expand as fast as new technologies develop.

Numerous other examples indicate that intrusive control and related technologies will increase in the near future in part because they reflect changes in America that are fundamentally related to the larger global economy, which, in turn, impacts our daily lives. It is understandable that current rights to be different and to make individual choices related to consumptive behaviors are becoming increasingly outmoded in the broader global context of increasing population growth and depleting natural resources. However, as we consider these global and national contingencies, our historical commitment to democratic principles, and our social contract with future generations, will we be able to rise above complacency and compliance to informed and critical consideration and action that can temper the emerging rush to regulate and control?

For today and tomorrow, Americans are and continue to be faced with a number of important challenges and questions related to the growing culture, business, and technology of control. While it is clear that the world and our country are undergoing rapid change, it is very unclear how these changes will affect our everyday lives. In sum, there are many more unknowns than knowns. Although present indicators provide room for "doom and gloom," there are some indicators for tempered optimism as well. For example, in late October 1999, President Bill Clinton issued an executive order that established guidelines and rules to protect the privacy of individual medical records that are stored electronically. Under this executive order, doctors, hospitals, and other health care related organizations are prohibited from releasing personal medical information not related to treatment or payment without the patient's permission. The order includes civil and criminal penalties for misusing such personal medical information. This executive order addresses important individual rights and privacy concerns that have been dramatized in recent years. For example, one HMO (health maintenance organization) stored thousands of individual medical records on a public Internet site for two months in early 1999. Moreover, the use of private medical records by employers and direct marketers has posed numerous threats to individual privacy. What has occurred in recent years is that, because of the absence of enforceable privacy rules and public fear of disclosure, countless numbers of Americans have withdrawn from full participation in needed health care because of fear that their personal medical records would be publicized. This includes persons with HIV, AIDS, cancer, heart disease, and other health problems ("Clinton Orders New Privacy Rules," 1999). Moreover, in May 2000, President Clinton and presidential candidate Al Gore unveiled a plan that would extend various privacy rules beyond medical to include banks, insurers, and other corporations that share information about their customers. Clinton stated, "In this information age we can't let new opportunities erode old, fundamental rights. We can't let breakthroughs in technology break down the walls of privacy" (Gearan, 2000).

We cannot be complacent or assume that the emerging culture and technology of control serve only positive goals, such as the need to control and prevent crime, improve health, improve productivity, or advance the quality of our lives. We must recognize how little we do know about the full set of consequences of these continual technological advances and control capacities. Our notions of privacy and individual rights are changing with far too little public and legislative attention, scrutiny, or understanding. As we come to recognize how little we know, we must begin to address the overriding and fundamental question: Can we live with these new levels of technology and accompanying control while simultaneously maintaining our commitment to fundamental democratic values?

Advances in technology and control do not necessarily indicate an abrupt end of life as we know it, or merely another challenge that democratically minded Americans will overcome. While the future is uncertain, advancing technology and control will, no doubt, provide society and the individual with gains and losses. Precisely what these will be remains to be seen. What is essential is that each of us recognizes these mixed gain and loss potentials and that we not assume that businesses, corporations, or the government will regulate or protect us from these fast-developing technologies. The message is clear: We cannot ignore our individual responsibilities—technology's spread applies to all of us. Neither fear nor complacency will suffice; we must play a part in confronting technology, be it through active education, greater awareness, or direct action. Nonetheless, while each of us may be able to temper some of the impacts of technology upon our daily lives, it should be evident from this book's arguments about penology and the culture of control that the future does appear to hold more of the same, namely, more visibility, regulation, and control. Our traditional values concerning the primacy of the individual and individual rights are at risk. While the notion of American society becoming like a maximum security prison is not imminent, it is increasingly evident that autonomous individualism is fading.

References

Adams, K. 1983. Former mental patients in a prison and parole system. *Criminal Justice and Behavior, 19*(3), 358–84.

Adams, K. 1986. The disciplinary experience of the mentally disordered inmate. *Criminal Justice and Behavior, 13*(3), 297–316.

Adams, K. 1993. Who are the clients? Characteristics of inmates referred for mental health treatment. *Prison Journal, 72,* 120–41.

Aday, R. H. 1994. Golden years behind bars: Special programs and facilities for elderly inmates. *Federal Probation, 58*(2), 47–54.

Allen, F. 1964. *The borderland of criminal justice: Essays in law and criminology.* Chicago: University of Chicago Press.

American Correctional Association. 1993. *Female offenders: Meeting needs of a neglected population.* Laurel, MD: Author.

Ashford, N. 1990. The conservative agenda and the Reagan presidency. In J. Hogan (Ed.), *Back to the 1970s: The context of the Reagan presidency* (pp. 3–20). New York: Manchester University Press.

Austin, J., Clark, J., Hardyman, P., & Henry, D. A. 1999. The impact of "three strikes and you're out." *Punishment and Society, 1*(2), 131–62.

Austin, J., & Irwin, J. 2001. *It's About Time: America's Imprisonment Binge* (3rd ed.). Belmont, CA: Wadsworth.

Austin, J., & Krisberg, B. 1981. Wider, stronger and different nets: The dialectics of criminal justice reform. *Journal of Research in Crime and Delinquency, 18*(1), 165–96.

Ayers, K. 1999. Should incarceration of pregnant women be avoided? In C. B. Fields (Ed.), *Controversial issues in corrections* (pp. 90–98). Needham Heights, MA: Allyn and Bacon.

Aylward, A., & Thomas, J. 1984. Quiescence in women's prisons litigation: Some exploratory issues. *Justice Quarterly, 1,* 253–76.

Baird, C., & Wagner, D. 1990. Measuring diversion: The Florida community control program. *Crime and Delinquency, 36*(1), 112–25.

Bales, W. D., & Dees, L. G. 1992. Mandatory minimum sentences in Florida: Past trends and future implications. *Crime and Delinquency, 38*(3), 309–29.

Barnes, H. E. 1972. *The story of punishment.* Montclair, NJ: Patterson Smith.

Baron, R. 1977. *Human aggression.* New York: Plenum.

Baron, R., Feeney, F., & Thornton, W. 1973. Preventing delinquency through diversion. *Federal Probation, 37*(1), 13–18.

Baskins, D., Sommers, I., & Steadman, H. 1991. Assessing the impact of psychiatric impairment on prison violence. *Journal of Criminal Justice, 19,* 271–80.

Bates, E. 1998. Private prisons. *Nation, 266,* 11–19.

Beccaria, C. [1764] 1963. *On crimes and punishment.* Translated with an introduction by Henry Paolucci. New York: MacMillan.

Becker, H. S. 1963. *Outsiders: Studies in the sociology of deviance.* New York: Free Press.

Beckett, K. 1997. *Making crime pay: Law and order in contemporary American politics.* New York: Oxford University Press.

Belden, E. 1920. *Courts in the United States hearing children's cases* (Publication No. 65). Washington, DC: U.S. Children's Bureau.

Belknap, J. 1996. *The invisible woman: Gender, crime, and justice.* Belmont, CA: Wadsworth.

Benekos, P. J., & Merlo, A. V. 1994. *Three strikes and you're out: The political sentencing game* (National Institute of Justice Research Report). Washington, DC: U.S. Department of Justice.

Bennett, W. J. 1994. *Index of leading cultural indicators.* New York: Simon and Schuster.

Bentham, J. 1789. *An introduction to the principles of morals and legislation.* London: T. Payne.

Berger, D. E., Lipsey, M. W., Dennison, L. B., & Lange, J. M. 1977. *The effectiveness of the sheriff's department's juvenile diversion projects in southeast Los Angeles County.* Claremont, CA: Claremont Graduate School.

Berecochia, J. E. 1982. *The origins and early development of parole in california.* Ph.D. dissertation, University of California, Berkeley.

Binder, A. 1976. *Diversion and the justice system: Evaluating the results.* Mimeograph. Irvine: University of California.

Birdsall, R. D. 1970. The second great awakening and the New England social order. *Church History, 39*(September).

Blomberg, T. G. 1977. Diversion and accelerated control. *Journal of Criminal Law and Criminology, 68*(2), 274–82.

Blomberg, T. G. 1978. *Social control and the proliferation of juvenile court services.* San Francisco: R. and E. Research Associates, Inc.

Blomberg, T. G. 1987. Criminal justice reform and social control: Are we becoming a minimum security society? In J. Lowman, R. J. Menzies, & T. S. Palys (Eds.), *Transcarceration: Essays in the sociology of social control* (pp. 216–18). Aldershot, UK: Gower.

Blomberg, T. G., Bales, W., & Reed, K. 1993. Intermediate punishment: Extending or redistributing social control. *Crime, Law, and Social Change, 19*(2), 197–201.

Blomberg, T. G., & Cohen, S. (Eds.) 1995. *Punishment and social control: Essays in honor of Sheldon L. Messinger.* Hawthorne, NY: Aldine de Gruyter.

Bloom, B., & Steinhart, D. 1993. *Why punish the children: A reappraisal of the children of incarcerated mothers in America.* San Francisco: National Council on Crime and Delinquency.

Blumberg, M. 1990. *AIDS: The impact on the criminal justice system.* Columbus, OH: Merrill.

Blumberg, M., & Langston, D. 1995. The impact of HIV/AIDS and tuberculosis on corrections. In K. C. Haas & G. P. Alpert (Eds.), *The dilemmas of corrections* (3rd ed., pp. 572–84). Prospect Heights, IL: Waveland.

Blumer, H. 1969. *Symbolic interactionism: Perspective and method.* Englewood Cliffs, NJ: Prentice-Hall.

Blumstein, A. 1995. Stability of punishment: What happened and what next? In T. G. Blomberg & S. Cohen (Eds.), *Punishment and social control: Essays in honor of Sheldon L. Messinger* (pp. 259–74). Hawthorne, NY: Aldine de Gruyter.

Bok, M. 1992. *Civil rights and the social programs of the 1960s.* Westport, CT: Praeger.

Bonomi, P. U. 1986. *Under the scope of heaven.* New York: Oxford University Press.

Boorstin, D. J. 1983. *The discoverers: A history of man's search to know his world and himself.* New York: Random House.

Bortner, M. A. 1984. *Inside a juvenile court: The tarnished ideal of individualized justice.* New York: New York University Press.

Bradford, W. [1793] 1972. *Reform of criminal law in Pennsylvania: Selected inquiries 1787–1819.* New York: Arno.

Bradley, R. C. 1990. Judicial appointment and judicial intervention: The issuance of structural reform decrees in correctional litigation. In J. J. DiIulio (Ed.), *Courts, corrections, and the Constitution* (pp. 249–67). New York: Oxford University Press.

Braithwaite, J. 1989. *Crime, shame, and reintegration.* Cambridge: Cambridge University Press.

Branham, L. S., & Krantz, S. 1994. *Sentencing, corrections, and prisoners' rights* (4th ed.). St. Paul, MN: West.

Brien, P. M., & Beck, A. J. 1998. HIV in Prisons. In T. J. Flanagan, J. W. Marquart, & K. G. Adams (Eds.), *Incarcerating criminals* (pp. 158–60). New York: Oxford University Press.

Brockway, Z. R. 1997. The American reformatory prison system. In J. R. Marquart & J. R. Sorensen (Eds.), *Correctional contexts.* Los Angeles: Roxbury. (Reprint of original from *Prison reform: Corrections and prevention* published in 1910.)

Burgess, E. W., & Bogue, D. J. (Eds.) 1967. *Urban sociology.* Chicago: University of Chicago Press.

Burnett, C., & Chaneles, S. (Eds.) 1989. *Older offenders: Current trends.* New York: Haworth.

Byrne, J. M., & Pattavina, A. 1992. The effectiveness issue: Assessing what works in the adult community corrections system. In J. M. Byrne, A. J. Lurigio, & J. Petersilia (Eds.), *Smart sentencing* (pp. 281–303). Newbury Park, CA: Sage.

Cahalan, M. W. 1986. *Historical corrections statistics in the United States, 1850–1984* (report no. NCJ 102529). Washington, DC: U.S. Bureau of Justice Statistics.

"California mental hospitals filling up with criminals." 1999. *Orlando Sentinel,* 1 May.

Carlen, P., & Tchaikovsky, C. 1985. Women in prison. In P. Carlen, J. Hicks, J. O. Dwyer, & D. Christin (Eds.), *Criminal women* (pp. 182–86). Cambridge, MA: Polity.

Carter, G. W., & Gilbert, G. R. 1973. *An evaluation progress report of the alternatives routes project.* Los Angeles: Regional Research Institute in Social Welfare, University of Southern California.

Carter, R. M., & Wilkins, L. T. 1976. *Probation, parole, and community corrections.* New York: John Wiley.

Cashman, S. D. 1988. *America in the age of the titans: The progressive era and World War I.* New York: New York University Press.

Catalano, R. F., & Hawkins, J. D. 1996. The social development model: A theory of antisocial behavior. In J. D. Hawkins (Ed.), *Delinquency and crime: Current theories* (pp. 149–97). Cambridge, MA: Cambridge University Press.

CEGA Services, Inc. 1992. *Corrections compendium.* New York: Edna McConnell Clark Foundation.

Center for Research on Criminal Justice. 1975. *The iron fist and the velvet glove: An analysis of U.S. police.* Berkeley, CA: Author.

Chesney-Lind, M. 1991. Patriarchy, prisons, and jails: A critical look at trends in women's incarceration. *Prison Journal, 71,* 51–67.

Chesney-Lind, M. 1997. *The female offender.* Thousand Oaks, CA: Sage.

Cicourel, A. 1968. *The social organization of juvenile justice.* New York: John Wiley.

Clear, T. R. 1994. *Harm in American penology.* Albany, NY: SUNY Press.

Clear, T. R., & Cole, G. F. 1993. *American corrections* (3rd ed.). Belmont, CA: Wadsworth.

Clear, T. R., & Cole, G. F. 2000. *American corrections* (4th ed.). Belmont, CA: Wadsworth.

Clemmer, D. 1940. *The prison community.* New York: Holt, Rinehart, & Winston.

"Clinton orders new privacy rules for medical records." 1999. *Tallahassee Democrat,* 30 October, B3.

Cloninger, C. R., & Gottesman, I. I. 1987. Genetic and environmental factors in antisocial behavior disorders. In S. A. Mednick, T. E. Moffitt, & S. A. Stack (Eds.), *The causes of crime: New biological approaches* (pp. 92–109). New York: Cambridge University Press.

Cloninger, C. R., Sigvardsson, S., Bohman, M., & von Knorring, A. 1982. Predisposition to petty criminality in Swedish adoptees: II. Cross-fostering analysis of gene-environment interaction. *Archives of General Psychiatry, 39,* 1242–47.

Cloward, R. A., & Ohlin, L. 1960. *Delinquency and opportunity: A theory of delinquent gangs.* Glencoe, IL: Free Press.

Coates, R. B., Miller, A. D., & Ohlin, L. E. 1978. *Diversity in a youth correctional system: Handling delinquents in Massachusetts.* Cambridge, MA: Ballinger.

Cohen, A. K. 1955. *Delinquent boys: The culture of the gang.* Glencoe, IL: Free Press.

Cohen, A. K., Lindesmith, A., & Schuessler, K. (Eds.) 1956. *The Sutherland papers.* Bloomington: Indiana University Press.

Cohen, L. E., & Felson, M. 1979. Social change and crime rate trends: A routine activities approach. *American Sociological Review, 44,* 588–608.

Cohen, S. 1985. *Visions of social control.* Cambridge, MA: Polity.

Corbett, R., & Marx, G. T. 1991. Critique: No soul in the new machine: Technofallacies in the electronic monitoring movement. *Justice Quarterly, 8*(3), 399–414.

Cornish, D., & Clarke, R. V. 1986. *The reasoning criminal: Rational choice perspectives on offending.* New York: Springer.

Correctional Association of New York. 1995. *Seeking justice: Crime and punishment in America.* New York: Edna McConnell Clark Foundation.

Corry, E. M. 1983. Receptive sites. In S. Kobrin & M. W. Klein (Eds.), *Community treatment of juvenile offenders* (pp. 120–35). Beverly Hills, CA: Sage.

Cressey, D. R., & McDermott, R. A. 1973. *Diversion from the juvenile justice system.* Ann Arbor: National Assessment of Juvenile Corrections, University of Michigan.

Criminal Justice Institute. 1997. *The corrections yearbook.* South Salem, NY: Author.

Cripe, C. A. 1990. Courts, corrections, and the Constitution: A practitioner's view. In J. J. Dilulio (Ed.), *Courts, corrections, and the Constitution* (pp. 268–86). New York: Oxford University Press.

Cullen, F. T., & Agnew, R. 1999. *Criminological theory: Past to present.* Los Angeles: Roxbury.

de Beaumont, G., & de Toqueville, A. [1833] 1997. On the penitentiary system in the United States and its application in France. In J. M. Marquart & J. R. Sorensen (Eds.), *Correctional contexts.* Los Angeles: Roxbury.

Dickens, C. [1842] 1972. *American notes.* Harmondsworth: Penguin.

Dilulio, J. J. 1990. Introduction: Enhancing judicial capacity. In J. J. Dilulio (Ed.), *Courts, corrections, and the Constitution* (pp. 3–11). New York: Oxford University Press.

Dilulio, J. J. 1993. Well-governed prisons are possible. In G. F. Cole (Ed.), *Criminal justice: Law and politics* (pp. 438–46). Belmont, CA: Wadsworth.

Diner, S. J. 1998. *A very different age: Americans of the progressive era.* New York: Hill and Wang.

Ditton, P. M. 1999. Mental health and treatment of inmates and probationers: Bureau of Justice Statistics Special Report, July, 1999. Washington DC: U.S. Department of Justice, Office of Justice Programs.

Donaldson, S. 1994. *Rape of incarcerated males in the U.S.A.: A preliminary statistical look* (5th ed.). Unpublished manuscript.

Duffee, D. E. 1989. *Corrections: Practice and policy.* New York: Random House.

Dugdale, R. [1877] 1979. The jukes: A study in crime, pauperism, and heredity. In J. E. Jacoby (Ed.), *Classics of criminology.* New York: MacMillan.

Dumond, R. W. 1992. The sexual assault of male inmates in incarcerated settings. *International Journal of the Sociology of Law, 20,* 135–57.

Durham, A. M., III. 1994. *Crisis and reform: Current issues in American punishment.* Boston: Little, Brown.

Edna McConnell Clark Foundation. 1995. *Seeking justice: Crime and punishment in America.* New York: Author.

Elkins, S., & McKitrick, E. 1993. *The age of federalism.* London: Oxford University Press.

Elliott, D. S. 1978. *Diversion: A study of alternative processing practices* (Final Report to the Center for Studies of Crime and Delinquency, NIMH.). Boulder, CO: Behavioral Research Institute, University of Colorado.

Ellis, L., & Hoffman, H. 1990. *Crime in biological, social, and moral contexts.* New York: Praeger.

Emerson, R. M. 1969. *Judging delinquents: Context and process in juvenile court.* Chicago: Aldine.

Empey, L. T. 1982. *American delinquency: Its meaning and construction.* Homewood, IL: Dorsey.

Erikson, K. T. 1966. *Wayward puritans: A study in the sociology of deviance.* New York: John Wiley.

Feeley, M. M., & Hanson, R. A. 1990. The impact of judicial intervention of prisons and jails: A review of the literature. In J. J. DiIulio (Ed.), *Courts, corrections, and the Constitution* (pp. 12–46). New York: Oxford University Press.

Feeley, M. M., & Sarat, A. D. 1980. *The policy dilemma: Federal crime policy and the law enforcement assistance administration.* Minneapolis: University of Minnesota Press.

Feeley, M. M., & Simon, J. 1992. The new penology: Notes on the emerging strategy of corrections and its implications. *Criminology, 30*(4), 449–74.

Feenberg, A. 1986. Paths to failure: The dialectics of organization and ideology in the New Left. In A. Reed (Ed.), *Race, politics, and culture: Critical essays on the radicalism of the 1960s* (pp. 119–44). Westport, CT: Greenwood.

Feinberg, G. 1984. White haired offenders: An emergent social problem. In W. Wilbanks & P. Kim (Eds.), *Elderly criminals* (pp. 83–101). Lanham, MD: University Press of America.

Ferrara, M., & Ferrara, S. 1991. The evolution of prison mental health services. In W. Wilbanks & P. Kim (Eds.), *Elderly criminals* (pp. 198–203). Lanham, MD: University Press of America.

Feuer, J. 1995. *Seeing through the eighties: Television and Reaganism.* Durham, NC: Duke University Press.

Fishbein, D. H. 1990. Biological perspectives in criminology. *Criminology, 28,* 27–72.

Florida Department of Corrections. 1994. *1993–1994 Annual report.* Tallahassee, FL: Author.

Flynn, E. 1993. The graying of America's prison population. *Prison Journal, 72,* 77–98.

Forward, J. R., Kirby, M., & Wilson K. 1974. *Volunteer intervention with court-diverted juveniles.* Boulder: University of Colorado.

Foucault, M. 1977. *Discipline and punish: The birth of the prison* (A. Sheridan, Trans.). New York: Pantheon.

Franklin, R. H. 1998. Assessing supermax operations. *Corrections Today, 60,* 126–28.

Friedan, B. 1963. *The feminine mystique.* New York: Norton.

Friedman, L. 1993. *Crime and punishment in American history.* New York: Basic Books.

Gabel, S. 1992. Children of incarcerated and criminal parents: Adjustment, behavior, and prognosis. *Bulletin on Academic Psychiatric Law, 20,* 33–45.

Garland, D. 1990. *Punishment and modern society.* Oxford: Clarendon.

Garland, D. 1998. *Eight propositions about the present.* Plenary presentation at the 1998 Southern Conference on Corrections, Palm Beach, Florida.

Gavora, J. 1996. The prisoners' accomplice. *Policy Review, 79,* 6–9.

Gearan, A. 2000. Clinton pushes privacy rules. *Tallahassee Democrat,* 1 May.

Giallombardo, R. 1966. *Society of women: A study of a women's prison.* New York: Wiley.

Glaser, D. 1966, March-April. The effectiveness of correctional education. *American Journal of Correction, 28*(2), 4–9.

Goddard, H. H. 1912. *The Kallikak family: A study in the heredity of feeble-mindedness.* New York: Macmillan.

Goddard, H. H. 1914. *The criminal imbecile: An analysis of three remarkable murder cases.* New York: Macmillan.

Goddard, H. H. 1915. *Feeble-mindedness: Its causes and consequences.* New York: MacMillan.

Goffman, E. 1961. On the characteristics of total institutions: The inmate world. In D. R. Cressey (Ed.), *The prison: Studies in institutional organization and change* (pp. 15–67). New York: Holt, Rinehart, & Winston.

Gomes, P. J. 1996. *The good book.* New York: William Morrow.

Gordon, D. 1990. *The justice juggernaut.* Newark, NJ: Rutgers University Press.

Gorringe, T. 1996. *God's just vengeance: Crime, violence, and the rhetoric of salvation.* Cambridge, MA: Cambridge University Press.

Gowdy, V. B. 1997. Should we privatize our prisons: The pros and cons. *Corrections Management Quarterly, 1,* 56–63.

Graham, H. D. 1992. *Civil rights and the presidency: Race and gender in American politics 1960–1972.* New York: Oxford University Press.

Greenberg, D. F. 1977. The dynamics of oscillatory punishment processes. *Journal of Criminal Law and Criminology, 68*(4), 643–51.

Greenfeld, L. A. and T. L. Snell. 1999. Women offenders: Bureau of Justice Statistics Special Report, December, 1999. Washington, DC: U.S. Department of Justice, Office of Justice Programs.

Gross, D. 1986. Culture, politics, and lifestyle in the 1960s. In A. Reed (Ed.), *Race, politics, and culture: Critical essays on the radicalism of the 1960s* (pp. 99–117). Westport, CT: Greenwood.

Gross, M. L. 1997. *The end of sanity: Social and cultural madness in America.* New York: Avon.

Haas, K. C. 1993. Constitutional challenges to the compulsory HIV testing of prisoners and the mandatory segregation of HIV positive prisoners. *Prison Journal, 73,* 391–422.

Hagan, J. 1973. Labeling and deviance: A case study in the sociology of the interesting. *Social Problems, 20*(4), 447–58.

Hammett, T. M., Harrold, L., & Epstein, J. 1998. Tuberculosis in correctional facilities. In T. J. Flanagan, J. W. Marquart, & K. G. Adams (Eds.), *Incarcerating criminals* (pp. 166–68). New York: Oxford University Press.

Haney, C. 1993. Infamous punishment: The psychological consequences of isolation. *National Prison Project Journal, 21,* 3–7.

Hansen, M. 1999, April. Going, going . . . gong; Support for minimum drug sentences hits new low. *American Bar Association Journal, 85-14*(1):14.

Harrison, B., & Bluestone, B. 1988. *The great u-turn: Corporate restructuring and the polarizing of America.* New York: Basic Books.

Hart, H. 1910. *Preventive treatment of neglected children.* New York: Russell Sage Foundation.

Hartstone, E., Steadman, H., Robbins, P., & Monahan, J. 1984. Identifying and treating the mentally disordered prison inmate. In L. Teplin (Ed.), *Mental health and criminal justice* (pp. 279–96). Beverly Hills, CA: Sage.

Heilbroner, R. L. 1980. *An inquiry into the human prospect: Updated and reconsidered for the 1980s.* New York: W.W. Norton.

Hellum, F. R. 1983. The deinstitutionalization of status offenders: The legislative mandate. In S. Kobrin & M. W. Klein (Eds.), *Community treatment of juvenile offenders* (pp. 19–38). Beverly Hills, CA: Sage.

Henderson, C. R. 1899. The relation of philanthropy to social order and progress. Proceedings of the National Conference of Charities and Corrections. In F. L. Faust & P. C. Brantingham (Eds.), *Juvenile justice philosophy* (pp. 24–35). St. Paul, MN: West.

Hibbert, C. 1963. *The roots of evil: A social history of crime and punishment.* Boston: Little, Brown.

Holt, K. 1982. Nine months to life: The law and the pregnant inmate. *Journal of Family Law, 20,* 523–43.

Holt, N. 1998. The current state of parole in America. In J. Petersilia (Ed.), *Community corrections* (pp. 28–41). New York: Oxford University Press.

Hunter, R. [1904] 1965. *Poverty: Social conscience in the progressive era.* New York: Harper & Row.

Hylton, J. H. 1982. Rhetoric and reality: A critical appraisal of community correctional programs. *Crime and Delinquency, 28*(3), 341–73.

Immarigeon, R., & Chesney-Lind, M. 1992. *Women's prisons: Overcrowded and overused.* San Francisco: National Council on Crime and Delinquency.

Irwin, J. 1970. *The felon.* Englewood Cliffs, NJ: Prentice-Hall.

Irwin, J. 1980. *Prisons in turmoil.* Boston: Little, Brown.

Irwin, J., & Austin, J. 1997. *It's about time: America's imprisonment binge* (2nd ed.). Belmont, CA: Wadsworth.

Irwin, J., & Cressey, D. R. 1962. Thieves, convicts, and the inmate culture. *Social Problems, 10,* 142–55.

Jacobs, J. B. 1997. The prisoner rights movement and its impact. In J. W. Marquart & J. R. Sorenson (Eds.), *Correctional contexts* (pp. 231–47). Los Angeles: Roxbury.

Jacoby, R. 1975. *Social amnesia: A critique of conformist psychology from Adler to Laing.* Boston: Beacon.

Jameson, F. 1981. *The political unconscious/narrative as a socially symbolic act.* Ithaca, NY: Cornell University Press.

Kagan, D. 1990. Landmark Chicago study documents rate of mental illness among jail inmates. *Corrections Today,* December, 164.

King, R. D. 1999. The rise and rise of supermax: An American solution in search of a problem? *Punishment and Society, 1*(2), 163–86.

Kitsuse, J. I. 1964. Societal reaction to deviant behavior: Problems of theory and method. In H. S. Becker (Ed.), *The other side* (pp. 87–102). New York: Free Press.

Klein, M. W. 1974. Labeling, deterrence, and recidivism: A study of police dispositions of juvenile offenders. *Social Problems, 22*(2), 292–303.

Klein, M. W. 1975. *Alternative dispositions for juvenile offenders.* Los Angeles: University of Southern California.

Klein, M. W. 1979. Deinstitutionalization and diversion of juvenile offenders: A litany of impediments. In N. Morris & M. Tonry (Eds.), *Crime and justice: An annual review of research* (pp. 145–201). Chicago: University of Chicago Press.

Kobrin, S., & Klein, M. W. (Eds.) 1983. *Community treatment of juvenile offenders.* Beverly Hills, CA: Sage.

Kratcoski, P. C., & Pownall, G. A. 1989. Federal Bureau of Prisons programming for older inmates. *Federal Probation, 53,* 28–35.

Ku, R., & Blew, C. H. 1977. A university's approach to delinquency prevention: The adolescent diversion project. Washington, DC: U.S. Government Printing Office.

Kuntz, W. F., II. 1988. *Criminal sentencing in three 19th century cities: Social history of punishment in New York, Boston, and Philadelphia, 1830–1880.* New York: Garland.

Kyle, J. 1998. The privatization debate continues. *Corrections Today, 60,* 88–93.

Lamb, S. 1996. *The trouble with blame.* Cambridge, MA: Harvard University Press.

Lawson, W. T., & Fawkes, L. S. 1993. HIV, AIDS, and the female offender. In *Female offenders: Meeting needs of a neglected population* (pp. 43–48). Laurel, MD: American Correctional Association.

Lemert, E. M. 1970. *Social action and legal change: Revolution within the juvenile court.* Chicago: Aldine.

Lemert, E. M. 1971. *Instead of court: Diversion in juvenile justice.* Washington, DC: U.S. Government Printing Office.

Lemert, E. M. 1981. Diversion in juvenile justice: What hath been wrought. *Journal of Research in Crime and Delinquency, 18*(1), 34–46.

Lemert, E. M. 1993. Vision of social control: Probation considered. *Crime and Delinquency, 39*(4), 447–61.

Levrant, S., Cullen, F. T., Fulton, B., & Wozniak, J. F. 1999. Reconsidering restorative justice: The corruption of benevolence revisited? *Crime and Delinquency, 45*(1), 3–27.

Lichtenstein, A. 1993. Good roads and chain gangs in the progressive south: The negro convict is a slave." *Journal of Southern History, 59*(1), 85–110.

Lilly, J. R., Cullen, F. T., & Ball, R. A. 1995. *Criminological theory: Context and consequences.* Thousand Oaks, CA: Sage.

Lilly, J. R. and P. Knepper. 1993. The corrections-commercial complex. *Crime and Delinquency, 39,* 150–66.

Lincoln, S. B. 1976. Juvenile referral and recidivism. In R. M. Carter & M. W. Klein (Eds.), *Back on the street: The diversion of juvenile offenders* (pp. 321–28). Englewood Cliffs, NJ: Prentice-Hall.

Lincoln, S. B., Teilman, K., Klein, M. W., & Labin, S. 1977. *Recidivism rates of diverted juvenile offenders.* Paper presented at the National Conference on Criminal Justice Evaluation, Washington, DC.

Lindsey, B., & Burrough, R. 1931. *The dangerous life.* London: Harold Shaler.

Lippke, R. L. 1997. Thinking about private prisons. *Criminal Justice Ethics, 16,* 26–39.

Lucken, K. 1997. Dynamics of penal reform. *Crime, Law, and Social Change, 26*(4), 367–84.

Lucken, K. 1998. Analyzing penal reform: Can theory and policy ever meet? In J. T. Ulmer (Ed.), *Sociology of crime, law, and deviance: Volume I* (pp. 85–103). Greenwich, CT: JAI.

Luke, T. W. 1986. The modern service state: Public power in America from the new deal to the new beginning. In A. Reed (Ed.), *Race, politics, and culture: Critical essays on the radicalism of the 1960s* (pp. 183–205). Westport, CT: Greenwood.

Lurigio, A. J., & Petersilia, J. 1992. The emergence of intensive probation supervision programs in the United States. In J. M. Byrne, A. J. Lurigio, & J. Petersilia (Eds.), *Smart sentencing* (pp. 103–19). Newbury Park, CA: Sage.

Lyon, D. 1994. *The electronic eye: The rise of surveillance society.* Minneapolis: University of Minnesota Press.

Mack, J. W. 1909. The juvenile court. *Harvard Law Review, 23,* 104–22.

Mahoney, R. 1974. The effect of labeling upon youths in the juvenile justice system: A review of the evidence. *Law and Society Review, 8*(4), 583–614.

Malabre, A. L. 1987. *Beyond our means.* New York: Random House.

Mannheim, H. 1940. *Social aspects of crime in England between the wars.* London: Allen and Unwin.

Marcus, D. L. 1999. File this under shock, future: Libraries enter the modern age. *U.S. News and World Report,* 12 July, 48–49.

Marquart, J. R., & Sorensen, J. R. (Eds.) 1997. *Correctional contexts.* Los Angeles: Roxbury.

Martin, B. 1980. Massachusetts' correctional system: Treatment or an ideology of control? In T. Platt & P. Takagi (Eds.), *Punishment and penal discipline* (pp. 156–64). Berkeley, CA: Crime and Social Justice Associates.

Martinson, R. 1974. What works? Questions and answers about prison reform. *Public Interest, 35*(2), 22–54.

Maruschak, L. M. 1999. HIV in prisons, 1997: Bureau of Justice Statistics Bulletin, November, Office of Justice Programs, Washington, D.C.

Marx, G. 1988. *Undercover: Police surveillance in America.* Berkeley: University of California Press.

Mauer, M. 1996. The truth about truth in sentencing. *Corrections Today, 58,* 51–59.

Mauer, M. 1990. *Young black men in the criminal justice system: A growing national problem.* Washington, DC: The Sentencing Project.

McCarthy, B. R. 1980. Inmate mothers: The problems of separation and reintegration. *Journal of Offender Counseling, Services, and Rehabilitation, 4*(3), 199–212.

McCorkle, R. C. 1995. Gender, psychopathology, and institutional behavior: A comparison of male and female mentally ill prison inmates. *Journal of Criminal Justice, 23*(1), 53–61.

McDonald, D., & Carlson, K. E. 1992. *Federal sentencing in transition* (U.S. Bureau of Justice Statistics Special Report, June). Washington, DC: U.S. Government Printing Office.

McKelvey, B. 1936. *American prisons.* Chicago: University of Chicago Press.

McShane, M. D. & Williams, S. P., III. 1990. Old and ornery: The disciplinary experiences of elderly prisoners. *Journal of offender therapy and comparative criminology, 34*(3), 197–212.

Mead, G. H. 1934. *Mind, self and society.* Chicago: University of Chicago Press.

Mednick, S. A. 1987. Genetic factors in the etiology of criminal behavior. In S. A. Mednick, T. E. Moffitt, & S. A. Stock (Eds.), *The causes of crime* (pp. 74–91). New York: Cambridge University Press.

Mednick, S. A., Gabrielli, W. F., & Hutchings, B. 1984. Genetic influences in criminal convictions: Evidence from an adoption cohort. *Science, 224,* 891–94.

Mednick, S. A., Volavka, J., Gabrielli, W. F., & Itil, T. 1981. EEG as a predictor of antisocial behavior. *Criminology, 19,* 219–31.

Melossi, D., & Pavarini, M. 1981. *The prison and the factory.* Totowa, NJ: Barnes & Noble.

Mennel, R. M. 1973. *Thorns and thistles: Juvenile delinquents in the United States, 1825–1940.* Hanover, NH: University Press of New England.

Merton, R. K. 1938. Social structure and anomie. *American Sociological Review, 3,* 672–82.

Merton, R. K. 1949. *Social theory and social structure.* Glencoe, IL: Free Press.

Michael, J., & Adler, M. J. 1933. *Crime, law and social science.* New York: Harcourt-Brace.

Miller, M. B. 1980. At hard labor: Rediscovering the 19th century prison. In T. Platt & P. Takagi (Eds.), *Punishment and penal discipline* (pp. 79–88). Berkeley, CA: Crime and Social Justice Associates.

Miller, W. B. 1958. Lower class culture as a generating milieu of gang delinquency. *Journal of Social Issues, 14*(3), 5–19.

Morain, D. 1994. California's prison budget: Why is it so voracious? *Los Angeles Times,* 19 October.

Morris, N. 1974. *The future of imprisonment.* Chicago: University of Chicago Press.

Morris, N., & Hawkins, G. 1976. Rehabilitation: Rhetoric and reality. In K. M. Carter & L. T. Wilkins (Eds.), *Probation, parole, and community corrections* (2nd ed., pp. 26–39). New York: John Wiley.

Mullen, J. 1975. *The dilemma of diversion: Resource materials on adult pre-trial intervention programs.* Washington, DC: U.S. Government Printing Office.

Nakell, B., & Hardy, K. A. 1987. *The arbitrariness of the death penalty.* Philadelphia, PA: Temple University Press.

Norton, M. B. 1991. Gender, crime, and community in 17th century Maryland. In J. A. Henretta, M. Kammen, & S. N. Katz (Eds.), *The transformation of early American history* (pp. 123–50). New York: Alfred A. Knopf.

O'Connell, J. P., Jr. 1995. Throwing away the key. *Spectrum: The Journal of State Government, 68*(1), 28–33.

O'Toole, P. 1998. *Money and morals in America.* New York: Clarkson Potter.

Obrien, K. E., & Marcus, M. 1976. *Juvenile diversion: A selected bibliography.* Washington, DC: U.S. Government Printing Office.

Pallas, J., & Barber, B. 1980. From riot to revolution. In T. Platt & P. Takagi (Eds.), *Punishment and penal discipline* (pp. 146–54). Berkeley, CA: Crime and Social Justice Associates.

Palmer, J. W. 1991. *Constitutional rights of prisoners* (4th ed.). Cincinnati, OH: Anderson.

Park, R. E., & Burgess, E. W. 1924. *Introduction to the science of sociology* (2nd ed.). Chicago: University of Chicago Press.

Parshall, G. 1998. Discovery: Makers of the 20th century. *U.S. News and World Report,* 17 August.

Paulsen, M. G., & Whitebread, C. H. 1974. *Juvenile law and procedure.* Reno, NV: National Council of Juvenile Court Judges.

Pessen, E. 1969. *Jacksonian America: Society, personality, politics.* Homewood, IL: Dorsey.

Petersilia, J. 1987. Georgia's intensive probation: Will the model work elsewhere? In B. R. McCarthy (Ed.), *Intermediate punishments: Intensive supervision, home confinement, and electronic surveillance* (pp. 15–30). Monsey, NY: Criminal Justice Press.

Petersilia, J., & Turner, S. 1990. Comparing intensive and regular supervision for high-risk probationers: Early results from an experiment in California. *Crime and Delinquency, 36*(1), 87–111.

Petersilia, J., & Turner, S. 1993. Intensive probation and parole. In M. Tonry (Ed.), *Crime and justice: A review of research, Vol. 17*. Chicago: University of Chicago Press.

Pezman, T. C. 1963. Untwisting the twisted. *Probation, camps, ranches, and schools* (pp. 1–2). Sacramento: California Probation, Parole, and Correctional Division.

Phillips, K. 1991. *The politics of rich and poor*. New York: Random House.

Pisciotta, A. W. 1994. *Benevolent repression: Social control and the American reformatory prison movement*. New York: New York University Press.

Platt, A. M. 1969. *The child savers: The invention of delinquency*. Chicago: University of Chicago Press.

Platt, A. M. 1977. *The child savers: The invention of delinquency*. Chicago: University of Chicago Press.

Polk, K. 1971. Delinquency prevention and the youth service bureau. *Criminal Law Bulletin, 7*, 490–529.

Polk, K. 1981. *Youth service bureaus: The record and the prospects*. Mimeograph. Eugene: University of Oregon.

Powers, E. 1966. *Crime and punishment in early Massachusetts, 1620–1692: A documentary history*. Boston: Beacon.

Preyer, K. 1982. Penal measures in the American colonies: An overview. *American Journal of Legal History, 26*, 326–53.

Radzinowicz, L. 1994. *Adventures in criminology*. New York & London: Routledge.

Rafter, N. 1990. *Women, prison, and social control*. New Brunswick, NJ: Transaction.

Ralph, P. H. 1997. From self-preservation to organized crime: The evolution of inmate gangs. In J. W. Marquart & J. R. Sorenson (Eds.), *Correctional contexts* (pp. 182–88). Los Angeles: Roxbury.

Reiman, J. 1990. *The rich get richer, the poor get prison*. New York: MacMillan.

"Religion was 'salt that flavored' colonial life." 1998. *Orlando Sentinel*, 5 July, A7.

Rhine, E. 1990. The rule of law, disciplinary practices, and Rahway State Prison: A case study in judicial intervention and social control. In J. J. Dilulio (Ed.), *Courts, corrections, and the Constitution* (pp. 173–222). New York: Oxford University Press.

Rhode, D. L. 1989. *Justice and gender*. Cambridge, MA: Harvard University Press.

Richmond, M. 1917. *Social diagnosis*. New York: Russell Sage.

Ringel, C., Cowles, E., & Castellano, T. 1993. *The recasting of parole supervision: The causes and responses of systems under stress*. Paper presented at the Academy of Criminal Justice Sciences Conference, Kansas City, Missouri.

Robbins, I. P. 1987. Privatization of corrections: Defining the issues. *Vanderbilt Law Review, 40*, 813–28.

Rosenfeld, R., & Kempf, K. 1991. The scope and purpose of corrections: Exploring alternative responses to crowding. *Crime and Delinquency, 37*(4), 481–505.

Rosenfeld, R., & Messner, S. F. 1999. Crime and the American dream. In F. T. Cullen & R. Agnew (Eds.), *Criminological theory: Past to present* (pp. 141–50). Los Angeles: Roxbury.

Rosenheim, M. 1969. Youth service bureaus: A concept in search of definition. *Juvenile Court Judges Journal, 20*, 69–74.

Rosica, J. L. 2000. Eyes in the sky will keep cons square. *Tallahassee Democrat*, 8 May.

Rossell, N. R. 1991. *Older inmates.* Tallahassee: Florida House of Representatives.

Rossiter, C. 1971. *The American quest 1790–1860: An emerging nation in search of identity, unity, and modernity.* New York: Harcourt-Brace.

Rothman, D. J. 1971. *The discovery of the asylum: Social order and disorder in the new republic.* Boston: Little, Brown.

Rothman, D. J. 1980. *Conscience and convenience: The asylum and its alternatives in progressive America.* Boston: Little, Brown.

Rotman, E. 1995. The failure of reform: United States, 1865–1965. In N. Morris & D. J. Rothman (Eds.), *The Oxford history of the prison* (pp. 169–97). New York: Oxford University Press.

Rowe, D. C. 1985. Sibling interaction and self-reported delinquent behavior: A study of 265 twin pairs. *Criminology, 23,* 223–40.

Rowe, D. C., & Osgood, D. 1984. Heredity and sociological theories of delinquency: A reconsideration. *American Sociological Review, 49,* 526–40.

Rubin, J. 1971. *We are everywhere.* New York: Harper and Row.

Rusche, G., & Kirchheimer, O. 1939. *Punishment and social structure.* New York: Columbia University.

Rutherford, A., & McDermott, R. A. 1976. *Juvenile diversion.* Washington, DC: U.S. Government Printing Office.

Ryan, T. A., & Grassano, J. B. 1992. Taking a progressive approach to treating pregnant offenders. *Corrections Today, 54,* 184–86.

Ryerson, E. 1978. *The best laid plans: America's juvenile court experience.* New York: Hill and Wang.

Sarri, R. C. 1983. The use of detention and alternatives in the United States since the Gault decision. In R. R. Corrado, M. LeBlanc, & J. Trepanier (Eds.), *Current issues in juvenile justice* (pp. 315–34). Toronto: Butterworths.

Sarup, M. 1993. *An introductory guide to post-structuralism and postmodernism* (2nd ed.). Athens: University of Georgia Press.

Sassoon, T. 1995. *Crime talk: Citizens construct a social problem.* Hawthorne, NY: Aldine de Gruyter.

Scheingold, S. A. 1984. *The politics of law and order: Street crime and public policy.* New York: Longman.

Schlossman, S. L. 1977. *Love and the american delinquent: The theory and practice of "progressive" juvenile justice, 1825–1920.* Chicago: University of Chicago Press.

Schlossman, S. L. 1995. Delinquent children: The juvenile reform school. In N. Morris & D. J. Rothman (Eds.), *The Oxford history of the prison* (pp. 363–89). New York: Oxford University Press.

Schulhofer, S. J. 1993. Rethinking mandatory minimums. *Wake Forest Law Review, 28,* 199–222.

Schupak, T. 1986. Women and children first: An examination of the unique needs of women in prison. *Golden State University Law Review,* 455–74.

Schur, E. M. 1971. *Labeling deviant behavior: Its sociological implications.* New York: Harper and Row.

Schwendinger, H., & Schwendinger, J. R. 1974. *The sociologists of the chair: A radical analysis of the formative years of North American sociology (1883–1922).* New York: Basic Books.

Scull, A. 1977. *Decarceration.* New Brunswick, NJ: Rutgers University Press.

Seiter, R. P. 1998. A rebirth of rehabilitation: The responsibility model. *Corrections Management Quarterly, 2,* 89–92.

Sewall, G. T. 1997. *The eighties.* Reading, MA: Addison-Wesley.

Shaw, C. R. 1930. *The jackroller.* Chicago: University of Chicago Press.

Shaw, C. R. 1931. *The natural history of a delinquent career.* Chicago: University of Chicago Press.

Shaw, C. R. 1938. *Brothers in crime.* Chicago: University of Chicago Press.

Shaw, C. R., & McKay, H. D. 1972. *Juvenile delinquency and urban areas* (Rev. ed.). Chicago: University of Chicago Press.

Sheppard, R. A. 1996. Closed maximum security: The Illinois supermax. *Corrections Today, 58,* 84–88.

Simon, J. 1993. *Poor discipline: Parole and the social control of the underclass, 1890– 1990.* Chicago: University of Chicago Press.

Skolnick, J. H. 1969. *The politics of protest.* New York: Ballantine.

Skolnick, J. H. 1995. Sheldon L. Messinger: The man, his work, and the carceral society. In T. G. Blomberg & S. Cohen (Eds.), *Punishment and social control: Essays in honor of Sheldon L. Messinger* (pp. 15–28). Hawthorne, NY: Aldine de Gruyter.

Smalley, S. 1999. Slamming the slammers: A stir over private pens. *National Journal, 31,* 1168–75.

Smart, C. 1976. *Women, crime and criminology: A feminist critique.* London: Routledge & Kegan Paul.

Smith, C. E. 2000. *Law and contemporary corrections.* Belmont, CA: Wadsworth.

Snell, T. L., & Morton, D. C. 1994. *Women in prison.* Washington, DC: U.S. Bureau of Justice Statistics.

Soderstrom, I. R. 1999. Is it still practical to incarcerate the elderly offender? In C. B. Fields (Ed.), *Controversial issues in corrections* (pp. 72–80). Needham Heights, MA: Allyn and Bacon.

Sommers, I., & Baskin, D. R. 1990. The prescription of psychiatric medications in prison: Psychiatric versus labeling perspectives. *Justice Quarterly, 7*(4), 739–55.

Specter, D. 1994. Cruel and unusual punishment of the mentally ill in California's prisons: A case study of a class action suit. *Social Justice, 21*(3), 109–16.

Spierenburg, P. 1984. *The spectacle of suffering: Executions and the evolution of repression.* Cambridge, MA: Cambridge University Press.

Staples, W. G. 1997. *The culture of surveillance: Discipline and social control in the United States.* New York: St. Martin's.

Steadman, H. J., Monahan, J., Duffee, B., Hartstone, E., & Robbins, P. C. 1984. The impact of state mental hospital deinstitutionalization on U.S. prison populations, 1968–1978. *Journal of Criminal Law and Criminology, 75,* 474–90.

Steelman, D. 1987. *The mentally impaired in New York's prisons.* New York: Correctional Association of New York.

Stratton, J. G. 1975. Effects of crisis intervention counseling on pre-delinquent and misdemeanor juvenile offenders. *Juvenile Justice, 26,* 7–18.

Sutherland, E. H. 1947. *Principles of criminology* (4th ed.). Philadelphia: Lippincott.

Sykes, G. 1958. *The society of captives.* Princeton, NJ: Princeton University Press.

Sykes, G. 1995. The structural, functional perspective on imprisonment. In T. G.

Blomberg & S. Cohen (Eds.), *Punishment and social control: Essays in honor of Sheldon L. Messinger* (pp. 77–84). Hawthorne, NY: Aldine de Gruyter.

Sykes, G., & Messinger, S. L. 1960. The inmate social system. In R. A. Cloward (Ed.), *Theoretical studies in the social organization of the prison* (pp. 5–20). New York: Social Science Research Council.

Tannenbaum, F. 1938. *Crime and the community.* New York: Columbia University Press.

Teplin, L. 1990. The prevalence of severe mental disorder among male urban jail detainees: Comparison with the epidemiologic catchment area program. *American Journal of Public Health, 80*(6), 663–69.

Thomas, J. 1988. *Prisoner litigation.* Totowa, NJ: Rowman and Littlefield.

Thompson, R. 1986. *Sex in Middlesex: Popular mores in a Massachusetts county, 1649–1699.* Amherst: University of Massachusetts Press.

"Thousands of eyes for state police." 1994. *New York Times,* 19 May, A8.

Tittle, C. R. 1995. *Control balance: Toward a general theory of deviance.* Boulder, CO: Westview.

Toch, H. 1977. *Living in prison: The ecology of survival.* New York: Free Press.

Tonry, M. 1999. Why are U.S. incarceration rates so high? *Crime and Delinquency, 45*(4), 419–37.

Torrey, E. 1995. Editorial: Jails and prisons—America's new mental hospitals. *American Journal of Public Health, 85*(12), 1611–13.

U.S. Bureau of Census. 1975. *Bureau of Census Statistics* (bulletin). Washington, DC: U.S. Government Printing Office.

U.S. Bureau of Justice Statistics. 1995a. *Prison sentences and time served for violence.* Washington, DC: U.S. Government Printing Office.

U.S. Bureau of Justice Statistics. 1995b. *Prisoners in 1994.* Washington, DC: U.S. Government Printing Office.

U.S. Bureau of Justice Statistics. 1996. *Correctional population in the United States, 1996.* Washington, DC: U.S. Government Printing Office.

U.S. Department of Justice. 1979. *Evaluation of the Des Moines community-based corrections replication programs: Summary report.* Washington, DC: U.S. Government Printing Office.

U.S. Office of National Drug Control Policy. 1995. *National drug control strategy: Budget summary.* Washington, DC: Office of National Drug Control Policy, Executive Office of the President.

U.S. President's Commission on Law Enforcement and Administration of Justice. 1967a. *The challenge of crime in a free society.* Washington, DC: U.S. Government Printing Office.

U.S. President's Commission on Law Enforcement and Administration of Justice. 1967b. *Task force report: Juvenile delinquency and youth crime.* Washington, DC: U.S. Government Printing Office.

Unger, I., & Unger, D. 1977. *The vulnerable years: The United States, 1986–1917.* Hinsdale, IL: Dryden.

Venables, P. H. 1987. Autonomic nervous system factors in criminal behavior. In S. A. Mednick, T. E. Moffitt, & S. A. Stack (Eds.), *The causes of crime: New biological approaches* (pp. 110–36). New York: Cambridge University Press.

"Vermont sterilized people." 1999, August 8. *Orlando Sentinel.*

Vitale, A. 1980. Inmate abortions: The right to government funding. *Fordham Law Review,* 550–67.

Vito, G. F. 1995. The penalty of death in the next century. In J. Klofas & S. Stojkovic (Eds.), *Crime and justice in the year 2010* (pp. 251–66). Belmont, CA: Wadsworth.

Vlahov, D. 1990. Coinfection with tuberculosis and HIV-1 in male prison inmates. *Public Health Reports, 105*(3), 307–10.

Vogelman, R. P. 1971. Prison restrictions, prisoner rights. In L. Radzinowicz & M. E. Wolfgang (Eds.), *Crime and justice series,* Vol. 3: *The criminal in confinement* (pp. 52–68). New York: Basic Books.

Von Hentig, H. (1942). Degrees of parole violation and graded remedial measures. *Journal of the American Institute of Criminal Law and Criminology, 8,* 233–58.

Von Hirsch, A. 1995. The future of the proportionate sentence. In T. G. Blomberg & S. Cohen (Eds.), *Punishment and social control: Essays in honor of Sheldon L. Messinger* (pp. 123–45). Hawthorne, NY: Aldine de Gruyter.

Wald, K. 1980. The San Quentin six case: Perspective and analysis. In T. Platt & P. Takagi (Eds.), *Punishment and penal discipline* (pp. 165–75). Berkeley, CA: Crime and Social Justice Associates.

Walker, S. 1985. *Sense and nonsense about crime and drugs.* Belmont, CA: Wadsworth.

Wallace, D. H. 1992. Ruffin v. Virginia and slaves of the state: A non-existent baseline of prisoners' rights jurisprudence. *Journal of Criminal Justice, 20,* 333–42.

Wallace, D. H. 1994. The Eighth Amendment and prison deprivations: Historical revisions. *Criminal Law Bulletin, 30*(1), 5–29.

Wellford, C. 1975. Labeling theory and criminology: An assessment. *Social Problems, 22*(3), 332–35.

Wheeler, P. A., Trammell, R., Thomas, J., & Findlay, J. 1989. Persephone chained: Parity of equality in women's prisons. *Prison Journal, 69,* 88–102.

Wheeler, S. 1971. Socialization in correctional institutions. In L. Radzinowicz & M. E. Wolfgang (Eds.), *Crime and justice series,* Vol. 3: *The criminal in confinement* (pp. 97–116). New York: Basic Books.

Wheeler, W. M. 1999. Is it still practical to incarcerate the elderly offender? In C. B. Fields (Ed.), *Controversial issues in corrections* (pp. 72–80). Needham Heights, MA: Allyn and Bacon.

Wickham, D. S. 1999. Insane with no asylum: Mentally ill pack jails. *Orlando Sentinel,* 31 October, 18.

Wilbanks, W. 1984. The elderly offender: Placing the problem in perspective. In W. Wilbanks & P. Kim (Eds.), *Elderly criminals* (pp. 1–11). Lanham, MD: University Press of America.

Williams, W. A. 1966. *The contours of American history.* Chicago: Quadrangle.

Wilson, J. Q., & Herrnstein, R. J. 1985. *Crime and human nature.* New York: Simon and Schuster.

Wilson, W. J. 1987. *The truly disadvantaged.* Chicago: University of Chicago Press.

Wooldredge, J. D., & Masters, K. 1993. Confronting problems faced by pregnant inmates in state prisons. *Crime and Delinquency, 39,* 195–203.

Zedner, L. 1995. Wayward sisters, the prison for women. In N. Morris & D. J. Rothman (Eds.), *The Oxford history of the prison* (pp. 329–61). New York: Oxford University Press.

Index